Anonymous

**Moody Bible Institute Lectures**

Anonymous

**Moody Bible Institute Lectures**

ISBN/EAN: 9783337172886

Printed in Europe, USA, Canada, Australia, Japan

Cover: Foto ©ninafisch / pixelio.de

More available books at **www.hansebooks.com**

Delivered by Noted Speakers During the World's Fair Season

AT THE

BIBLE INSTITUTE

OF THE

CHICAGO EVANGELIZATION SOCIETY.

———

CHICAGO:
TUPPER & ROBERTSON, PUBLISHERS,
1896.

# CONTENTS.

| | |
|---|---:|
| The Epistle to the Romans—Prof. J. M. Stifler | 1 |
| The Holy Spirit.—Rev. J. H. Brookes | 31 |
| The Inspiration of the Old Testament.—Rev. J. H. Brookes | 39 |
| The Resurrection—Dr. L. W. Munhall | 51 |
| The Fullness of God.—Rev. A. C. Dixon, D.D. | 59 |
| Necessary Qualifications for Christian Work.—Rev. B. Fay. Mills | 65 |
| Soul Winning.—Rev. H. M. Wharton, D.D. | 71 |
| Working for Christ.—Rev. H. M. Wharton, D.D. | 75 |
| Authenticity of the Scriptures.—Rev. R. G. Pearson | 81 |
| Faith.—Rev. R. G. Pearson | 85 |
| The Baptism of the Holy Ghost.—Rev. G. H. C. Macgregor, M.A. | 91 |
| Walking With God.—Rev. G. H. C. Macgregor, M.A. | 99 |
| Humanity's Headlight.—H. L. Hastings | 107 |
| Jesus as Our Example in Preaching.—Major D. W. Whittle | 121 |
| Christ in the Old Testament.—Major D. W. Whittle | 127 |
| Public Reading of the Word of God.—Rev. Arthur T. Pierson, D.D | 151 |
| Methods of Studying the Word of God.—Rev. Arthur T. Pierson, D.D | 157 |
| The Unity of the Word of God.—Rev. Arthur T. Pierson, D.D | 165 |
| The Spirit and His Work.—Rev. Arthur T. Pierson, D.D | 183 |
| God's Independence of Man's Wisdom.—Rev. Arthur T. Pierson, D.D. | 195 |
| Jesus Christ in the Two Testaments,—Rev. Arthur T. Pierson, D.D. | 207 |

# Lectures on the Epistle to the Romans.

## By Prof. J. M. Stifler.

THE Epistle to the Romans was written by the Apostle Paul, at Corinth, A. D. 58. Its genuineness and authenticity have never been seriously questioned. It is the universal epistle, in that it presents the Gospel in a way suited to all nations and to all times. It is the Gospel of the Resurrection. The resurrection is mentioned in chapters 1:4; 4:17, 24, 25; 5:10; 6:4, 5, 9; 7:4; 8:11, 34; 10:9, and perhaps in 11:15, but these citations only show where the thought of the resurrection comes to the surface. It underlies every argument. It is the key to the epistle.

It is the fundamental epistle. It deals with the foundation of the faith. If the Epistle to the Ephesians carries the reader into the heights, this one permits him to peer into the depths.

The Epistle to the Romans, from first to last, is grounded on the Old Testament as no other is, not even Hebrews. See especially the fourth chapter and the fifth, with its parallel between Adam and Christ. The seventh chapter is more like Hebrews. Chapters nine to eleven have the Old Testament continually in view.

The Epistle embraces four great topics:

I. Sin—Chapters 1; 3:20.

II. Righteousness—Chapter 3:21, to the end of the eighth chapter.

III. The present and future relation of the Jews—Chapters 9–11.

IV. Hortatory matters—Chapter 12 to the end of the Epistle.

## LECTURE I.—CHAPTER 1.

This chapter contains three main divisions. First, the Salutation, verses 1-7; second, the Introduction, leading up to the theme of righteousness by faith, verses 8-17; third, the universal sinfulness of the Gentiles, verses 18-32.

In the Salutation the writer first of all identifies himself. As to his relation, he is a servant of Jesus Christ; as to his office, an apostle; as to his ground or authority, he is called. He is exclusively engaged with the Gospel.

After the identification of himself he begins the exaltation of his theme, the Gospel. (a) It was promised from ancient times by God's prophets and the Holy Scriptures. Note that he recognizes the prophets as God's, and that he calls the Scriptures holy. (b) The Gospel is concerned about One, the most Exalted, whether considered in His human or in His divine relations. Considered on the human side, Jesus is royal, the Son of David; considered on the divine side, He is higher than all angels. He is the Son of God. His Sonship is proven by His resurrection. Immediately upon the mention of the resurrection Paul mentions his apostleship, and this to show its character. It is from the raised Christ who is universal.

In this Salutation all the essential facts of the Gospel are assumed as true. The Gospel was promised in the Old Testament. The Old Testament is holy. Jesus was the Messiah, the Son of David. Jesus is Divine, the Son of God, and chief of all His resurrection from the dead is a fact.

Having addressed them officially, he now writes personally and with less formality. In this introduction he asserts first of all his thankfulness for them and his interest in them, as well as his desire to see them. It is no fault of his that he has not visited them before this time. He wishes to see them that he may impart to them some "spiritual gift." This gift, then, whatever it was, could not be conveyed by the letter. It depended on his presence. His failure to visit them hitherto is not because he was ashamed to preach the Gospel in Rome. He is not ashamed of the Gospel, because it is a power, and men are never ashamed of power. It is a power for salvation, and the reason of this efficacy is that the Gospel reveals a righteousness from God, a righteousness whose sole condition is faith.

The argument of the Epistle begins with the eighteenth verse. The opening statement is that God's righteous wrath is universally revealed against all unrighteousness and ungodliness of men. After this initial statement, he confines his view for the rest of the chapter to the Gentiles. God is angry with them because they know. They know because He, Himself, has revealed Himself. He has revealed Himself in nature in the things that He has made. His works are from the beginning and everywhere seen; therefore He has made Himself everywhere known from the foundation of the world. That which is known about Him is His eternal power and Godhead, so that if men sinned they are without excuse.

God's revelation of Himself did not fail. "They knew God," but in spite of their knowledge they refused to glorify Him as God. They turned from the light, and in their darkness fell, first, into idolatry; second, into sensuality; and third, into every species of immorality. A closing verse of the section shows their wantonness and defiance in their wickedness. "Who, knowing the judgment of God, that they who commit such things are worthy of death, not only do the same, but have pleasure in them that do them."

This section gives us the history of religion from the beginning. It asserts that, at the first, men knew God. From this point it exhibits a religious development downward. When men knew God they refused to worship Him, and degenerated into idolatry; hence men at the first were monotheists and not idolators. As the Scriptures elsewhere teach, idolatry is not as old as the race. Man did not grope his way through fetichism and polytheism to monotheism; his course was just the reverse, from the knowledge of the one true God to the worship of the many.

This section teaches that the heathen are responsible even without the Bible and without the Gospel. They have that older Bible, God's works in nature in which He reveals Himself, a Bible that is universal. The section declares that men are responsible and condemnable for their refusal of that light which nature gives about the character of God.

## LECTURE II.—CHAPTER 2; 3: 20.

Having shown in this section that the Gentiles are universally sinners, he proves the same about the Jews. In convicting the Gentiles the Apostle had but to point to their history. Facts were his arguments. Here the task is not so easy. The Jew is in covenant relations with God, and His professed worshiper. The Apostle first lays down a major premise in which he discusses the character of the judgment. There are four points: (a) the judgment would be according to truth; (b) it will be according to works; (c) it will be without respect to persons; (d) it will be according to "My Gospel" (2: 1-16).

A judgment according to truth means that in that final hour God will look upon men and their deeds just as they are. The Apostle does not argue that point, but makes a twofold appeal to his readers, first, against a false reckoning in the matter; and second, against contempt of God's goodness (2: 1-5).

A judgment according to deeds or works is one that does not turn upon dead faith and idle convictions. The Apostle does not argue this point, but presents a long, appositional sentence showing what the deeds are. These consist not in what are usually called works, but in the aim and persistence in that which is good or evil (2: 6-10).

A judgment without respect of persons means one in which the Jew will have no advantage because he is a Jew. If, just because he has the law, he can stand in the judgment, so also can the Gentile, for the latter had what is tantamount to the law. The Gentile shows the work of the law written in his heart (2: 11-15).

A judgment according to Paul's Gospel looks at the universal character of the truth as he preached it. The facts of the Gospel, whether proclaimed by Peter or Paul, are ever the same; but Paul presented them in a way fitted to the whole world; Peter, in a way suited more especially to the Jew (verse 17. See Gal. 2: 7).

After exhibiting the nature of the judgment in its fourfold elements, after this major premise, with the seventeenth verse he begins the direct application to the Jew. The order of his argument here is the same as that pursued in showing the sinfulness of the Gentile, first the Jew knows, for he has the law and he teaches it, and he who teaches another, does he not teach himself? Now Paul does not declare that the Jew is guilty of the same three sins charged against the Gentile—idolatry, sensuality, and general immorality. He simply asks the question, "Thou that preachest a man should not steal, dost thou steal?" "Thou that sayest a man should not commit adultery, dost thou commit adultery?" "Thou that abhorrest idols, dost thou rob temples?" Yes, for the name of God is blasphemed among the Gentiles through you, as the Scriptures declare. In these short, pointed questions the appeal is to the Jew's conscience. He could not deny his guilt in these three directions.

It is to be noticed that in speaking of these three sins, he reverses the order. In convicting the Gentile the order was from idolatry to immorality. Here it is from immorality to idolatry. The reason for the change is, first, that there he was giving a natural development. Here we have a religious development, but the chief reason for the reversal of the order is that Paul might make his statement climactic. To a Jew, idolatry was the acme of sin; therefore Paul framed his argument so as to bring it in last.

We have now reached the twenty-fifth verse. The Jew would claim that he had the shield of circumcision, and that, after all, he was a Jew. The Apostle tears away this refuge by showing the intent of circumcision. It was profitable if a man kept the law, otherwise it would be a premium on a bad life. Furthermore, uncircumcision was no disadvantage if a man did that which was right. To be a Jew was not simply to wear the name, but to be a Jew at heart.

Paul sees that this true exposition of circumcision raised a serious objection which must be removed before the argument can advance. He proceeds to do this in chapter 3: 1-8. If the uncircumcised man by keeping the law stands on a level with the follower of Moses, what advantage then has the Jew, and what is the profit of circumcision? His answer is, that the Jew has the oracles of God. He is embraced in the covenants. That the oracles of God were committed to him does not mean that he was simply the depository of the sacred books, but that he was involved in the blessing which they promised.

He might be an unbeliever, but his unbelief did not annul the faithfulness of God who would somehow make these promises good. The Apostle does not complete this argument until he takes it up anew in the ninth chapter. But the Jew's failure makes the faithfulness of God all the more conspicuous. The black background of the Jew's failure makes God's mercy toward him shine all the brighter. Thus the Jew, by his sins, seems to have done God a favor. Why, therefore, should he be punished for his sin? The question demands too much. If God may not punish the Jew for his sin, neither may he punish the world for the world's sin, sets out in bright colors the long-suffering mercy of God toward it. Indeed, the Jew's objection that God cannot righteously punish his sin because that sin enhances God's glory, comes to this absurd extreme that we may do evil in order that good may come.

At the ninth verse of the third chapter begins the scriptural argument that the Jew first, as well as all others, is a sinner before God. These quotations from the Old Testament Scriptures are methodically arranged so that they give:

1. State, 10-12.
2. Conduct, { Word, 13-14. Action, 15-17.
3. Source, 18.

As to man's state, there is no one righteous. It is his sin that he does not understand. It is his sin that he does not seek after God. He has left God's way and betaken himself to his own. The word "unprofitable" is powerful as well as picturesque. It means corrupt beyond any human power of recovery.

As to his conduct, we have an anatomical view proceeding from the throat outward to the tongue, the lips, and the mouth.

As to their action, their feet are swift to shed blood. That which is left in their track is destruction and misery. As the race has come down through the centuries, what has it left behind it? Though the search for peace and stability has been earnest, that way has not been found, "the way of peace have they not known."

The cause of all this sin and misery is that God's fear is not before their eyes.

That the Jew may not escape the point of these quotations the Apostle declares (3: 19, 20) that what is written in their law must apply primarily to themselves. The Jew having now been shown a sinner, the climax is reached that all the world is guilty before God. Guilty, because deeds of law cannot justify in His sight for, practically, the law simply brings about a knowledge of sin, a statement that will be unfolded when we reach the seventh chapter.

### LECTURE III.—CHAPTER 3:21; 4.

At chapter 3:21 the discussion of salvation begins. There are two main divisions. From 3:21 to the end of the fifth chapter we have the topic of justification. Chapters 6-8 give an exposition of sanctification.

To return to 3:21, we find *righteousness described*. It stands apart from law and is from God, but is witnessed by the law and the prophets. Its condition is faith in Jesus Christ. In its actual intent it is for all who believe. For all, because there is no difference among men. All have sinned, and though not to the same extent, yet all are coming short of the approbation or glory of God. They are justified, that is, accounted righteous without cost to themselves, or freely. The source of this righteousness is God's grace. Its means is the redemption which is in Christ Jesus. This redemption is not found outside or apart from Him (Eph. 1:7). This redemption is in Him because God set Him forth on the cross as a propitiatory sacrifice by means of faith, setting Him forth thus in His blood. This sacrificial spectacle took place to declare God's holiness in passing over past and present sins, so that God is now just in justifying the man who believes in Jesus. Now (verses 27-31) since men are all sinners and are justified, when they are justified alone by God's grace no man can boast. The Jew has no exclusive claim on God, for He is one, and is God of both Jew and Gentile, and justifies all by the same means, namely, faith.

The fourth chapter looks at the same subject from the Old Testament point of view. The Old Testament seems to make a difference between Jew and Gentile, and on the face of it to teach salvation by works of law. Therefore, does not justification by faith make the Old Testament, or in other words the law, to be of no effect? To answer this question the Apostle looks into the Old Testament to see how Abraham was saved. He was justified not by works, for the Scripture says he believed God, and it was reckoned to him for righteousness. Paul shows that this means that Abraham did not work, but believed on Him who justified, that is held guiltless, the ungodly. He understood that God's mercy was intended to save sinners. Salvation by grace excludes all works. David, in the Thirty-second Psalm, teaches the same doctrine when he describes the blessedness of the men to whom God reckons righteousness without works (4:1-8).

This is the first point showing that Abraham was justified by faith. The second is that he was justified when still uncircumcised, that is, while yet a heathen. Verse eleven shows that his circumcision, instead of making him righteous before God, was a seal of the righteousness which he already had. He had a righteousness in both conditions, circumcised and uncircumcised, that he might be the father, that is, the racial head of both believing Jews and believing Gentiles (4:10-12).

In the third place, Paul shows that he received the promise of the heirship of the world, *not* on the ground of law, but on the ground of faith. Only thus could the promise be realized. Had it been conditioned on works of law, first, faith would have been out of the question, and the promise would have been nugatory. Law cannot realize any promise, but invariably brings down God's wrath; but where there is no law, as there was not in the case of Abraham's promise, there is of course no transgression, and so, no wrath. Hence, the promise can be realized as a gracious, free gift to a justified sinner (4:13-17).

The last point to prove, that faith does not make void the law, stands in this, that the faith demanded by the Gospel is of the same character as that exercised by Abraham. He had to believe in God as one who makes alive the dead, and the believer in the Gospel believes that same thing, that the Jesus who was delivered for our offenses was raised again for our justification. "If thou shalt confess with thy mouth the Lord Jesus, and shalt believe in thine heart that God hath raised Him from the dead, thou shalt be saved. (Rom. 10:9; 4:17-25.)

## LECTURE IV.—CHAPTER 5.

Having shown that men are justified by faith, and that this is in harmony with the Old Testament Scriptures, the fifth chapter shows that this justification is permanent. It affords a sure hope.

That this hope is well founded is demonstrated, first, by the effect of tribulations, which make this hope a tried hope (verses 3, 4). Secondly, this hope, strengthened by trial, does not make ashamed because it is swathed in love from God shed abroad in the heart by the Holy Spirit (verse 5). Without this gift of love the justified sinner's hope would seem like madness. What would be thought of the obscure, untitled young man, who should say that he has a certain hope of being son-in-law to the good Queen of England? He would be considered daft. But if at the same time he could exhibit on his finger one of the crown jewels, the "Kohinoor," given him by the Queen, we would admit his claim. The justified sinner has in his heart the jewel of God's love toward him. With that in his possession, unworthy man though he is, his hope does not put him to shame. To bring out the strength of this argument the character of this love is shown (verses 6-8). It surpasses anything known in human history. At the best men can die for the good. But God commendeth His love in that while we were yet sinners Christ died for us. The conclusion comes then in the ninth verse — he who is justified by this blood, provided by God, will surely be saved. This conclusion is again supported (verse 10) by a statement in the form of a triple antithesis, like that in Mark 7: 8.

Laying aside....commandment....of God.
Ye hold...........tradition.......of men.

Here it stands:—
Enemies....reconciled to God....death
Reconciled........saved..........life.

If God could do so much for His enemies what can He not do now for those who are in a reconciled state? Again, if God could become reconciled with men when enemies, can He not remain reconciled (which insures ultimate salvation) now that they have become friends? And once more, if the death of

Christ, a negative power, could do so much, what will not His life, His active energy on high in their behalf, what will not such life insure? Why, it gives more than hope, it gives "joy in God" (verse 11).

This completes the second argument for hope. This hope is supported by a love of such a character that it provided a Saviour not only to die, but to live on high for the believer (8: 32).

The third argument is found in the parallel between Christ and Adam, "who is the figure of Him that was to come." Adam was so related to men that his one sin involved all his posterity in death, even without any sin of their own; for, though men sinned from Adam to Moses, the individual's own sin could not be charged against him, for there was no law from Adam to Moses by which to convict men of a sin, at least no law like that against which Adam transgressed. Men died for Adam's sin. Through the offense of the one the many died. (Verse 15. See Rev. Ver.)

Now just such a relation exists between Christ and His followers, so that life is assured to them not by any good which they may do, but by the one righteous act which He has done. The hope of eternal life is not based on any human act, but on an unfailing relation to Christ, Death never fails to come to those in Adam. How can life fail to those in Christ? "Therefore as by the offense of one it (the offense) was to all to condemnation (of death), even so by the righteousness of the One it (the righteousness) was upon all men unto justification of life" (verse 18). The parallel in the relation between those in Adam and those in Christ to their respective heads is complete, and something more. For the argument stops in verses 15-17 to show how "much more" certainly men in Christ will be saved than men in Adam will die; and yet the latter is certain. The power for life in Christ is both stronger (verse 15) and broader (verses 16, 17) than the power for death in Adam.

It follows, then, that hope cannot make ashamed for trials, only root it deeper. God's love toward the justified man cannot fail, and his union with his Saviour cannot be broken. That hope stands not on a foundation of flesh but in the love and power of God.

## LECTURE V.—CHAPTER 6.

When Paul concluded the discussion of the permanence of justification by faith he glanced at the law. It came in, not at all, to save men, but that the "trespass might abound," but where sin abounded grace superabounded. This suggests the inquiry: "May we not continue in sin that grace may abound?" He gives a twofold answer in the negative. (a) We are dead to sin (6:2-7), and (b) we are alive with Christ (8-11).

To die to sin does not mean that evil passions and desires perish from the heart. Christ died to sin, and the moment any one accepts Him, that same divine power operates on his heart; so that instantly the believer finds himself possessed of a power over sin. This power is not in man except when he is *in Christ*. Baptism signifies the same thing. It is a burial with Christ into death, but it is more. It is also a resurrection with Him to a new life. Paul now (verse 6) changes his figure to say that our old man was crucified with Him. The old man is the former unregenerated self. He that is crucified with Christ has met sin's penalty, and so is free from sin.

On the other hand, if one dies *with* Him, the emphasis is on the word "with," he shall also live with Him. The assurance of this turns on the deathlessness of Christ, hence verses 8-10 prove that Christ once raised dies no more. The word "reckon" is all-significant. The ability to lead a good life lies in *reckoning* ourselves to be what the Gospel declares we are, dead to sin, but alive to God in Christ Jesus our Lord.

An exhortation follows in verses 12-14. In saying, "Let not sin reign that we should obey its desires," it is to be noted that he admits that sin's desires are still present in the believer's heart, but their reign is broken, and they are uncrowned when one reckons himself dead, etc. It is by this reckoning of faith, and not merely by prayer and watchfulness and the like, that the "let not" is attained. The concluding assertion is, that sin cannot dominate because we are not under law, but under grace (verse 14).

This starts a second inquiry, whether we may commit an act of sin. The answer is found in the nature of sin, and in the nature of righteousness. He who sins becomes enslaved to sin, the end of which is eternal death. One cannot sin, and by repentance and forgiveness step back to the same freedom that he had before he sinned. Though the guilt of a sin may be removed, its other consequences may remain. But it is also blessedly true, that he who practices righteousness becomes, so to speak, enslaved to righteousness, the end of which is eternal life. Therefore he exhorts them to follow righteousness.

For this metaphor, "servants of righteousness," he gives an explanation. They are really not servants, but he speaks in this fashion on account of the feebleness of their spiritual apprehension.

Continuance in sin, as well as sinning, is prevented, not by mere force of will, not by religious activities, useful and proper as these may be in their place, but by an *intelligent faith* in Jesus Christ. To believe in Jesus may mean anything, or perhaps, nothing profitable; and therefore we say "intelligent" belief. This intelligence is gained in the Scriptures, which teach us what Christ has become to us. His death is our death, His crucifixion is our crucifixion, His resurrection is our resurrection; not yet the resurrection of the body, but that our spirit is touched and strengthened with resurrection power. Hence, when it is said, "Reckon yourselves dead," and, "Reckon yourselves alive," this means that we must *account* ourselves to be *in Christ* just what the Scriptures declare we are. And he who can so reckon himself, whether he can understand the Gospel or not, finds sin's power broken in his heart.

## LECTURE VI.—CHAPTER 7.

This chapter deals with the nature of law and with the believer's relation to it. The law has already been mentioned several times. In chapter 3: 20 the law was said to give a full knowledge of sin. In 5: 20 the law was said to be added that the fall might abound. In 4: 14 it was said, "Ye are not under law but under grace." In the chapter now before us these fragmentary assertions are amplified, and the whole subject of law considered; but the immediate reference is to the passage in 4: 14. First of all in chapter 7: 1-6, Paul shows how and why the Romans were delivered from law. He begins with the assertion of the perpetual validity of law. It has dominion over man as long as he lives. He illustrates this feature of law: The woman who has a husband is bound by the marriage law as long as he lives. If he dies she is at liberty to be married to another man. There seems at first sight to be a lack of correspondence here between the principle and Paul's illustration. He said that the law bound the man while he lived, but in the illustration it is the man who dies, but the woman is thereby set free. This lack of correspondence, however, gives the very point of the matter; for when the husband died, the wife died too, since by the nature of marriage they were one. The wife died, but the woman remained. Such is his illustration. The application is found in the fourth verse, so that ye also, my brethren, died to the law by the body of Christ as the wife died to the marriage law in the death of her husband, in order that as she may now be married to another, ye also may be married to Him who is raised from the dead. This very simple and almost commonplace illustration is after all most profound. The illustration implies two husbands. In the case of the Christian what corresponds to the two is the Christ before the tomb and the Christ after the tomb. The latter is significantly called the "other," to which the Romans were wed. The believer's Christ is far more than the Christ of the Gospels. It is union with the raised Christ that saves. (See II Cor. 5:16). Salvation is very much more than an imitation of Christ. It is union with Him—"That ye might be married to another, even to Him who is raised from the dead." To believe *in* Christ is to take the present living Christ, just as a woman takes a man for a husband. It is this union that is the source of fruitfulness, love, joy, peace, etc. Service to God is not service in the oldness of the letter of the law, but in the newness of the spirit, given in this marriage relation with Christ.

The teaching that we must be delivered from the law to be fruitful, raises the objection, "Is the law sin?" Paul declares it is not, and his argument is that it reveals sin. He refers to the Tenth Commandment. He declares that he would not have known desire if the law had not said, "Thou shalt not desire." As the law laid its restraining hand upon his will, so he found it also restraining all his desires. The result was that every kind of desire was roused up within him. When he was told to want nothing, he found he wanted everything; that is, his heart rebelled against the Tenth Commandment, and before it he found himself a dead man. He was alive before he knew what the law meant, that is, before it "came," but when he found its deep spiritual significance he died before it, and this is his experimental argument. The law showed him that he was a sinner. He concludes, therefore, that the law is holy and the commandment is holy and just and good.

A new and apparently unanswerable objection (verse 13) arises now—"Was that which is good made death to me?" Does pure water poison? Does wholesome food kill? No, he adds, but the moral disease within seized upon that which was good and slew me. How desperate then must be the disease which works death by that which is good. Sin is exceeding sinful, in that it destroys a man by the law which is holy.

Paul has now reached the point (verse 14) in which he can show man's conduct under the law. Man is carnal or natural; the law it spiritual. They differ in their nature. It is as impossible for man to keep the law as it would be for him to fly. He is not adapted to skim the air; the law of gravity is against him.

There has been no little controversy as to the character of the person here contemplated. Is he regenerate or unregenerate? The Bible never leaves vital questions unanswered, and since this question cannot be determined, we may be sure that it is not vital. Any earnest man, saved or unsaved, who undertakes to keep God's law apart from Christ, is sure to have the experience here detailed.

It has been questioned, also, whether or not Paul is here giving his own experience. It may have been his own experience, but most likely he is himself personating the character of one who should attempt to obey the law, without knowing, or without believing the Gospel.

The section shows in three dirges the experience of a resolute seeker after righteousness under the law. The first dirge (verses 15-17) teach such a man that he is under sin, which is his master. The second dirge (verses 18-20) shows that the master occupies the whole house, "For I know that there dwells in me, that is, in my flesh, no good thing." The third dirge (verses 21-24) drops all figurative language, and states plainly the sad condition of the man seeking righteousness under the law. He approves God's law (chapter 2 : 17-20), but he sees another law in his members enslaving him to the law of sin and death within his members. The condition is so painful it wrings from him the cry, "Oh, wretched man that I am, who shall deliver me from the body (his own body) of this death?" The answer is, "Jesus Christ," stated briefly in verse twenty-five because it has been fully unfolded before.

To sum up, then, the teaching of these three dirges, it comes to this, that I myself, apart from Christ, unconscious of the spirituality of the law, with my mind do homage to the law, but with my flesh am enslaved to sin, a divided state whose fruit is spiritual wretchedness.

This seventh chapter teaches then clearly why man must be delivered from the law to be saved. It teaches the office of the law and its holiness. It also shows that the most earnest efforts to keep its behests show the impossibility of keeping them.

## LECTURE VII.—CHAPTER 8.

This is the chapter that begins with no condemnation and ends with no separation. If the last chapter taught the misery of a man under law, this chapter gives the happy condition of a man in Christ. Its idea is not wholly unlike that of the fifth chapter. There it was the certainty of justification in itself considered. Here it is the same certainty in the midst of every conflict. Conflict with the flesh within, and the world about.

This chapter has four main divisions: It shows, first, how the man in Christ is delivered from the flesh (verses 1-11); secondly, it shows his sonship (verses 12-17); thirdly, it teaches how he is sustained in a life of trials (verses 17-30); fourthly, it concludes with a pæan of victory (verses 31-39).

I. Since in the preceding chapters he has shown the redemption in Christ Jesus, he can now easily say there is *no* condemnation to the man who is in Christ Jesus. The emphasis is on the word "no." Christ overcomes not only the guilt of sin, but also its power in the flesh. There is therefore no condemnation from either law or conscience. In the second verse he is looking only at the sinfulness of the flesh when he says, "The law of the spirit of life in Christ Jesus has set me at liberty from the law of sin and death." The law of the spirit of life is the Holy Spirit in His delivering power. He is found only in Christ Jesus. The law of sin and death is that force which the seventh chapter of Romans shows to be too great even for an earnest man to conquer. It is the law in the members bringing the man into captivity. This law or force is overcome in the man in Christ Jesus by the law of the spirit found in him. A man could fly over a broad, deep chasm, but that the law of gravity drags him down. If, however, he enters a balloon, another law operates there, by which he may safely cross the chasm. While he is in the balloon gravity is not dead, but it can not operate. While a man is in Christ, the law of sin and death in his members has no power.

All this, however, is true only of those "who walk not after the flesh but after the spirit," for they who live in accordance with the flesh, mind the things of the flesh. They cannot do otherwise, for the mind of the flesh is enmity against God, because it cannot subject itself to his law. This inability is the very acme of wickedness, that a man cannot do what a holy God commands.

At the close of this first section he looks briefly at the resurrection of the body. He declares that the Romans are not in the flesh, but in the spirit, because God's spirit dwells in them. He asserts that if one have not the Spirit of Christ, which is the Holy Spirit, he does not belong to Him, but when Christ dwells in one, the body is still dead on account of sin, but the spirit is alive on account of righteousness; and He who raised up Jesus from the dead will ultimately bring life to the mortal body, the same happy life which the Spirit already has.

II. To live after the flesh is to live for death, but if by the power of the spirit in Christ the deeds of the body are destroyed, "Ye shall live." Note that the deeds of the body cannot be destroyed but by the Spirit. The emphasis is on the words "by the Spirit." They that are thus led by the Spirit, putting to death the deeds of the body, are the sons of God, who have not received the old legal spirit of bondage, but the new spirit of adoption, whereby the first word of the Lord's Prayer, "Our Father," becomes real and significant. Union with Christ by the Spirit gives sonship, and from sonship everything else follows, heirship, heirship jointly with Christ who is also Himself the Son.

III. Why should the sons of God suffer? Suffering is the one path that leads to glory. If we suffer with Him, it is that we may be glorified with His glory.

Suffering is inevitable, but there are three considerations for those who follow Christ amidst sorrows and trials akin to His:

1. First, the follower of Christ is sustained by hope. However great the sufferings, they are not worthy to be compared with the glory which is going to be revealed for us. Paul proceeds now to give an idea of the vastness of this glory. It is so very great that the creation is represented as awaiting it on the tiptoe of expectation. But why speak of the glorification of creation? Because it was made subject to vanity and is personified as groaning and travailing in pain, and it is to be delivered from its bondage of corruption, girt about it by the pristine curse, into the glorious liberty of God's sons. Therefore it awaits their glorification, because it will be permitted to share in it.

Not only does material and irrational creation groan in suffering, but we also, who have the first fruits of the glory to come, namely, the Spirit. We also groan in expectation of the completion of our adoption, viz.: the redemption of the body. "For we were saved in hope" (verse 24). This signifies that when saved from sin we were not saved from all the conditions of sin, for if we now saw the whole of our salvation there would be nothing to hope for; but since we do not see all, we are animated by patient hope. (Compare in I Peter 1:5, 9).

2. Secondly, Christ's follower is sustained by the Holy Spirit, (verses 26, 27). He helps in our weakness. Though He helps in every way, only one point is mentioned, prayer. This is the simplest of all Christian exercises, and yet we do not know what we should pray for as we ought, but in the intensity of His desire in the heart He makes intercession for the saints, with groan-

ings which cannot be expressed in words. But while there are no words, God knows the meaning of His groans, and answers accordingly, for this intercessor in the heart pleads only according to God. Doubtless it was this passage that gave birth to the hymn,

> "Prayer is the soul's sincere desire,
> Unuttered or expressed."

The Scriptures teach, then, that the follower of Christ has two intercessors, one in the heart and the other in the presence of the Father (I John 2:2). The Holy Spirit, who is the intercessor in the heart, has to do especially with trials, afflictions, and sorrows.

3. The Christian, in his sufferings, is sustained by the Providence of God, and his gracious purposes toward him. "All things work together for good to those who love God." The word "all" can be received only by faith. It embraces all sufferings, all trials, indeed all the powers of opposition mentioned in the close of the chapter. Again, it is to be noticed that there are no accidents in the believer's life, for all things work harmoniously together, under the Divine guidance, and there is nothing effecting the believer which does not conduce to his ultimate good. The reason for all this is that those whom God foreknew, that is, those with whom he entered into saving relations, he also predestinated to be conformed to the image of His Son. This means that His own people, whom He chose from eternity, were so chosen that ultimately they might be like Christ. It is because God has determined this high destiny for them that He preserves them and keeps them, and turns every vicissitude of their life toward their good. God's providence, from the eternity of the past to the glory of the future, attends a believer at every step. The very ones whom He predestinated, these He also called; the ones whom He called, He also justified; and whom He justified, these He also glorified. God's grace toward His own is like a five-link golden chain, reaching from the beginning of His purpose toward His people to its consummation in their glory.

IV. With the thirty-second verse Paul begins a strain of triumph: "What shall we say to these things?" "If God is for His people who can be against them?" It is not God in His might, but God in His infinite grace. He spared not His own Son in His purpose of love toward His people, which is a pledge that with the giving of Him He will surely give all the rest necessary to bring them to glory; for having given the Son all else, sweet and necessary as it is, is yet small in comparison. He who should make a present of a costly and precious stone would not hesitate to give with it the case that inclosed it. How can anyone lay anything to the charge of God's elect after God has declared them guiltless? Can anyone condemn? Against such condemnation Christ is a fourfold answer. He died, He rose, He is at the right hand of God, He intercedes for us. Here we have the other intercessor. He is mentioned once again in Heb. 7:25.

Paul asks one more triumphant question: "Who shall separate from God's love toward us in Christ Jesus?" In the pain of tribulation, in the sorrow of distress, in the tumult of persecution, in the suffering of famine, in the shame of nakedness, in danger, in judicial punishment by the sword, God's love is still toward His people, so that they are more than conquerors through Him that loved them. What is it to be more than a conqueror? To be unconquerable? These Romans had an illustration in their own history. Hannibal held their country in his grip for some years and surrounded their city, but though he was conqueror the Romans defeated him by being unconquerable. Neither death with its terrors, nor life with its perils and temptations, nor bad angels, nor Satanic principalities or powers, nor the things about us, nor the things to come,—the future is often contemplated in fear—nor height, nor depth, nor any other created thing shall separate us from the Creator in His love toward us in Christ Jesus our Lord.

## LECTURE VIII.—CHAPTERS 9, 10, 11.

This section is peculiar in the New Testament. It belongs appropriately to the fundamental and universal epistle. The Old Testament, on which Paul has grounded this epistle, knows nothing about a church in which Jew and Gentile came together on a level, a church which gave the Jew no preference and blotted out every national distinction. The Old Testament promised the salvation of the Jew and of the Gentile, but the

Jew was to have the leadership and the pre-eminence. This is to be noticed everywhere, but see especially Isaiah, chapters 2 and 61, and Zachariah, chapter 14.

Another difficulty confronted Paul. The Old Testament promised that when the Messiah came He would redeem the Jew, give him his pre-eminence and headship in the earth. This was the burden of the song of Zacharias (Luke 1: 67-79). Now, how is it that this Jesus whom Paul preaches is the Messiah, if as is the fact the Jews are not saved nationally? To firmly establish the Messiaship of Jesus, and to vindicate the scripturalness of the Gospel as he unfolded it, Paul must answer this question. In this section he addresses himself to this task.

### PART I.

In chapters 9 and 10 he deals with the failure of the Jew. In chapter 9: 1-29, it is shown that his failure is after all not a failure of the Old Testament scriptures. In chapter 9: 30, to the end of the tenth chapter, Paul shows why he failed. We have thus two sections in this first part.

In the first section (9: 1-29) Paul begins by vehemently asserting his interest in those who are his own flesh and blood. In the Spirit of Christ he could wish himself accursed on their behalf. He recites their seven magnificent privileges: theirs was the adoption. Of all the nations of the earth, God chose them alone to be His. Theirs was the glory of the presence of God. Theirs was the covenant, made first with Abraham and renewed to his descendants. Theirs was the giving of the law. Theirs was the service of leading God's worship in the world. Theirs were the promises that seem now not to be realized. Theirs were the fathers, Abraham, Isaac, and Jacob. And they had one more honor, but this not exclusively theirs. The language varies to say that from them came the Christ according to the flesh, that Christ who is God over all and blessed forever.

But in spite of these glorious privileges Israel has failed. At this point (verse 6) he takes up the proposition of the section that after all the word of God has not failed. For, first, the promises of the Old Testament were not made to them on the ground that they were the natural descendants of Abraham. "Neither because they are Abraham's seed are they all children." It was in Isaac that the true seed was called. This little phrase "in Isaac" is very significant; it not only excludes Ishmael, but more than all it shows the character or condition of the true seed. Isaac was a supernatural child, born through the aid of divine power, and in consequence of God's promises to Sarah. And such are all the true seed, not natural but supernatural children.

That only the promised supernatural children are the heirs is proved further by the case of Rebekah. Here, unlike the story of Ishmael and Isaac, there were twin children, and before they were born or could possibly have done anything good or evil, God again reversed nature, and asserted his purpose that "the older should serve the younger." He did this that his purpose of salvation might stand not on human works but on His own inscrutible choice. The sharp word of Scripture is, "Jacob have I loved and Esau have I hated."

This assertion of God's interference, to establish His own purpose, raises the serious objection (verse 14), "Is there unrighteousness with God?" That He chose Jacob for no assignable reason, chose him not because He foresaw his faith and the suitableness of his character for the divine purpose, is put beyond doubt by the raising of this question; for if any reason could be given for His choice of Jacob and rejection of Esau, that reason precluded this painful inquiry, "Is there unrighteousness with God?" In answering the question he cites first of all two very striking Old Testament instances. When Moses sought a blessing (Ex. 33: 19) God taught him that he gained it not because he was Moses, but because God would have mercy on whom He would have mercy, and would have compassion on whom He would have compassion. This corresponds to Jacob's case. The other instance is more striking, that of Pharaoh, in regard to whom the Scripture says, that God raised him up to show His power in him, and that His name might be announced in all the earth. Pharaoh's history corresponds thus to Esau.

These Scripture citations throw the objection into another form: "Why then does He still find fault, for who resists His will?" If Pharaoh became the means for the display of the divine power, and for the spreading abroad of God's name, why should God be angry with him and punish him? Why should God choose Jacob and reject Esau before they had done anything good or bad? Why to-day should God take one man and leave out another equally as good?

In answer to this question, Paul in the most weighty manner asserts what is often called "the sovereignty of God." But what this really means is, that the Creator is the Creator, or that God is God. The very idea of God is that of a being who need not give any reason for anything which He does. If He must give a reason, that necessity is higher than He, and destroys His divinity. The idea of a God is that whatsoever He does is necessarily right. There can be no higher standard than His own pleasure.

This is Paul's answer to the question about the unrighteousness of God. He enforces it powerfully by the illustration of the potter. He intimates also that to ask it is impious: "Nay, but O man, who art thou that repliest against God?"

This simple and unmistakable teaching of the Scripture is hard to receive for three reasons: first, there lies back in the human heart the irreverent thought that really God ought not do so—that He has no right to choose after His own pleasure; secondly, it is vainly thought that by His sovereign purpose, man's opportunity for bliss is circumscribed, and that human rights are needlessly interfered with; thirdly, human reason cannot comprehend how there can be one absolute sovereign free will and other free wills. This third point is the only real difficulty; it has not been solved, it cannot be, but it is not peculiar to Christianity, but belongs to every religion that owns a personal God.

In the twenty-second verse, Paul shows that God has exercised His sovereignty in the greatest mercy. Though willing to show His wrath and to make His power known, He has after all borne in much long suffering with vessels of wrath fitted to destruction, and done this in order to make the riches of His glory known upon the vessels of mercy which He prepared beforehand for eternal glory. These vessels of mercy are selected from among both Jews and Gentiles.

In proof (verses 25-29) that God has His people both among the Jews and the Gentiles, in proof that He has exercised His sovereign mercy for salvation, he quotes the Old Testament Scriptures, first, to show that the Gentiles, who were not a people, and had no more right than Jacob to his favor, were yet taken for a people; and, secondly, to point out what Esaias says, that though the natural descendants of Abraham were numerous as the sand of the sea, only a remnant should be saved. He brings the argument for salvation by God's sovereign mercy alone. He brings this argument to a climax by another quotation from Isaiah, that but for God's electing grace Israel would have come to the condition of Sodom and Gomorrah. God's election keeps *no one* out of heaven. It is the sole reason why anyone even wishes to reach heaven, for in the third chapter we were taught of men that there is "none righteous, no, not one." "There is none that seeketh after God."

The second section (chapter 9:30; 10:21) shows why Israel failed. That reason is not because God did not elect them, but because they did not elect God. To be sure without His election they would not choose Him (Acts 13:48). But He was under no obligations to elect them, since He can be under none, and they were under obligations to follow Him, and it is their wickedness that they did not.

He gives five items in their perversity to account for their failure: first (10:30-33), the Jews failed to attain to righteousness because they sought it in the keeping of the law, and not by faith. They stumbled at that stumbling stone, the offer of Christ. They failed to see the significance of their own Scriptures which read, "He who is believing upon Him shall not be put to shame."

Secondly (10:1-4), they failed to see that Christ was the end or completion of the law, with a view to righteousness, to every one who believes on Him. When one accepted Christ by faith for righteousness, he had no further need of the law for the same purpose. In giving this item Paul stops again to show his affection for his own fallen people. Their failure was the more painful because they had a genuine and earnest zeal for God. But earnestness and zeal in religion can never take the place of intelligent obedience to the will of God.

Thirdly (10:5-11), the Jew failed because he did not see the gratuitous character of salvation. It does not impose some hard condition, or demand some impossible work, like ascending into heaven or descending into the deep, to find Christ; but it is like the air, "in thy mouth and in thy heart," to breathe which gives life. "With the heart man believes to righteousness and with the mouth confession is made to salvation." He concludes this point by again quoting the Scripture, "Whoever believes on Him shall not be put to shame."

Fourthly (10:12-18), the Jew failed because he did not see the universal character of salvation. It has been already shown in chapter three, and it is now repeated, that "there is no difference between the Jew and the Greek." "There is one Lord over all," and he is more than beneficent, "He is rich to all who call upon Him." Men cannot call upon Him without hearing of Him, but He has taken the means to make His truth universally known.

Fifthly (19-21), the Jews failed to see that all these things, together with their rebellion, were predicted in their own Scriptures. Even Moses foretold the acceptance of the Gentiles, and Esaias repeated it, in bold fashion, in saying that God "was found by those who did not seek Him." He also foretold the stubbornness and apostasy of Israel, in declaring that all the day long God "had stretched out His hands to a disobedient and caviling people."

## PART II.

In chapter eleven Paul deals with the present condition and future of the Jew. There are two main divisions: first (verses 1-10), the fall of the Jews is not total, and, secondly, their fall (verses 11-32) is not final. The chapter closes with a profound doxology (verses 33-36).

In the first section, in the question, "Has God cast away His people," it means Israel according to the flesh. Paul answers in the negative because he is himself a pure-blooded Israelite, of the seed of Abraham, of the tribe of Benjamin, and he is not cast away but is an example of many. Next he reiterates the denial, God has not cast away the descendants of Abraham whom He foreknew. The argument is in the word "foreknow," which means that He entered into relations with them, and He is not fickle like man to change (Mal. 3:6).

While to all appearance, even in the estimation of good men, the nation was in utter apostasy, the case was yet not so bad as that. It was now as in the days of Elijah. He thought himself the last and only worshiper of God in the whole nation, but God had at that time seven thousand who had not bowed the knee to Baal. The incident is typical. What God once does He will do again in a similar case. Hence Paul rightly infers that at his time of writing all were not lost, but there was a remnant according to the election of grace. The rest were hardened as the Scripture predicted it and explained it.

With the eleventh verse he takes up the second idea which is concerned with the larger but fallen portion of Israel. Did they stumble in order that they might fall? Was this the whole of the divine intent in their failure? By no means. By their fall salvation went to the Gentiles. The history of the case is given in the Book of Acts, beginning with chapter six. The Jews refused the Gospel, stoned Stephen and scattered the church, which went everywhere preaching the word. Since the Jews would not have the Gospel, and the believers in it were so full of the Spirit that they must speak, some of them (Acts 11:19-21) offered the Gospel to the heathen. It was thus that the Jews' obstinacy drove the Gospel into foreign lands.

But this acceptance of the Gospel on the part of the Gentiles will have a reaction (verse 14) on unbelieving Israel to provoke them to emulation, and if a few of them carried the word to all nations, what a spread of the Gospel there must be when they are all received to God's favor again. With verse sixteen, Paul begins what amounts to an exhortation and a warning to the Gentiles. He declares that if the root is holy, that is, if Abraham, Isaac, and Jacob are holy, so are even the fallen branches. Holy not in the sense of righteous, but holy in that they are in unalterable relations with God, and still involved in His purpose of mercy. The branches were broken off that the wild, sour Gentile scion might be grafted in. The figure is contrary to the custom of grafting and for a purpose. The Gentile may say that these branches were broken off that he might be grafted in. That must be admitted, but now follows the significant warning, that by unbelief they were broken off, and the Gentile stands alone by faith. He has no occasion to boast, but every reason to fear, for if God spared not the natural branch, why should He spare the unnatural one, the wild scion in the holy stock. God was severe toward them, but kind toward the Gentile if the latter continues in God's kindness; otherwise, he also shall be cut off, and they, if they remain not in their unbelief (II Cor. 3 : 14-16), shall be grafted in again. This is not beyond God's power (verse 24); for if He could take a wild olive branch, and place it in the sweet, natural tree, how much more reasonable to think that He can regraft the natural branches in their own olive tree.

Everything belonging to the establishment of Christianity in the world is Jewish; the Saviour was a Jew, the Bible was written by Jews, the first Christian Church was wholly Jewish, and the first preachers were Jews. The churches of to-day have accepted the God, and the sacred writings, and the worship of another nation. The warning that the Gentile churches stand by faith, and only by faith, may well make one tremble when he sees the faithlessness of the churches of to-day. The letters to the seven churches of Asia (Revelation, chapters 2, 3) ought to be solemnly and prayerfully pondered.

After speaking of the naturalness of the restoration of fallen Israel, Paul now (verse 25) boldly and clearly predicts it. He declares their blindness has a limit. That limit is "until the fullness of the Gentiles is come in." He declares all Israel shall be saved. The elect remnant is already within the fold. The fallen branches shall be restored to the tree from which they were cut out; and so the promise, the glorious promise so often given in the Old Testament Scriptures, that in the seed of Abraham all nations should bless themselves, shall be realized. "There shall come out of Zion the Deliverer, and shall turn away ungodliness from Jacob." Their sins shall be forgiven. If now they are enemies, it is not because God has cast them off, it is for the good of the Gentiles.

In the Lord's dealing in this way with Jew and Gentile to reach ultimately the salvation of both, the writer sees the depth of the divine riches and wisdom and knowledge, and concludes with a doxology that ascribes everything to God "from whom, and through whom, and for whom all things are, and will be."

# The Holy Spirit.

## By Rev. J. H. Brookes, D.D.

---

PART I.

Mr. Torrey read in the morning prayers that Samson "wist not that the Lord was departed from him." It never occurred to him—he did not know it. He thought he was just as strong as ever. We read that the Spirit of the Lord came upon him and he met a lion and rent him as he would a kid; and again, after being tied with new chords, the Spirit of the Lord came upon him and he break them as tow touched with the fire, and he seized the jawbone of an ass and slew a thousand men. You will notice that it is not a new jawbone but a moist. You cannot serve the Lord with a dry jawbone, you must have a moist jawbone.

He slept upon the lap of Delilah and told her the secret of his great strength. "It is a shame for a man to wear long hair" and he was occupying the place of humility before Jehovah. He said if this long hair of mine be cut off I shall be weak. He was leaving the place of shame and contempt. I will be like anybody else. So he was. Delilah said: "The Philistines be upon thee." And he arose and shook himself. There is no use shaking yourself if the Spirit of God is grieved; it will not do a bit of good. "He wist not," did not know that the Lord had departed. This is the saddest picture of that sad story. How many there are who wist not that the Lord has departed, and they are powerless. You may imagine that you are safe because you are in this Institute. I do not know of a place more dangerous to spirituality than to be engaged in constant study. I went to Princeton Theological Seminary with the idea that there was an atmosphere of prayer, and that I would not have any trouble in maintaining my fellowship with God, surrounded with so many Christian men preparing for the ministry; but I found by sad experience that I was mistaken.

I have learned in an experience of forty years as a pastor that it is the easiest thing in the world to slip into the place of formality. We have given ourselves to studies, but the most dreadful thing about it is that the Lord will depart from you, if you are careless, and you will not know it. "Wist not that the Lord was departed." In this first lecture I want to be very practical and very simple.

Let us look at the Holy Spirit in the Gospel of John. The Spirit is revealed there as quickening, making alive, imparting spiritual life (John 3:5). How many seem to have life as the Church at Sardis. The water mentioned here, as in the Old Testament, is a symbol of the Word of the Lord Jesus Christ. It as no reference to baptism in any form administered by any person, because if it does, it is inconceivable that the Lord Jesus did not baptize any one. He never preached about baptism, and when He did refer to it, it was not until after His resurrection. It is inconceivable that the Lord Jesus Christ should never talk about that which is essential to eternal life or salvation—of regeneration—if the new birth comes through water. It is also inconceivable if he meant baptism that the Apostle Paul, in writing to the Corinthians, should say: "I thank God that I baptized none of you." In the next place, in fourteen of the inspired epistles, baptism does not occur once, while faith and believe occur five hundred and sixty times in the New Testament. In the next place let us see if the Lord himself does not make a comment upon the verse. John 6:63: "It is the Spirit that quickeneth, the flesh profiteth nothing. The words that I speak unto you they are Spirit and they are life." No matter what you do, elevate it, culture it, do what you may, the flesh profiteth nothing. "Except a man be born of water and of the Spirit he cannot see the kingdom of God." Again, James 1:18, "Of His own will begat He us with the word of truth." Are there two or more ways of being born? Peter 1:23, here we have an inspired comment on our Lord's statement to Nicodemus. "Being born again, not of corruptible seed, but of incorruptible, by the Word of God which liveth and abideth forever." Is not that plain enough? I Cor. 4: 15: "Begotten through the Gospel." The means used by the Holy Spirit to bring about this new birth is to beget us into newness of life by the Holy Ghost through the Word.

In the Old Testament water is used as a symbol of the Word. Now we have these statements which we can understand more clearly in the light of what has been said. John 1:12-13. By believing on Him we have the right to be made the children of God. Gal. 3:26, "Ye are all the children of God by faith in Christ Jesus." Also I John 5:1. In my pastoral work among inquirers I find this one of the most helpful texts to use among those who want to be saved. I was preaching in Dublin years ago; a tall, gray-haired man was among the inquirers, and my host came and asked me to let all others go and talk with this one man. He proved to be an Irish lord, an intelligent, fine-looking man. He said: "I want to be a Christian; I have lived long enough the life of sin." "Well," I said, "we can go to the Word of God in regard to that," and I turned to I Cor. 12:3: "You cannot say that Jesus is Lord but by the Spirit." I then turned to I John 5:1, and said to him: "Do you believe that Jesus is the Christ?" He said: "I do most sincerely." I said: "Are you born of God?" He did not answer but looked down upon the floor. I said: "Please read it again." He read: "Whosoever believeth that Jesus is the Christ is born of God." I said, again: "Are you born of God?" Still he did not answer. I said: "Please read it again," determined to fasten his attention upon the Word of God. He read it again very slowly and deliberately. I said: "If you say that you believe that Jesus is the Christ, and you are not born of God, you make Him a liar. Is there any sin so great as to make God a liar?" He sat in perfect silence for a moment. Looking up he said: "Lord Jesus, I believe that thou art the Christ, and I am born of God—let us pray," and he dropped on his knees. His mind had to be diverted away from himself to Christ. "That which is born of flesh is flesh." Until they lay hold of this truth they are like a corpse. Every one of us must go through that in his own experience. If you come to say, I am a lost, ruined and helpless sinner, and Jesus Christ came to save sinners, and you receive Him, you are saved.

John 4:14: Here again we have the water connected with the Spirit. Water connected with the Spirit is the symbol of the Word.

John 14:17: I am sure it is needless to say to you here that you ought never to speak of the Holy Spirit as "it," but you will find a great many Christians who do. The Lord Jesus always spoke of the Holy Spirit in the use of the personal pronoun. You often hear good people in their prayers speak of the Spirit as "it." The Lord says He shall be "in you." Mark it. A divine person is dwelling in you.

Rom. 8:9-11: "Ye are not in the flesh but in the Spirit." "He dwelleth in you."

I Cor. 3:16-17: "Know ye not that ye are the temple of God." This was addressed to the entire Church. "If any man mar or deface it, him will God mar, for the temple of God is holy, which temple ye are."

I Cor. 6:19: "Know ye not that your body is the temple of the Holy Ghost which is in you?" Here is a business man hurrying along the street, here is a woman going through the routine of household duties, here is a Christian lying upon a sick bed, what a blessing to remember that this body is the temple of the Holy Ghost. A dear fellow in St. Louis, a Christian and an officer in the church, but not thoroughly taught in the truth of God, attended a Bible reading one afternoon when this thought was brought out; namely, that the body of every believer is the temple of the Holy Spirit. He said afterwards that this thought almost lifted him from his feet. Dr. Mason, at Lafayette College, at the funeral of his son, said to the young men who bore the casket: "Tread lightly, for you are bearing the temple of the Holy Ghost." If that thought would fill us what an impression it would be. You are bearing the temple of the Holy Ghost. The Spirit of God dwelling in you.

How are you going to test it? I John 4:2. I wrote to a dear brother who sent me some little thing he had written out speaking of the time when Jesus Christ, at the beginning of His ministry, became convinced that He was the Son of God, and my reply was that the Lord knew that when He was twelve years of age.

## PART II.

I John 4:13: "*Hereby know we*." How do we know? Because the Spirit of God dwells in us. I do not wonder at this Scripture when you go into the next epistle of John and read of the spirit that is not of Christ. II John 10, I do not see how those Christians could take part in that Parliament of Religion.

Here, in I John 4:13, observe, is *the indwelling of the Spirit*—the Spirit dwelling in the body in the believer. When that thought takes full possession of a young Christian they will have a safe walk.

The *third thing in the Gospel of John: The Spirit Outflowing*. John 7:38-39: "He that believeth on me, out of him shall flow rivers of living water." This is a marvelous statement in the light of the fact that from the first chapter of Genesis to Malachi, the Spirit was really bestowed. There is communication of the Spirit for power, outflowing like rivers of water, and therefore if we are filled with the Spirit He will dwell in us to the exclusion of everything else, that every one may bear witness with power.

What is required of a witness? That he shall be a man of high social position. It is required that he shall know whereof he witnesses. The poorest laborer can go into court before the judge and say: I witnessed the deed and I am here to testify to what I saw. His testimony is received because he is a witness. You can never be a witness for Jesus Christ in the power of the Holy Ghost until you have known Jesus. When our Lord arose from the dead he breathed on his apostles. But the Holy Spirit came in power on the Day of Pentecost.

Acts 2:4: They were gathered in one place. The place of weakness, of helplessness; the place of prayer. Suddenly there came a sound from heaven as of a mighty breathing. The Lord breathed before, but here comes another breathing. Well, how men can read a passage like that and then deny verbal inspiration I cannot understand. The apostles spoke fifteen or sixteen different languages which they had never heard and which they did not know anything about. What would we think if a man stood up here and began speaking all the modern European languages which he had never learned. There was a direct communication of the Holy Spirit. "They began to speak with other tongues as the Spirit gave them utterance." The result was that three thousand souls were converted. We need these Pentecostal days. Men are going out proclaiming the Gospel with apparently feeble results. Why can we not have such a day as the Day of Pentecost. "They were all filled with the Holy Spirit," and when a man is full there is no room for anything else; and if the Christians of this city would put away sin and get filled with the Holy Ghost Chicago would be shaken from center to circumference.

II Cor. 6:14: "What fellowship hath righteousness with unrighteousness? or what communion hath light with darkness?" Ye are the temple of the living God, as God said: "I will dwell in you." This poor narrow heart will be large enough for the infinite God to walk in. "Come out from among them, and be ye separate." "Touch not the unclean thing."

Ezek. 47:9-12: As the prophet went out to look at the river it greatly enlarged. Whithersoever the rivers came everything that had life grew upon the bank, and only the marshy places were left. The power of the believer in Jesus Christ is in being filled with the Holy Ghost.

*Next thing revealed in John's Gospel is* COMFORTING. John 14:16: "I will pray the Father and He shall give you another Comforter." Observe, I have not seen it noticed, the first promise concerning this important fact of the Holy Ghost is in answer to prayer, and in every recorded instance of the giving of the Holy Ghost in the New Testament it is preceded by prayer. I am greatly afraid we are failing in prayer. Remember that all the education you get here and all the training in the Bible will amount to nothing unless you are men and women of prayer. The Comforter was sent in answer to prayer. Paraclete is one called to the aid of another. I shall give you another Advocate that He may abide with you forever. It was expedient for us that Jesus went away. Acts 9:31. Has it ever occurred to you the contradiction between fear and comfort? The churches "walking in the fear of the Lord, and in the comfort of the Holy Ghost, were multiplied."—II Cor. 1:3-4. Also Rom. 8:15. Some years ago a man whose wife was dead had an only child that was deaf and dumb, and he sent her to a deaf and dumb school. He loved the child very much, and some time after he wrote to the superintendent saying that he must see her. On the day that he was to arrive, the child watched for him at the window, and when he appeared she rushed up to him and said "Papa." On hearing her say this he rolled on the grass in the agony of his joy. It is not a question about your talents, but your personal devotion to God by the Holy Ghost. What comfort to look at the Lord and say "Father." Chalmers was found lying on his bed dead one morning, and then his family remembered that the night before, when he seemed perfectly well, he was walking in the garden, and he was heard repeating "Father! O my Father!" What a comfort to be able to say that. If there is anything in your life that keeps you from saying that get rid of it at once.

*Teaching*, John 14:26: "But the Comforter, the Holy Ghost, whom the Father will send in my name, He shall teach you all things." We all need teaching. A man never gets beyond the need of the divine teacher. As in John 6:45: "They shall be all taught of God."

John 14:23: "We will come unto him and make our abode with him," by the Holy Spirit. Oh, my friends, can we enter into that practically — the indwelling of the Holy Spirit as teacher?

Rom. 8:26: "*The Spirit maketh intercession for us with groanings.*" A dear friend who was very ill and in great pain once said: "I cannot pray, I can only groan." "Never mind, dear sister," I said, "that is prayer. God knows the meaning of our sighs." "The Spirit helpeth our infirmities." In my experience I have seen people that would have died broken-hearted if it had not been for the Holy Spirit.

*The Holy Spirit shows things to come.* John 16:13: "When He, the Spirit of truth, is come, He will guide you into all truth." There is no man wise enough to predict the events of a single day. The greatest philosopher on earth cannot. The future is absolutely unrevealed.

I Cor. 15:42-44: "The resurrection of the dead. The Spirit shows you this. The body is laid away in the grave in corruption, in weakness, but it shall be raised in glory.

II Cor. 5:1.

I Cor. 2:9-10: Many people stop at the ninth verse; but in the tenth verse, "God has revealed them by His Spirit." The opinions of the wisest scholar on earth are not worth a single straw when He comes to tell you about the future. He does not know anything about the future, and no man knows until the Spirit of God teaches.

I Thes. 4:14: There will be a great reunion. I do rejoice that the time is coming when death will be cast into the lake of fire. There is going to be a glorious victory. The Holy Spirit reveals that Jesus is coming back. he Lord himself shall descend from heaven with a shout and the dead will rise first. "Then we which are alive and remain shall be caught up together with them in the clouds to meet the Lord in the air; so shall we ever be with the Lord."

Cherish this doctrine of the Holy Spirit for your own comfort and joy. Do not let your experience interfere. These lectures will be absolutely of no value to you unless they bring you nearer to Jesus Christ.

# The Inspiration of the Old Testament.

### By Rev. J. H. Brookes, D.D.

---

I have no views of my own to present to you. I have no opinions on the subject; I simply wish to aid you in ascertaining what is the testimony of the Bible to itself.

II Peter 1:21: "For the prophecy came not in old time by the will of man, but holy men of God spake as they were moved by the Holy Ghost." A prophet is one who speaks for another; in the Bible sense, he is one who speaks for God. Prophecy, therefore, is a communication from God through men to men — in a single word, revelation—God's revealed will. The testimony of the Apostle Peter is that no prophecy came by the will of men. That is, man's will did not originate it — had nothing to do with it. If so, the testimony of Peter would not be true. The prophecy came not of old or at any time by the will of men, but holy men of God spake, being borne along by the Holy Ghost. You probably know that this is the correct reading. It does not say that the holy men of God thought. It does not concern us what they thought; but holy men of God spake, being borne along by the Holy Ghost. If Peter's testimony is to be believed, then prophecy or revelation is far above man's will. It is a direct communication from God to men. That settles the question.

I Peter 1:10-11: Here the Apostle had been speaking of the salvation which they had received, and of which salvation the prophets — the Old Testament prophets who spake for God inquired — searched diligently. "What or what manner of time the Spirit of Christ which was in them did signify," etc. Stop and ask yourself a question — what were these old prophets doing? Sitting down and perusing the prophecy or revelation which they did not understand, the same as an amanuensis would write from dictation and afterwards try to learn the meaning of what he had written.

As if a dozen amanuenses were employed by some great statesman and took down just the words he dictated, then if he should disappear they would pore over these words to ascertain his views. Searching. What did they search? The prophecies, the revelation, the communication from God through holy men of God. What for? To discover what the Holy Spirit had revealed to them concerning the sufferings of Christ and the glory that should follow:

II Tim. 3:15-17: The Apostle writes to his son Timothy that from a child he has known the Holy Scriptures, and refers to his mother and grandmother in the first part of the book. If the Scriptures are full of errors and mistakes could Paul have spoken of them as holy? "Which are able to make thee wise unto salvation." Is it possible that that which is full of errors and mistakes makes wise unto salvation? "All scripture is given by inspiration of God," or God breathed; or, if a word might be invented—God-spirited—"and is profitable"—meaning all God's words. The word furnished here is really a nautical term, and has reference to the furnishing of a vessel—complete in every particular and ready to face the storm. But if the scripture was corrupt, how could one be thoroughly furnished? Some one will say that the revised version reads "Every scripture." Dean Burgon, of the Committee on Revision, pronounced this translation "a stupendous blunder"; it does not make good English. In Acts 2:36 you have exactly the same form of expression. What sense would there be in saying that every house in Chicago had been built? All the houses in Chicago have been built. These scriptures which are God-spirited are the scriptures which the Apostle refers to. Timothy knew in his childhood the Holy Scriptures. Dr. Lightfoot, the chairman of the Committee on Revision, defended the new translation on the ground that it gave greater emphasis to every part of the scripture. Every part is God-breathed. You often hear loose talk about Gladstone, Shakespeare, and others being inspired. They were not God-breathed. It was the scripture, not the men; and all scripture, or every scripture, was God-breathed—God inspired. Hear the testimony of two apostles as to the inspiration of the writings. You known the word scripture means writing, and writing is made up of words; therefore the words are God-breathed, or spirited, or inspired.

Matt. 22:31-32: The testimony of the Lord Jesus. The Sadducees came to perplex Him in regard to the question of resurrection. Jesus says in these verses that "God spake." Was it a mistake? Some say "there are so many difficulties we cannot understand." I do not care what difficulties may present themselves to your mind. There will always be difficulties. Take any one of the facts of your own daily observation and there will be just as many difficulties. One day while Mr. Moody was in St. Louis an old gentleman was among the inquirers, and Mr. Moody asked me to take him alone into a room in order to have a personal talk with him. There followed him into the room a young lady whom I afterwards discovered to be his daughter. I commenced opening the word to this anxious old sinner. During the conversation the young lady spoke up, saying: "I want you to understand that I do not believe anything that I cannot see the reason for." I went on with the old gentleman. Again she spoke: "I do not believe anything I cannot understand. I am educated; I recently graduated from college." Finally I spoke to her: "You blew your nose just now; how did you do it?" She said: "My intellect took knowledge of the condition of my nose and my volition communicated itself to the muscles of my arm and hand and I lifted my hand to my nose. I said: "What is your volition?" She said: "My will." I said: "What is your will?" She said: "My volition." Then I said: "Your will is you volition and your volition is your will, but how did your immaterial will or volition communicate itself to your arm?" She said she did not know. Then I said: "You do not know how you blew your nose. Keep still till you understand this, while I address your father."

Can one explain how it is that the same grass eaten by sheep, calves, pigs and geese makes wool, hair, bristle, and feathers respectively? And how can one refuse to accept the statement that God has inspired the Scriptures until he understands the question of inspiration?

Mark 12 : 36. "David himself said by the Holy Ghost," so Jesus Christ tells us; but in Psalm 110 : 1, to which he refers, we do not find any allusion to the Holy Ghost. Here we have the testimony of two apostles and the testimony of Jesus Christ concerning the old Scriptures.

Ex. 4 : 10-12. Moses had been attending God's theological seminary in the solitude of Horeb for forty years, and now he is ready for work, and God says, "Go to Pharaoh." In his youth he went without being sent, but now he is humble and does not want to go; he was not eloquent, etc. But what is God's reply? "Who made man's mouth?" Observe, God does not say who made man's mind. "Go and I will be with thy mouth, teaching thee what thou shalt say." He did not promise to be with his head. I do not care what Moses thought, but I want to know what Moses said. God promised to be with his mouth and teach him what to say. The words, "The Lord said unto Moses," and "The Lord spake unto Moses," occur five hundred and sixty times in the Pentateuch. Is that true? If not, then do not believe anything in the Bible. Accept or reject it.

Ex. 32 : 16. Moses had been on the mount in communion with God, and when he descended the people had fallen into idolatry, and he threw down the tables of the law, breaking them to pieces in his wrath. Note that "the tables were the work of God, and the writing the writing of God graven upon the tables." Not the work of man.

Deut. 4 : 2, 10, 12. Forty years had passed since God had written upon the tables of stone, and the people are about to enter the promised land, and He said: "Ye shall not add unto the word." Mark it. "Neither shall ye diminish ought from it." It is a perfect, infallible word, and it would be a shocking sin to add to or diminish from it. It would be no sin to add to the writings of Gladstone or Shakespeare. Is it strange that the Bible stands unique and glorious above all other books? The tenth verse tells us why. These words were to be written down and put into the ark of the covenant where they were to be kept as a memorial.

Let us go to the second division where David is the great actor. Remember Jesus Christ said: "David himself said — by the Holy Ghost." Turn to II Sam. 23 : 1 and 2 : "These be the last words of David." If a man is ever honest it is when he comes to die. "What are they, David?" We stand by the bedside to hear the last words of so illustrious a monarch and poet. "The Spirit of the Lord spake by me, and His word was in my tongue." Not the Spirit of the Lord thought by me, but He spake by me. Not His concept in my mind, but "His word was in my tongue." I do not care for the concept. It is invisible, intangible ; I cannot grasp it. It is all folly.

Take Psalm 19 : 7-11. Here are six different titles of the word which is declared to be true and absolutely perfect.

Take Psalm 119 : 105, 130, 151, 160. The word is a light and a lamp (verse 105). Can that be true of anything that is full of errors and imperfections? Verse 130 : Can that which is full of errors and mistakes give light and understanding? Verse 151 : "All Thy commandments are true." Verse 160 : "Thy word is true from the beginning," or from the first word.

Prov. 30 : 5 : "Every word of God is pure." "Add thou not unto His words, lest He reprove thee and thou be found a liar." The present-day trifling with the word of God is simply shocking in the light of such verses as these.

Take the next division — the prophetical books. More than two hundred times we find the expression : "The word of God came" to such a man, and "God said unto" such a man. When the Bible says this it is a fact. We do not understand it ; you do not understand how the divine Son of God was a babe on the breast of a human mother; nor how he stood at the tomb of Lazarus and called him forth from death.

Jer. 1 : 6-9. As an illustration of the rest of the prophets, Jeremiah was a young man, and, like Moses, recoiled from the mission on which God was about to send him. What was God's reply? You have all read the Book of Jeremiah, I presume. From that moment his life was like a grand, solemn refrain of music— wherever he went he was simply repeating God's words. When thrown into prison and exposed to death, how did he encourage himself? It was by "Thus saith the Lord," I have no message of my own to give you; I am simply telling you what God says. You say this does not include the written revelation. Read Jer. 26:2. He must not add nor diminish a word. He proclaimed God's word and any who would not listen did so at their own peril.

Jer. 30:2. Jeremiah was commanded to "Write thee all the words that I have spoken in a book." "Holy men of God spake as they were moved by the Holy Ghost," and the words were recorded in a book.

Zech. 7:12. This brings us to the close of Israel's history. They would not listen to the word of God, and are sold into captivity, and the wrath of God falls upon them like a lightning flash. They refused to hear the word which the Lord of hosts sent in His Spirit by the hand of the prophets. And that which is going to curse the church of Great Britain and America is this refusal to listen to and receive the word of God. It will bring dissolution and fury. The pride and presumption of men, some of whom boast of their intellectuality and talk about inspiration of concept and dynamic inspiration; it is dynamic nonsense. God inspired every word, every syllable, and let us bow our wills to it.

## Lecture 2.

Matt. 1:22: Read in the revised version—"Which was spoken by the Lord through the prophet." Now if we are to believe any part of the Bible at all, why not believe this? If we do believe this, then it was the Lord who spoke through the prophet. It is just as when you send a message to your friend by a messenger, and you put the very words you wish your friend to hear into the mouth of the messenger.

"Matt. 2:5, 15, 17, 23. Verse 5: The wise men of the east had come to inquire about the birth of Jesus—"And they said unto him, in Bethlehem of Judea; for thus it is written through the prophet." Somebody is therefore back of the prophet; who was the medium or agency to transmit the message.

Verse 15: "Spoken by the Lord through the prophet." There are such things in the Bible as immediate fulfillment of prophecy and ultimate fulfillment. From this verse you will find that prophecy has an immediate fulfillment and an ultimate fulfillment. The Holy Ghost dictated these words to Hosea (chapter 11:1), and afterwards informs us that the ultimate fulfillment of that scripture is in Jesus Christ. All scripture is about Him.

Verse 17: "Spoken through Jeremiah." Somebody back of Jeremiah, and that person was God Himself, the Holy Ghost. What Jeremiah said was spoken through him; not by him, but through him.

Verse 23: "Spoken through the prophets." Not prophet. If you will undertake to look this verse up as the commentators struggle over it you will be surprised. In the south where I came from the darkies call potatoes " taters "—" common taters," and what the commentators say about this verse is simply common taters. They do not see the difference between the singular number prophet and the plural number prophets. If it had been said through the prophet, that would be another thing. There is no carelessness in the Bible in the use of the singular or plural number. It simply means that the whole of the Old Testament prophets say that "He shall be called a Nazarene."

Matt. 15:4: "God commanded." God gave the command, according to the testimony of our Lord Jesus Christ. I do not care if it was through Moses any more than if it is a question of prime importance whether you send a message to your friend through one agent or another; the agent is not responsible, you are the responsible one. Although Moses wrote these words God commanded them, so Jesus Christ testifies. You may avoid the commands of God, but it is a solemn sanction that Jesus Christ gives to the inspiration of the Old Testament.

Matt. 22:32: "I am the God of Abraham," said Jesus. "God is not the God of the dead, but of the living." Observe that the blessed Lord makes the whole of this tremendous argument about the resurrection to depend upon the present and past tense of the verb. If He had said, I was the God of Abraham, Isaac, and Jacob, then there might have been some objection, but he said: "I am the God of Abraham, Isaac, and Jacob." Observe that Jesus Christ put it distinctly upon the ground that "God said"; and if you believe Jesus Christ at all, why not believe this.

Luke 1:68-70: Here clearly and distinctly it was God who made the prophets and spake by them. The reference is to all the Old Testament prophets from first to last since the world began.

John 10:35: Jesus Christ says that "the scripture cannot be broken." "All scripture is given by inspiration of God"—God-breathed, God-spirited. He had reference to the Old Testament scripture. It cannot be broken. It is infallible—God's Word—and you cannot break the least chapter, verse, word or syllable; you must not add to or diminish from it, because it is God's Word, and you will be wise and effective workers for the Master just in proportion as you bow your will to the Master in every particular. "God spake by the mouth of His holy prophets since the world began," and "the scripture cannot be broken."

Acts 1:16: "Which the Holy Ghost by the mouth of David spake." If I believe anything in the Bible I am going to believe that. You cannot play fast and loose with God's Word. "The Holy Ghost by the mouth of David;" therefore the responsible author of that statement concerning Judas is the Holy Ghost. I do not see how a man with a fair mind, and who wants to know the truth, can get around such a statement.

Acts 4:25-26: The assembly of the apostles had met with a great persecution and had gathered for strength and prayer. "Who by the mouth of thy servant David hast said, why did the heathen rage." Who said it? God said it—by the mouth of David. What do men mean when they say they do not know whether or not the Scripture is verbally inspired?

Acts 28:25: "Well spake the Holy Ghost by Isaiah." Observe the point is this, that Paul's testimony as well as Peter's is that it was the Holy Ghost who said, or spake by Isaiah. Isaiah was therefore the mouthpiece of the Holy Ghost. It was in that same connection that Isaiah, when he saw the glory of the Lord Jesus Christ, tells us distinctly that the divine Being in the temple filling the holy place with His glory was the Lord Jesus Christ. Isaiah had been prepared for service by recognizing himself as utterly undone. "Woe is me for I am undone." He does not say there is something a little wrong about me; but the Lord took a coal of fire and touched his lips. Then came the voice, and John tells us this was the voice of Christ. "Who shall I send and who will go for us?" Why say "for us?" Then read that last quotation in Acts 28:25. It was the Father, Son, and Holy Ghost. Every young man or woman must either believe that or reject the whole book. You have no more right not to believe that than not to believe the birth of Jesus Christ in Judea. You cannot believe one more than the other. I am so anxious that you should go forth from the Bible Institute to your work permeated with the truth of God's word, and remembering that you are not called to present your own views or opinions to men, but that you stand upon the authority of God's word.

Now for the Epistles. Rom. 1:2. Paul, the bondservant or slave of Jesus Christ, says: "Which He promised afore by His prophets." How did God promise by the prophets? Where did He promise in the Holy Scriptures? Why did Paul say "Holy Scriptures?" Because he knew they were from God. But if they contained errors and mistakes Paul would not have called them holy. It is nonsense on the face of it. They were holy because from God.

Rom. 15:4: "Written aforetime," in the Old Testament. "Might have hope." Hope through that which is full of errors and mistakes—which is not divinely inspired—through that which is some invisible "concept" darting about in the dark— hope in that which is called dynamic inspiration? It is nauseating to hear these men use such words. The great fad nowadays of these false teachers is "character building." It is building on a heap of manure. You cannot build a very good house on that foundation. It is a rotten, stinking mass. A friend of mine who is a great scholar said: "Whenever I hear a man talking about character building, I go out and spit." "Through patience and comfort of the scripture might have hope." The young man who goes from the Institute with the firm conviction that this is true will be led of God.

A young man said: "I am glad I came here because I have been convinced of God's truth." I cannot tell the joy of my own experience when I discovered out of the Scriptures that peace with God is not a feeling, but a state or a condition. I was in a theological seminary and did not dare to go to the professors with my difficulties because I knew they were sent to teach theology. I thought, "I am a lost sinner, and there is no help." Then it was revealed to me that peace was a state or condition, not feeling. Christ is our peace. He is our righteousness, our life. Oh to be deeply read in the oracles of God — that is the secret of your power.

Gal. 3:8, 16, 22: Prof. Briggs says this blessed book cannot any more stop a bullet than a pack of cards. Can a pack of cards foresee? The Scriptures foresee. Why? Because instinct with the life of God divine attributes are ascribed to the Scriptures.

Verse 16: Now, to Abraham and his seed were the promises made. It does not say "seeds" "as of many; but as of one." "Thy seed which is Christ." I have heard of some of these chaps who say Paul was not a good grammarian — he did not know "seeds" does not admit of the plural. The audacity and impudence of these fellows is out of sight. The Holy Ghost not a good grammarian? The whole of that great argument concerning justification of Abraham by faith, before circumcision, before the giving of the law, was that God gave the promise unto his seed. But the law which came four hundred years after could not annul or make void that promise.

Verse 22: "Scripture hath concluded." The Greek word for "concluded" means to shut up as in prison—into the power of sin. The Scripture does that. Then is the Scripture not something more than a common book?

Heb. 1: 1-2: How did He speak? He did it by the prophets and in His Son. Who was the speaker? God. If you do not believe that do not believe anything. Do one thing or the other. God spake unto the fathers by the prophets. "In these last days — spoken unto us by His Son." And since then nothing can be added or taken from, and all the pretended revelations of these cranks are but the dreams of an insane brain.

Heb. 3: 7: "Wherefore the Holy Ghost says." Who said it? The Holy Ghost. Where? In the Ninety-fifth Psalm. Do you read anything about the Holy Ghost there? No. How do I know that the Holy Ghost inspired it? Because the inspired writer declares that it was the Holy Ghost. What a power it will give you when you say this is not my opinion, the Holy Ghost said it—when you are back of the Holy Ghost, behind the word. "To-day if ye will hear his voice, harden not your hearts." What a dreadful solemnity it imparts to that solemn admonition and warning!

Heb. 12: 27: "This word." Does not Paul build a great argument or doctrine upon the force of one word? Do not get into the habit of saying "Pauline writings" and "Petrine writings," the Holy Ghost says. Of course there are differences of style in the Bible. Sir Walter Scott had a very different style in his different works, but it was Sir Walter Scott all the time. Mr. Gladstone has a very different style when he writes on the "Iliad" and when he writes for his political followers. These young ladies may have very different styles when playing the piano, yet it is one hand that controls the keys and produces all this different music. The Lord Jesus Christ and His inspired apostles uniformly attribute the Old Testament to the immediate inspiration of God, and there are more than three hundred and twenty direct repetitions of Old Testament texts in the New Testament on the doctrine now being discussed. One day Prof. Briggs said, "Paul does not care anything about the Old Testament." The gentleman he was speaking with called a young man to bring a Bible, and he opened at Romans and read: "What says the Scripture." Eighteen times in the Epistle to the Romans alone we find the words, "It is written." That was Paul's respect for the Old Testament. One brother quoted this Scripture in his prayer: "That the Father of our Lord Jesus Christ give you the Spirit of Wisdom—opening the eyes of your understanding." It is the "eyes of your heart" to be opened. God wants the eyes of your heart fixed upon Him and upon the inspired revelation, that you may know more and more of God's revealed will in this blessed Book, that you may go out to do valiant service for Him.

---

PUBLISHER'S NOTE:—The copy for these lectures was sent to Dr. Brookes for revision, just as he was preparing for a journey, which his physician said he must take for his health; consequently he could not give the matter thorough and complete revision, which he would gladly have done had it been possible.

# The Resurrection.

## By Dr. L. W. Munhall.

### PART I.

I want to call your attention to the doctrine of the resurrection of the dead. I want first to call your attention to something that is very often lost sight of by Bible teachers and students.

Gen. 13: 14-17: This covenant and promise made unto Abraham, repeated to him and reiterated to Jacob, and it appears all the way along the line of prophecy to the very close of the canon of the Old Testament scriptures; no subject is so frequently referred to excepting the deliverance from Egyptian bondage. The covenant and promise were made to Abraham and to his seed. We know this promise and covenant have never yet been fulfilled. In Acts 7: 5, mark it carefully, the Holy Spirit declares through Stephen that the promise made to Abraham away back in history had not yet been fulfilled. What are you going to do about it? The seed of Israel in the earth at the present time is only about twelve million. But if you take the generations that have lived you can see how literally it will be that they are as the dust of the earth and the stars of heaven. Now this promise made unto Abraham was for all the seed; the promise and covenant not yet fulfilled is to be fulfilled, for the strength of Israel cannot lie. Some people think that because of the lapse of centuries therefore the promise stands for nothing, but that promise is specific. The length and breadth of the land was described to Abraham. Of course, during Solomon's reign there was a sense in which his reign extended over this land, but not according to the covenant and promise, and therefore not fulfilled. When will it be fulfilled? Read Ezek. 37 : 12-14. This covenant and promise will be fulfilled, therefore, at the resurrection of the Jews. You are obliged to believe this or believe that the covenant and promises of God are not worth the paper they are written on. There must be a resurrection from the grave.

I want first of all to call attention to the resurrection of Jesus Christ.

Psalm 16 : 10. Here is a definite prophecy concerning the resurrection of Jesus Christ. There are some people nowadays calling themselves Christians and occupying orthodox pulpits who tell you that there is no prophecy in the Old Testament scriptures. They have accepted a theory from the rationalistic school of Germany called the Near Horizon theory, and they hold that man could not see beyond his own horizon, and therefore they deny the Messianic prophecy. But here is a definite prophecy written by King David. But some say that David never wrote the Psalm. If you believe that, you cannot believe the Bible, and you will never amount to much as a teacher of God's word. Read John 2 : 19-21; also Acts 2 : 29-31. The Holy Ghost says that David was a prophet. But some tell us there were no prophets. David saw beforehand; but some people tell us that the old prophets were not foreseers. Note the testimony of the Holy Ghost that King David wrote that Psalm. The critics say that David did not write that Psalm. I believe they lie. You must believe that or disbelieve the Word of God altogether. Here is a definite prophecy by the great king of Israel that Christ should not see corruption; here is a prophecy by the Lord Jesus that agrees with it, and here is a statement made by Peter that that very prophecy was fulfilled. There are many people who profess to believe in the resurrection of the Lord Jesus, but do not really believe in their own resurrection. In I Cor., fifteenth chapter, we are told that if the dead rise not then is Christ not risen. Do you see how the resurrection of Jesus Christ is identified with the resurrection of the saints? If you deny the resurrection of the saints you deny the resurrection of Jesus Christ. We are identified with Christ's resurrection. He is the first fruits. Whenever a man begins to philosophize and speculate in regard to the resurrection of the dead he gets beyond his depth. There is absolutely no information in regard to the resurrection of the dead save what is in the Word of God. Nobody ever died and came back or looked into the other world and saw for himself. You may go into the natural world and find there much that will illustrate the doctrine of the resurrection, but you will find no authoritative teaching save in the Word of God. A worm out of himself spins his own winding sheet, lies still for a season, but finally the winding sheet bursts and a beautiful butterfly soars away. This illustrates the doctrine of the resurrection, but does not teach it authoritatively. A gold ring may be placed in certain chemicals and be dissolved, and then certain other chemicals may be deposited into the solution and the gold of the ring be reassembled and the ring reproduced. This illustrates but does not teach authoritatively the doctrine of the resurrection. I have heard a great many sermons and read many books upon the resurrection, and some of them have made me very sad. I heard a distinguished scholar speak on the subject twice. He said a man's body is like that of a horse. He is born under precisely the same laws as the horse; he develops from babyhood under the same laws that the horse develops under from colthood; he gets hungry, so does the horse; he gets weary, so does the horse; he grows old, so does the horse; he gets sick, so does the horse; he dies, so does the horse; he goes back into dust, so does the horse; a man's body is like a horse's body. I say it is not so. There is one kind of flesh of men and another kind of beasts. I know my body is not like that of a horse: you may think yours is if you like; this is a free country.

Let us come to the Bible and see what it says: It is to the law and the testimony. We can do nothing against the truth, but for the truth, and our business at all times is to search the Scriptures.

Look at Dan. 12:2. I read Dr. Tregelle's translation. There is no such thing taught in the Bible as a simultaneous resurrection of the good and bad. Absolutely nothing goes into the dust of the earth but the body; therefore the Scripture says that they that sleep in the dust of the earth shall awake unto everlasting life, the rest of the sleepers unto shame and everlasting contempt. Reference is made to the resurrection of the body. The Bible does not teach by a single statement the unconscious state of the dead. There is nothing in the earth but the body, and if the body does not come out of the earth there is no sense in that scripture.

John 5: 28-29: "The hour is coming." Hour, here, is the same word as used in thet wenty-fifth verse, and means all the time that has elapsed since the time of Jesus Christ; therefore that hour is now more than eighteen hundred years long. What is it in the grave? Nothing but the body, and therefore without bodily resurrection that scripture is meaningless.

Turn to I Cor. 15: 19-23, and read God's exposition of the doctrine of the resurrection of the dead. This does not teach universal salvation or annihilation. The wicked dead are raised by the same power as the righteous dead, but already we have seen a difference. Some to everlasting life and some to shame and everlasting contempt.

### PART II.

Phil. 3: 20-21: Our citizenship is in heaven. These vile bodies, bodies of humiliation, bodies so full of weakness and infirmities, are going to be changed and fashioned like unto His glorious body. If you say that does not refer to my literal body, I say that it does not refer to Christ's body either.

Rom. 8: 11: Quickened means to make alive again. I Peter 3: 18. I am alive again by the Holy Spirit, the only person of the Godhead present on earth — the executive of the Godhead in all the administration of the affairs of God; and here we see Him in the resurrection of Jesus Christ from the dead. He quickened Jesus Christ and He will do the same work for you.

Eph. 1: 13-14: The Holy Spirit is the earnest of our inheritance. In law the earnest is the first payment. If I buy a man's farm and pay ten dollars, that makes the bargain good — it is earnest money, and the farm is mine. The Holy Spirit dwelling in you, that is God's earnest of the final resurrection of the redeemed. It is made sure to you. It is the first payment of the resurrection and makes the bargain good. Rom. 8: 11. I Thess. 4: 13. I would not have you ignorant. I John 3: 2. You see the logic of these numerous Scripture quotations. Jesus Christ was born into this world, developed from the Babe of Bethlehem to the perfect physical Man of thirty-three years of age, according to the same laws by which we were developed. He was very man as very God. When thirty-three, his body having no infirmities was nailed upon the accursed tree. He was taken down from the cross, prepared for burial according to the customs of those times, and laid in Joseph's new tomb. A stone was placed upon the mouth of that tomb and it meant death to the man who broke the seal; soldiers were placed there to keep guard. On the morning of the third day he arose from the grave — that very same body that was born of Mary, that developed, that was crucified and buried. The women who arrived first at the sepulchre recognized him. This latter is a proof to my mind that we shall recognize one another in resurrection life. He said to the women: "Go tell my disciples that I ascend." Directly He ascended and returned again. And they held Him by the feet, but He suffered them not. Why did He not let them touch Him? You understand that under the ceremonial law for a woman to touch a priest was pollution. The blood was not yet offered. When the priest shed the blood it was not efficacious until put upon the altar, and though Jesus had shed His blood He had not yet offered it unto God. Therefore He ascended that first Easter morning unto God and there offered His blood in the presence of God; and then He returned in His glorified body. You will see the reason for it all in the Scripture. The disciples met and discussed the question of philosophy and metaphysics, and they could not understand how this could be. Thomas said, I will not believe unless I can put my fingers into the nail prints; and while they were talking the Lord appeared; and He said to Thomas — John 20: 27-29: This is the same hand that was born of my mother Mary once. My dear mother used to play with that hand; it grew to be full grown according to the laws of natural physical development, and it was nailed upon the accursed tree. Here is the same side where the cruel Roman spear was thrust into the throbbing heart. A spirit has not flesh and bones as you see me have. Notice that He does not say blood, for He had offered His blood. Some people jump at conclusions and say: "How could

He come into a room with the doors shut if he had a body of flesh and bones?" But He did so. Prof. Christlieb said the constituent elements of the resurrected body were not altered as to its essential component parts, but in resurrection He stood under other than natural laws. I could not go through that wall without first making a hole. When I get my resurrected body, don't you think I could get out of Chicago in less than half an hour? I could go to Jupiter in a moment of time. Thomas said: "My Lord and my God." Some men have to be knocked down before believing the Word of God. The Lord Jesus was seen frequently during a period of forty days after the resurrection. No fact in history so abundantly attested, no fact so clearly proven as the resurrection of the Lord Jesus Christ.*

The Lord appeared to His disciples thirteen times after the resurrection. And here are five hundred witnesses, not one of whom was ever known to lie, except Peter, and he repented and always told the truth after that, and they testify to the most important fact in history; these five hundred bear uniform testimony. Now if twenty-five men who are careful in making examinations on that which they testify of, and have never been known to lie but once in ten times, if their testimony is accepted, surely if you take five hundred, excepting one, who have never been known to lie, there is no room whatever to doubt that the Lord was raised from the dead. The only thing not to be forgotten is that He was not seen of any one but His own disciples. The five hundred saw Him and went everywhere preaching Jesus and the resurrection. There can be no doubt as to the resurrection. On the fortieth day as He was walking to Bethany they saw Him go up into heaven. Who were the two men that appeared after His ascension? Evidently Moses and Elijah. They were with Him on the Mount of Transfiguration. Remember Elijah was translated, and Moses died on Nebo; although the devil tried to get possession of the body He was not able, for the

---

*NOTE.—Babbage in Bridgewater, Treatise IX, shows by mathematical calculation that the concurrent unbiased testimony of only twenty-five men, who tell the truth ten times as often as they lie, in matters of sufficient importance to make them careful, is enough to outweigh antecedent probability of a billion to one against the event they testify.

Archangel buried it, and therefore it is no surprise that they were with Jesus on the Mount of Transfiguration. In I Thess. 4: The last generation of Christians will not die at all. They will be changed only as to their physical bodies.

Jesus will so come—come in His glorified body, and therefore He must have had His glorified body before that. When He comes He will change these vile bodies and fashion them like His own glorified body. As He went away in the body of flesh and bones He will come back in the body of flesh and bones, and when He appears the second time in His body of flesh and bones I will be like Him. There is only one thing for you to do and that is to spiritualize the whole thing away, and if you do that there is an end of all significance of language. We shall rise again, death and the grave shall not always dominate. The sting of death is sin. The honey bee can sting but once. Death stung into the heart of the Son of God once, so He cannot sting you and me. "Oh grave, where is thy victory?"

You have a living Christ to teach, and therefore you have a living hope to impart. The early disciples went everywhere teaching Jesus and the resurrection. One trouble with our preaching is that we do not have resurrection enough. Let us have more and more of the risen Jesus from the dead and his living power will transform human life.

---

NOTE.—For a more complete treatment of this subject, see "The Lord's Return, and Kindred Truth," by the same author, published by Fleming H. Revell & Co., Chicago, Ill.

# "The Fullness of God."

### By Rev. A. C. Dixon, D.D.

"That ye might be filled with all the fullness of God."—Eph. 3:19.

Standing on the deck of a ship in midocean, you see the sun reflected from its depths. From a little boat on a mountain lake you see the same sun reflected from its clear, shallow waters. Looking into the mountain spring, not more than six inches in diameter, you see the same great sun. Look into the dewdrop of the morning, and there it is again. The sun has a way of adapting itself to its reflectors. The ocean is not too large to hold it nor the dewdrop too small. So God can fill any man, whether his capacity be like the ocean, like the mountain lake, like the spring, or like the dewdrop. Whatever, therefore, be your capacity, the text opens to you the possibility of being "filled with all the fullness of God."

Our purpose now is to show you the kind of man God will fill, and we need but to study this prayer of Paul's to see the elements of his character.

1. *The God-filled man must be Strong in a Conscience ruled by the Spirit.* "That he would grant you, according to the riches of His glory, to be strengthened with might by His Spirit in the inner man." Conscience is not all of the "inner man," but it is such a part of it that there can be no strength of character without it. Strength of reason, or imagination, even of faith and love, will not atone for lack of conscientiousness. If a man's faith and affections are full of Christ he will be conscientious; and if his conscience is ruled by the Spirit, his faith and love are apt

to be all right. Conscience must have a ruler. It is of itself not a sufficient guide. The heathen mother's conscience makes her throw her child to the crocodile. A nail near the compass on a Cunard steamer caused her to be thrown out of her course, and almost upon the breakers. The iron freight on vessels sometimes so affects the compass that it cannot be implicitly relied upon. And there are many things in us and about us that affect our conscience. One has a conscience ruled entirely by the law of the state. To him, whatever the state approves is right. Another man's conscience is ruled by public sentiment. What the people approve is to him right. God cannot fill such people. Their "inner man" must be strengthened, not by statute law or public sentiment, but by the Spirit. What the Spirit approves we must approve; what the Spirit opposes we must oppose, if we would be "filled with all the fullness of God." To be God-filled, therefore, we must be in perfect harmony with the Word of God. More than that, we must know it, and be suffused with its Spirit. The mind of the Spirit must be our mind.

Note the measure of strength we may have. "Strengthened according to the riches of His glory." The riches of grace come to us through the death of Christ, and no one can be poor who has them. The riches of His glory come to us through the resurrection and ascension of our Lord, and no one can be as rich as he should be who does not appropriate them. Through the death of Christ we are saved; through the life of Christ we are enriched with power. Away with the crucifix which represents the dead Christ as the object of worship. Let the throne with its living Christ take its place. If the Spirit rules in the holy of holies within us, we are filled with God's fullness and have already entered upon the first stage of an experience of glory. We have not to await our going to heaven; heaven has come to us.

2. *The God-filled man is one in whose heart Christ abides and feels at Home.* "That Christ may dwell in our hearts by faith." One would expect the phrase "by love." But no; Christ dwells in our love by faith. We love Him by faith, and we have faith in Him through love. Christ cannot abide where He is not trusted, and where He is trusted He is sure to be loved. Now if we would have God fill us, we must make Christ at home in our hearts.

There must be nothing in them that He cannot live with. We must consult His pleasure in all the company we invite into our heart-house; and we must let Him have access to every room. If I take a friend into my house as a guest for a few days, I give him a room and insist that he make himself at home; but he knows what that means, and confines himself to a few rooms specially set apart for company. But I go into my house with a bunch of keys in my hand, and there is not a nook or corner in it I do not enter if I wish. I go into the cellar, or garret, and into every room that lies between. Lord Jesus, here are the keys to every room of my soul. Enter and make Thyself at home. Thou ownest the whole establishment from cellar to garret. If there is a person or thing in the house that Thou dost not like, cast it out.

3. *The God-filled man must have the proper idea of dimensions.* "That ye, being rooted and grounded in love, may be able to comprehend with all saints what is the breadth and length, and depth and height." The true Christian conception of "breadth and length, and depth and height, is one thing; the world's conception is quite another. If we would be filled with God, we must have the Christian conception—"with all saints"; if we comprehend with the world, we will, of course, be filled with the world. Our idea of breadth must accord with God's idea. A broad theology usually means a theology that boasts of being a little broader than God's thought as expressed in the Bible. And a broad theology is a barren theology, for God does not fill the men who would be broader than Christ.

Jesus was broad in His sympathies, so broad he took in the whole world; but Jesus was narrow in His spirit of obedience. Every jot and tittle of the law He fulfilled. A breadth of sympathy that cultivates a sentimentalism which dispenses with obedience to Christ really narrows men and pushes God out. The narrowest men I ever met were those who boasted most loudly of their breadth. Show me a man who says: "No matter what one believes, provided he is honest," and, depend upon it, he is a man who is bitterest in feeling toward those who refuse to agree with him. God's idea of breadth is the conquest of the whole world, and only those who have drunk in this broad missionary spirit can be filled with God. The Church has ever been weak or strong in proportion to her breadth of view on this subject. The men who have shown that they were most filled with God have been those who took into their prayers and efforts the conversion of the whole world to Christ. The world's idea of breadth is "the survival of the fittest." "Let the struggle go on and those who are fit to live will survive." Christ's idea is the survival of the unfittest through the suffering of another. This Spirit, filling the followers of the Man of Calvary, builds home for the weak in body and mind, and seeks to help all who cannot help themselves. The Lord save His Church from the narrow view of those who think that only the fittest should be saved. Where that spirit prevails, there can be no fullness of God.

God's idea of length is eternity. The man whose idea of length is time will, of course, live for what time can give. He lays up treasures only on earth. He prizes life, but not eternal life. He fears death, not eternal death. Christ cannot be at home in such a man's heart. Two objects cannot occupy the same space at the same time. He is full of the world, and of course God is shut out.

The man, on the other hand, who looks at things unseen and eternal; who regards himself as a pilgrim through time to eternity; who uses this world as not abusing it, not letting it use him; who is in the world but not of it, because he seeks a better country,—such a man God can fill, because he is self-emptied.

Men have false conceptions of "depth and height." To be high is to rise above others. To be low is to lack the elements which raise them above others. Now Christ's conception is the opposite of this. With Him the place of honor is at the feet of others, girded with a towel and serving them. His "Excelsior" means helping some one else to the top of the mountain. Faithfulness, not position or acquisition, is His standard of honor. The man who is trying to rise God cannot fill. He is already full of self. The man who is trying to help others rise, and whose ambition is to see Jesus Christ exalted, has a heart in which He who "Made Himself of no reputation, and took the form of a servant," can feel at home.

In a word, God's measure of all things must be accepted if we would be filled with all His fullness. In order to have this conception we must be "rooted and grounded in love." Between the foundation of a house and the house itself there is no living connection. The foundation simply rests upon the earth, and the house simply rests upon the foundation. But the tree's foundation is rooted. There is a flow of life from the root to trunk and branches. The substance of the earth is carried by this life into the tree. The tree is filled with the fullness of root and earth. If we have this living connection with Christ, it is easy for God to fill us. The life forces in us carry the very substance of that in which we are "rooted and grounded" into our souls. God's thought becomes our thought; God's desires become our desires; God's purposes become our purposes. We live upon His life.

4. *The God-filled man must know the unknowable.* "To know the love of Christ which passeth knowledge." I know the English language, that is, I know the alphabet and a few books. I can read English, and yet when I go into the Peabody Library and look around me, I feel that I know nothing of the English language; and what is more, with the time and capacity I have, I can never know much of it. It holds treasures I can never gain. I know the love of Christ. That is, I have learned the alphabet. I am a poor sinner and He is a great Saviour. I love Him because He first loved me; and yet there are volumes in this love I cannot read. My little dewdrop nature is trying to take in an ocean vastness. I simply gaze and weep.

> "Oh for such love let rocks and hills
> Their lasting silence break,
> And all harmonious human tongues
> The Saviour's praises speak."

An inward look discourages the best of us. We do not seem to ourselves to be full of God. Can we ever attain to it? We can at least offer ourselves day by day to His inspection, and pray that every hour may bring us a little nearer to the realization of our desire. Mr. Morse, while studying in London, painted a picture for the inspection of Benjamin West. After he had finished it, as he thought, he spent two weeks more on it, hoping to detect faults and make it better. When he showed it to Mr. West, the great painter looked at it for a moment, and then said: "Your picture is very good, but why don't you go on and finish it?" "I have finished it," replied the young artist. "Look here," continued West, as he touched it with his brush and showed how much better it could be made. Three weeks more the young painter labored to perfect his picture, and brought it again to the master for inspection, confident of his approval. "Your picture is better, but go on and finish it." "I have done all I can do to it," said the now discouraged Mr. Morse. But with a few touches of his brush Mr. West showed him that it could be greatly improved. We work under the eye of a master who can help us every hour. Our discouragements often arise, not from failures on our part, but from the enlarged conception of the perfection of our ideal. Let us thank God for such discouragement while we "Go on and finish" what He tells us to do. In due time we shall be "Filled with all the fullness of God."

---

PUBLISHERS' NOTE.—The substance of this address was given in Central Music Hall at one of Mr. Moody's meetings, held during the Gospel campaign of 1893. Dr. Dixon kindly consented to write the address out in full for publication in this volume.

# Necessary Qualifications for Christian Work.

### By Rev. B. Fay Mills.

---

Sidney Smith is reported to have said that if you would give him the luxuries of life he would do without the necessities. There are some of us that perhaps have been trying to live upon the luxuries of the Christian life without the necessities. I believe we each ought to be witnesses for Christ in life and testimony; but I believe still further, that God has especially called some to proclaim His message.

I. In the first place, if a man is to proclaim God's message, he must be conscious that God has called him. A man never becomes a prophet simply by wishing to be a prophet. I suppose we need as much as anything else a John the Baptist. The men of old who spoke by the Holy Ghost were men called of God — such men as Noah, Elijah, Samuel, and Elisha; men that God called for a special work; men who knew they had a commission from the highest court and were not afraid of the tribunals of earth. You remember what a definite commission was given to Elisha, and you remember what a double portion of power there fell upon him.

Dr. Parkhurst, in speaking of this, said: "It must have been a great testing time for Elisha when he came down to the water," for there were from fifty to one hundred theological students — or "sons of the prophets"— on the other side of the Jordan looking at him. He further said, that he thought it would have been quite a natural thing for him to want to get down back of some bush and try the experiment first to see whether it would work or not. He went out into the face of all and smote the waters as his predecessors had done.

Men that God wants to-day are men who know that they are commissioned of God, and who know that God will perform what He says He will.

II. The next thing for a man or woman is a complete knowledge of what God has tried to teach through His word, and such communion with God that He may teach us His truth by the personal revelation of the Spirit. You know Jesus said: "I have many things to say unto you but you cannot bear them now." He might have revealed some of these things after the resurrection.

There is no Christian experience that may not be testified to and proven by this word of God, yet it is a terrible thing in this day to note the ignorance of Christians in regard to the written word of God. You hardly dare say to one in a meeting: "Are you a Christian?" and if so ask him to sit down and point an inquirer to Christ.

I wish we could get them to come to this word as though it were an entirely new book, and then let Christ be the only teacher.

There are things, if you ever learn them, you will have to receive yourself in the Holy of Holies, and into which wife or mother cannot enter with you. This word will have to become a part of your soul.

I remember, when a boy, a young man walked up and down in front of the governor's house all night. In the morning the news came that the governor was dead. This young man, who was a drug clerk, gave himself over to the officers and said he had been the cause of the governor's death, for on the day previous he had made a mistake in putting up the prescription, by getting one of the ingredients wrong.

Oh friends, we need to realize that one man's medicine may be another's poison. Our work will be worse than fruitless, and a curse rather than a blessing, unless we are taught of God.

A few years ago there was a train running through a blizzard on a northern railway. The trainmen knew well the stations and stopped as they came to them. The people would get out into the blinding storm, and the train would move on. One passenger, a woman, was afraid she would not get off at the right station, but was assured by a gentleman, who said he knew perfectly every station on the line; that he would tell her when they arrived at her home. The train stopped at the station before hers; the passengers got out into the storm; the train went on and presently stopped again. "This is your station," said the gentleman, and he hurried her out into the blinding blizzard. After they had run on some distance, he heard the brakeman call out the station at which he supposed he had put the woman off. "What do you mean?" he asked the brakeman. "I thought that was the last stop." "Oh, no, that was only something the matter with the engine; that was away out on the prairie." The train was run back to the spot, and there they found the woman and her child frozen and dead. How much more awful for any of us to misdirect a soul and leave it to die.

III. Entire consecration to the Lord Jesus. Beloved, if the ordinary measure of consecration that we find among Christians of to-day is what God wants, then the church of Christ was never intended to be a witness for Jesus Christ. A life of consecration is entered into by a single momentary act in which the life of an individual is changed from what it always was. Someone says: "Do you believe in a second blessing?" I believe in all the blessings there are. What difference does it make what the number of the blessing so long as you have not given yourself entirely to God. I believe there is a place where we can say, "I have given everything to God."

Abraham was called "the friend of God," but I believe he never received the fullness of blessing until he put his knife to the throat of Isaac. The people around Abraham were giving their children to their gods, and I think that this thought had come to Abraham over and over again. He had come to that last place of testing, and when he came to that, he came to the last limit. He had done other things. He had gone out from his home at the call of God, and gone hither and thither in obedience to God's command. When he had done this last thing, God said: "Because thou hast done *this* thing" (the last test of God), "in blessing I will bless thee," etc. God is after the last thing in us. Like the soldiers looking for the fugitives in the South: They went to the place beyond which the pursued could not have gone; searched through the house but could not find them; then they searched the barn, but they were not there; then they tramped over the haystack, and as a last effort took the bayonets of their guns and ran them down into the hay, and back to them came the shrieks of the men for whom they were looking. Oh let the bayonet of God's truth down into the depths of your heart and test you to the uttermost.

IV. A definite, conscious baptism of the Holy Ghost. In the early days of this dispensation, it was just as much expected that a man should be baptized with the Holy Ghost as with water, and to have this power upon him as that he should be regenerated; and ever since the apostolic times the men and women that have been used of God have been conscious of a filling and refilling of the power of the Holy Ghost. This baptism of power does not necessarily make us all preachers, however. A colored brother once rose in a meeting and said: "Brethren, I've got my commission. When I was coming to church I looked up and saw the letters G. P. C.—*Go preach Christ.*" Another brother arose and said: "I do not doubt the brother's sincerity, but I think it may be that he should go pick cotton." Maybe some of us would be more in our place if we should "Go pick cotton." I heard of a man in Minneapolis, who, seventeen years ago, was a maker of violins. He was impressed one day that he ought to pray about one violin. He did so, and never worked on it unless he was in a prayerful spirit. His other violins sold at from three to four dollars, but this one brought him over $300. You would think he would have learned the lesson, but he did not. Ten years rolled by and he had the same impression with the same result, but still he failed to get the lesson. Three and one-half years more went past, and one day he thought, why should I not pray over my work all the time. From that time he has not sold any violins for less than $300.

A seminary student, just settled over a congregation, and knowing nothing of personal work, went down to Indianapolis where there were some evangelistic meetings. After the meeting the evangelist said: "Every one of you get up now, and try to bring a soul to Christ." He came personally to this young minister three times with this injunction, and at last finding that he was a minister, said: "Great God, a minister of the Gospel letting souls go to hell all around you." The young man went out of the meeting and home to his closet, and there he stayed for forty-eight hours. Then the church was called together, and within twenty-four hours one hundred received Christ as their Saviour.

# Soul Winning.

## By Rev. H. M. Wharton, D.D.

---

I have chosen for my subject this morning one that is of intense interest to every one of us. A subject that filled the heart and hands of our Saviour, and a work in which you and I have entered for life,—" Soul Winning."

In Prov. 11: 30 you find these words: " He that winneth souls is wise." Not long since I was on the coast and I visited one of these life-saving stations; and when I looked into the faces of those brave men of the life-saving crew, it seemed that there was something more than human in them that they would so risk their lives in saving their fellow-men from watery graves. But when you think of your work of saving souls you see how much greater an estimate God puts upon your work than theirs. There was an old hulk lying there that had floated in from a wreck. The people had been out in the ship and it had become damaged and was fast going to pieces. Many attempted to escape and were drowned, and those remaining, as a last resort, took a cask and tied a rope around it and threw it into the sea. It floated about until it was cast upon the shore. The men seized it and made the rope fast. The other end being fast to the ship the people made their escape over the rope, and reached the land in safety over a sea which was too rough even for a life-saving crew. I felt like taking off my hat to that cask, and I just looked up to God and asked Him that I might be like it, and float the life-line of Jesus Christ into the harbor for some poor, perishing sinner.

In carrying out the plan of salvation the idea is this, that every soul won shall become a soul winner. "Let him that heareth say come." In traveling in the East sometimes pilgrims get out of water, and they begin to separate in search of some spring or lake. They go just far enough apart that they can still hear each other's voice, and then begins the search for the water. As soon as one has found it he shouts to the one nearest him, "Come," and he takes it up and passes it to the next, and so on down the line until every one comes and takes of it. So Jesus says, "Let him that heareth say come." It is your bounden duty to say to the one next to you, "Come." The Christian who lives in this world and fails to win a soul to Christ fails in his mission. The souls that we win for Christ will be our reward. Those of us who fail in winning souls fail in the object of our ministry.

The two great keynotes of the Gospel are "come" and "go." "Come unto Me all ye that labor and are heavy laden and I will give you rest;" and, "Go ye into all the world and preach the Gospel to every creature." You perhaps have all read the pretty little poem written on the dream of a young lady. She was so happy over her conversion that she prayed that God would take her right to her home in heaven. She went, and the angel was taking her around showing her the beautiful things, and they came to some crowns. Some had one star and others had many; but they came to one that had none, and she asked the angel what that meant; and the angel replied: "That is yours, for you wished to be brought right to heaven, and you had never won a soul to Christ." The young lady awoke from her dream and resolved that by the help of God she would not go to heaven without some of those precious stars in her crown.

You cannot take anything into heaven with you but souls. You cannot take money, nor houses, nor fine clothes, nor anything else. You must leave them all here. A wealthy man died in our country and some one asked how much money he left, and they said: "He left all he had." He could not do anything else. But if you win souls you will have them forever.

Winning souls is the best thing we can do for others. If you wish to do a person a favor, just win him to Jesus. It is the best thing a mother can do for her child, or a father for his son.

He that winneth souls for Christ is doing what pleases Christ, and there is nothing we can do for Him that will please Him more. Every time you bring a soul you bring an eternal treasure. Some one says that in this world the Christian digs for diamonds, and in the eternal world he sees them shine.

He that winneth souls must be wise. You are not only wise for going into this business, but you must be wise as you engage in it.

Many men don't want to be saved. It is a strange characteristic of a horse that the only way you can get him out of a barn on fire is to blindfold him and back him out, and if you take the blindfold off when you get him out he will rush back in. He has lived in there all his life and knows nothing else, and thinks that old barn will protect him from the flames.

How gentle, sympathetic, and helpful we must be in this work.

1. Use great carefulness. You cannot rush into the presence of an unsaved soul carelessly. You must find out the disposition. You have heard of the preacher who was riding through the woods and invited a peddler whom he overtook to ride with him. After a short distance, thinking of his duty as a soul winner, he shouted out, "Are you prepared to die!" "No," said the frightened man as he jumped out, leaving his pack and running off into the woods. The preacher cried, "Come back! I only meant to do you good; I'm a preacher." "You can't fool me," said the man. "You can have the pack, but you can't have me."

2. You need tact. That's what a woman has. Your wife leads you around where she will and yet you don't know it. She does it by tact.

You meet a person with doubts and you can display tact by telling him that you have had the same trouble.

3. Sympathy—suffering with them. Going through a street in Baltimore one rainy day I noticed a young sparrow sitting on a step, and another was chattering away, up in a tree, and it seemed to say, "Come up here and you'll be all right." After it had chattered for a long while and the little one did not move, the mother flew down from the tree and came right up close to the little thing, as much as to say, "Well, if you cannot come up into the tree I will stand by you down here." That's sympathy.

4. Help. Sympathy will not always be enough; we must sometimes render temporal assistance. I do not mean that we

must always render substantial help, although it is necessary sometimes.

A tramp went to a house and asked for something to eat, and the Christian woman gave him a tract and he tore it up and went away cursing. If she had given him a meal of victuals and then the tract it might have had some effect on him.

5. Earnestness. Let us seek souls as men seek money, as pleasure-lovers seek pleasure, as a mother seeks for her lost child.

6. Knowledge of God's word. Let us seek out those things which tell us how they worked in olden times. So long as human nature is the same you need the same help.

Acts 8. The case of Philip and the eunuch. There you have both sides of the history of a conversion. Generally you only hear the human side. You hear testimonies like this: "I was converted through the influence of my mother." Another says: "I just chanced to drop into a meeting and was converted." You also have the human side in the case of the eunuch. He chanced to meet Philip there in the road. Then you have the divine side, where God spake to Philip to "Arise, go toward the south," etc. Haven't you often felt led to do things in this way? Suppose he had said, "That's a desert place and hard traveling; I guess I'll not go." Did you ever say no when you felt that God wanted you to speak to one about his soul?

This man was a rich man, and God often sends us to the rich as well as the poor.

God prepared the way for Philip, and He is continually preparing the way for us.

Philip began "at that same Scripture, and preached unto him Jesus." Begin right where you find a man, and talk to him about Jesus.

I have found in my experience of twenty years in the ministry that the unsaved are more anxious to be talked with on the subject of religion than the saved are to talk with them.

Last and greatest of all: You must have the Holy Spirit, for even God's word has not the power without the Spirit. Ask Him that the Spirit may go with you; yea, go before you.

# Working for Christ.

## By Rev. H. M. Wharton, D.D.

---

I believe that one of the greatest privileges Christ has given to us is to work for Him — not that He needs us, but that we need Him. He could get along without us. He could let the angels come down and do this work He has given us; but no, he has had us in mind all the time.

I think one of the loveliest traits of character in a human being is gratitude. If you are sick and some kind-hearted one comes and ministers to you in your sickness, and sits by your bed during the long nights and nurses you back to health and strength, one of your first thoughts will be, what can I do for that kind one? So when you and I have been brought from darkness to light, and from the power of sin and Satan unto God; and when we know that Jesus died for us, what a proof of our thanksgiving it is for us just to spend our lives working for Him.

Our Lord himself was a great worker. You remember when He was sitting by the well of Sychar and a woman came out for a pitcher of water and He talked with her. The well of Sychar is about one-half way from the city to the fertile fields. The city is well watered and she had no need to carry water there, but she had probably come up out of these fertile fields, where there were a great many men at work, for the purpose of getting water and carrying it back to the hands in the field. There at this well she met Jesus, and after the conversation she hurried away to the city, leaving the waterpot behind, for she had no need of carrying water to the city, and there she spread the news of the Gospel Jesus had just given her. Women are the best spreaders of news I know of. They can spread other news and why can't they spread the good news of the Gospel? Then the disciples came and He made that most marvelous statement: "My meat is to do the will of Him that sent me." Then pointing to the field down below Him He said: "Say not ye there are yet four months and then cometh the harvest," then pointing to the people that were coming out of the city He said: "Look on the fields for they are white already to harvest."

Turn to John 3:16, and you will find the Gospel in a nutshell. It is just a condensed form of the Gospel. Two old ladies were sitting knitting, when one said: "Suppose the Bible were destroyed, and that you could only have one verse, what one would you choose?" The other old lady said: "Oh, I could not think of the Bible being destroyed." "Yes, but just suppose it was." "Well," said the good old lady, "I think I would choose that verse that says, "For God so loved the world that He gave His only begotten Son, that whosoever believeth in Him should not perish, but have everlasting life." She knew where the verse lay that contained the most precious truth.

John 9. Here you find a great long chapter telling about giving sight to a blind man. He does not do things as we think He would. In one place He puts so much in one verse and in another He talks so much about one poor man.

Christ said among other things: "I must work the works of Him that sent me." Each one of us has a mission in this world. Write that down, and some of these days, when these meetings are all over, and you take up your notes to read them, you will come across it. And I will say another thing before I go on, and that is, that Jesus Christ sent us into this world to do our work just as much as God the Father sent Him to do His; and I believe that each one of us here to-day can feel as Jesus Christ did as He said: "I must work the works of Him that sent me." Have that on your heart. Say "must." When I was a boy I used to put a coal of fire on a terrapin's back to make it move, and it everlastingly moved as long as that fire was on it. Get the fire of God in your heart and you will move as you never did before. Feel that nobody can do your work and that you must do it. I stood on a principal street in Baltimore one day, and noticed all the people running from the center of the street to the sidewalk, and I looked up the street and there was a little gray horse hitched to a little buggy coming down street for all it was worth, and it seemed to say: "Get out of my way; I must get away with this old buggy." And he was getting away with it, and the people got out of his way and let him get away with it.

Another thing. Be dead in earnest. Be like the little boy; when they asked him how much he weighed, he said: "I weigh eighty pounds, except when I am dead in earnest and then I weigh a ton."

Look at the nature of these works. There are two great forces in this world — good and evil. All of us are on one side or the other. God and good are on one side and the devil and evil are on the other. Jesus said: "He that is not with me is against me." Those of us who think we are neutral, as the moralist does, are on the side of evil. I remember a prominent man who once thought himself not on the side of evil, and yet there were a number of young men who refused to become Christians, saying: "Why can't we be just as good as he and not be in the church?" He was not in the church and was keeping others out, and such people can't be on the side of Christ. When the devil is showing you his pile of corn he will call your attention to the finest and plumpest ear in the pile; but when he comes to show you the Lord's pile he picks out the worst old mildewed nubbin he can find. He uses his own fine specimens to lead people away from Christ. You know the hunter when he is going out to hunt for ducks takes along a lot of decoy ducks and puts them on the pond while he gets in the "blind" and hides. Then the live ducks come flying over and see the decoys, and say: "Oh, there is no danger here," and fly down into the water, and the sly old hunter gets as many as he wants. These fine moral ladies and gentlemen are the devil's decoys which he sets to catch people, and he is catching them. Are you wholly on the Lord's side, and have you committed yourself soul and body, out and out, to the good and to God? That was Christ's work. He came into the world to destroy the works of the devil, and wherever you find any of those works strike them. A country man once came up into the city to a show. They took him in the side-show first, and in going around he came across a glass case of live snakes. He raised his cane and smashed it through the glass case, when some one made an effort to stop him; and he said: "Stand back, gentlemen; I kills 'em wherever I finds 'em." That's just the way you want to be in your Christian work.

If you go to work for Christ you must begin on your own self first. That is the hardest place to work, too. Any man hates to figure up his accounts when he knows they will figure up against him. I do not think it is a good thing to keep looking at yourself all the time, but it is a good thing once in a while. Suppose you were sick, and would sit before the glass with your tongue out three or four inches, and your finger on your pulse all the time. The doctor would say "Stop that," the very first thing. It's good to know you are sick when you are, but don't keep it before the mind all the time. It's a good thing to see your heart, but not a good thing to think of it and nothing else.

When I came to this Institute I saw on the door of the wardrobe in my room these words: "Get right with God," and I have thought of them a good many times. We not only need to get right before men, but before God. A little boy going to Sunday-school noticed a hole in his shirt and told his mother, and she said: "I'll just put on your vest, and it will cover it up so no one will know it's there." "Yes," said the boy, "but I'll know it's there." We may cover up things from others, but we are conscious of their presence all the time.

Let me give you an important thing in your work — look after the sick. They are visited enough, but not in the right kind of a way.

1. Go into the sick room quietly and softly. Do not go in as though you were going to scare pigs out.

2. Go with a bright face.

3. No matter how emaciated they may be, express no surprise.

4. Don't speak discouraging words to the sick.

I was sick once, and a young preacher who was studying medicine, and was deeply interested in electricity, which was just beginning to be studied, called on me more as a physician than as a preacher, and after looking at my tongue and feeling my pulse he said: "Wharton, you are liable to go off with apoplexy or paralysis at any time. Do you know you need a battery?" Well, I would like to have had a battery turned on him.

5. Don't talk too much nor too solemnly about religion and death. Don't worry them with a dissertation about dying.

6. Don't stay too long. Even if the sick one urges you to stay don't do it.

7. Leave something as you go away. If they are well to do leave a flower or bunch of roses; and if they are not, better leave something more substantial. How nice it is to see a woman go in with a buttered roll and some nicely cooked chicken, and while the sick one eats she washes the children's faces. We are the ministers of God to the sick, and one of the greatest blessings we enjoy is ministering to them.

# Authenticity of the Scriptures.

### By Rev. R. G. Pearson.

---

Matt. 27:40: "If thou be the Son of God come down from the cross." These were the words spoken by those Godless, God-defying sinners at the crucifixion. As much as to say: "You said you were the Son of God; you said you came to save the world, and now, if you cannot save yourself, how can you save the world?" "If you are the Son of God, come down from the cross."

Why did He not come down from the cross if He were the Son of God? I suppose we all believe in the divinity of Jesus Christ. It is not enough simply to believe it, we ought to be grounded in it and be able to give a reason for the hope that is within us.

There are three propositions which I wish to lay down and discuss:

I. Unbelief requires proof of that which has had a reasonable demonstration.

II. Unbelief requires that the demonstration shall be made in such a way as involves a moral impossibility.

III. Unbelief requires such an amount of evidence as to destroy the ability to doubt.

I have not very much patience with a man that says, "I am a Christian just because my mother was." I like a man that says I want a reason for the hope that is within me; but when he asks for proof of a thing that has had a reasonable demonstration, then I demur.

I. Unbelief requires proof of that which has had a reasonable demonstration. I am satisfied that if I cannot show that

Jesus Christ gave a reasonable demonstration, then my proposition falls to the ground.

1. First in the fulfillment of Old Testament prophecies which pointed to Him. Let me illustrate. You have what is called an ancient document, that is, a document that has passed muster through the courts of the country for thirty years. Let us apply that to the Bible. Is it an ancient document?

We see the Council of Nice, in the fourth century, has this Bible practically as it is to-day. We see it pass muster at the Diet of Worms. Then we have King James bringing out the edition of the fifteenth century which we have to-day. We cross to this country and we find George Washington taking the oath of office with his hand on this book. Any man that says that is not an ancient document, and that it is not what it claims to be, upon that man, logically and legally, lies the burden of proof to show that his assertions are correct.

Let me give you an illustration to show that the burden of proof lies on this man. We will suppose Mr. Moody has had a clear title to this property for thirty years, and the owners before him held it clear for seventy-five years, or from the time the government gave the first deed. Now suppose some man from India or China comes here and whispers around that the title deed is not good. I say that upon that man lies the burden to prove that this title deed is not good.

Jesus Christ was prophesied of four thousand years before He came.

1. In Gen. 3:15, you have the prophecy that the seed of the woman should bruise the serpent's head, and in Gal. 4:4 you have it fulfilled.

2. In Gen. 22:18: He should be of the seed of Abraham, and in Acts 13:23 it is fulfilled.

3. Gen. 49:10: Of the tribe of Judah. In Matt. 2:6, fulfilled.

4. Micah 5:2: Born in Bethlehem; fulfilled in Matt. 2:6.

5. Isa. 11:1: Of the house of David; fulfilled in Luke 1:69.

6. Zech. 11:12; Psalms 41:9: Betrayal by Judas; fulfilled in Matt. 26:15.

7. Psalms 22:16: His death on the cross; fulfilled in Matt. 26:35.

8. Psalms 49:15: His resurrection; fulfilled in Matt. 27:63.
9. Psalms 24:7: His ascension; fulfilled in Luke 24:51.

Every one of these prophecies of the Old Testament was fulfilled to the letter.

2. Demonstrated in the miracles. The peculiarity of Christ's miracles was, that they were not done like modern seances. Their verdict to His work was: "We cannot deny it, for a notable miracle has been performed here in our midst."

3. The doctrines He preached were a demonstration of His divinity. John 7:17.

· (a) Universal brotherhood of man. Before Christ came the world was divided into cliques and clans, and they never thought of all men being brothers.

(b) The value of an individual man.

4. The life that He lived. The judge that tried Him said three times: "I find no fault in Him." The soldier at the cross said: "Surely this was a righteous man."

In the history of mankind there has been but one man that was not found fault with. He never did anything to make God or angels blush. This is a unique fact and what are you going to do with it?

When a fact is brought into court, it is disposed of in a way that is most free from objection. If Jesus Christ was not the Son of God then your faith is vain, and you are plunged into darkness. Now put these things together, and you find that Christ did them before He went to the cross. Then on the cross He is told to come down if He be the Son of God. If skeptics deny the claims, they must also deny these facts.

II. It requires that the demonstration be made in a way that involves a moral impossibility. It's all right to want a demonstration, but to try and involve Christ and God in an impossibility is preposterous.

The plan of salvation must be consummated. Away back in eternity He planned salvation. He selected a man, then a nation, and out of them brought the Redeemer. He gave types and symbols, and the great antetype, Jesus Christ, must fulfill all these. And just at this critical point they say: "If thou be the Son of God come down from the cross."

III. Unbelief concerning the divinity of Jesus Christ requires such an amount of evidence as to destroy the ability to doubt. Some one says: "I will believe no proposition in philosophy unless it is made so plain that I can see through it." You can't take the "milky way" and the "seven stars" and squeeze them up in your hand. God is infinite, therefore there are things in His salvation that you cannot crowd into your little intellect.

Whenever you raise evidence so high that you cannot doubt, then you eliminate faith. There is not a man that can doubt that five times five are twenty-five. So if there can be no doubt there can be no faith. As the soul rises in evidence to such a height that it is impossible to doubt, it then has full opportunity for the exercise of faith taken away.

Just so with the man in hell. He knows that Jesus Christ is the Son of God. He cannot doubt it, and consequently there is no more chance to exercise faith than there is in the multiplication table. "Now abideth faith, hope, and charity." *Faith*, in the eternal world, ends in sight; *Hope* ends in fruition, but *Charity* continues on as it has here.

# Faith.

By Rev. R. G. Pearson.

---

James 2 : 14-26. I wish to call your attention especially to the twenty-fourth verse: "Ye see then how that by works a man is justified, and not by faith only." You find in this text faith, works, and justification. These three are inseparably connected. Not simply in the text do you find this, but through God's word and in every well-regulated Christian life. It is a great thing to have a well-rounded and well-developed symmetrical grip upon the truths in God's word. Some men see one truth and press it too far. A heretic is a man that has pressed a truth too far. Some people are all faith and others are all works, and generally you find they are all one-sided. If you are going to row a boat and wish to go straight forward, the best way for you to do is to row with both oars. You drop one oar and go on pulling with the other, and you are sure to get out of line and go off to one side. Some people have the idea that it does not make any odds what they *do*, just so as they *believe* right; and others have the idea that it does not make any difference what they *believe* if they only *work right*. There is a little truth, and a great deal of error, in each.

There is a great difference in the world in the effect which these questions have. Skeptics say that Paul says we are justified by faith, and Peter says we are justified by works, therefore Paul and James contradict each other. Let us look at this.

There are just three questions I wish to ask:
I. How are we justified in the sight of God?
II. How are we justified in the sight of man?

III. What is the connection between faith and works?

Now to the law and the testimony.

I. How are we justified in the sight of God? Who are you talking about? I say the unsaved man, the unregenerate sinner. What is the present standing of an unsaved man in the sight of God? See what God says about it:

Rom. 3:23: "For all have sinned and come short of the glory of God."

John 3:18: "He that believeth not on the Son is condemned already."

Gal. 3:10: "Cursed is every one that continueth not in all things which are written in the book of the law to do them."

Put these together and you find the condition of an unregenerate man is one of guilt and condemnation, and he is under the curse of God's holy law. The question now is: How can a man that is under the curse of God's broken law be justified in God's sight? A more fundamental Bible question was never pressed upon a sinner's heart.

(a) Such a man is not justified in the sight of God by the law. Gal. 3:11: "But that no man is justified by the law in the sight of God, it is evident; for the just shall live by faith." From this scripture it is as clear as a sunbeam, for it is said by God that no man is justified by the law. That settles the question.

(b) Rom. 3:20: "Therefore by the deeds of the law shall no flesh be justified in His sight." The province of God's law is not to justify a guilty sinner. A law cannot justify. It's purpose is to give a knowledge of sin. A man that tries to be justified by God's law is perverting it. Let me illustrate. We will suppose a case. Here is a man building a house. He wishes to know if the walls are perpendicular, so he gets a plumb-line and hangs it by the wall; now that plumb-line is not to straighten the wall, but to show where it is crooked. God's plumb-line is not to straighten a crooked heart, but to show how much out of plumb and how crooked it is. You take God's law and swing it up and down your soul and let it come to perpendicular, and you will see how crooked it is. Notice that wonderful statement in Rom. 8:3. The law could not straighten a crooked sinner, so God sending His own Son in the likeness of sinful flesh, and for sin, condemned sin in the flesh. The guilty man is not to look to the law for justification, but to Jesus Christ.

(c) We are not justified by works or deeds of the law. Paul tells in Galatians, that by the deeds of the law shall no flesh be justified.

Rom. 4:5: "To him that worketh not, but believeth on Him that justifieth the ungodly, his faith is counted for righteousness."

Eph. 2:8-9: You have a great many self-made men here in Chicago, but I tell you there is not a self-saved man here in Chicago or in heaven either. The poor deluded moralist says: "I expect to get to heaven, because I pay my debts and live an honest, moral life." Dear, dying man, no one can be saved that way.

(d) In the sight of God a man is justified by faith first, last, and all the time. Acts 13:38-39; Rom. 3:28. A man to be justified, must come and put his faith in the Lord Jesus Christ, God's Son, and not in the law. As the lawyer would say: "Let us go back and get a precedent." Take that wonderful character — Abraham. Read Rom. 4:2, 3, and you find: "Abraham believed God, and it was counted unto him for righteousness." Then further on you find that "he staggered not at the promise of God." Then notice how the fourth chapter glides right into the fifth: "Therefore, being justified by the faith, we have peace with God through our Lord Jesus Christ."

II. How are we justified in the sight of men? Who are we talking about now? I am speaking of men inside the church, and what we technically call professing Christians. First, last, and all the time He is justified by works, and works only.

Jas. 2:24: That word "only" is suggestive. James' idea is this: "Brethren, Paul has been showing that a sinner is justified by faith," and that is right, but there is another way. We are justified by works. You cannot see a man's faith, but you can see his works, and you can see that a man is justified before *men* by his works.

Matt. 7:20: "By their fruits *ye* shall know them." God can look down into men's hearts and see if they are justified, but we only can see by works. Let us go again and get a precedent that illustrates and emphasizes the principle laid down here. Take Abraham. Paul uses him to show that a man is justified by faith, and James that a man is justified by works. God says to Abraham: "Take thine only son Isaac and offer him upon an altar." It was not a promise of God's, but it was His specific command. Abraham did what God commanded him in will and intention. Hence we have the statement, "Justified by *works*." When? When he offered Isaac upon the altar.

Paul was taking Abraham as a guilty sinner before God, and he says: "He believed God and it was counted to him for righteousness. James was talking about him some years afterward when he offered Isaac upon the altar. Is there any conflict? Paul is talking about the justification of a sinner by faith and James is talking about the justification of a Christian by works. Let me give you another illustration.

We are having a meeting here, and in the church we will suppose next Sunday night I preach and give an invitation for all who believe that God, for Jesus Christ's sake, forgives them to come forward. Up come half a dozen. I do not know anything about their hearts and just take their word. Next year I ask Mr. Hyde how they are getting along. I say: How about Jones? Well, Jones is drinking just like he did before. He goes to balls and on Sunday excursions, just as he did before. What do I know then? I know that that night when Jones came up and gave me his hand he was either a deluded simpleton or an out and out hypocrite.

Then I say: Well, Mr. Hyde, how about Smith? Mr. Smith! I am glad to be able to tell you that he has not been in a saloon nor cursed his wife since. He is a regular old Saint Paul Christian. There, you see he was justified before God by faith, and then he proved it before men by his works.

I want you to get from God's word the right exposition of works — good works. Here is a man that says: "I pay my debts and live a moral, upright life." Is that the Bible idea of good works. Jas. 2:22. Abraham was justified by works when he offered Isaac. It was his obedience to a plain command. I say these are good works and only good works that are done in obedience to God's commands. Are you a moral, upright man out of pride of reputation and character? Mr. Ingersoll does it out of pride of character, and he tells the truth except when he is talking about the Bible. If you keep the Sabbath and live a sober life because God commands it then it is good works.

Let us get an explanation of what faith is. It is not this namby-pamby, twiddle-twaddle sentimentalism. Oh, yes; of course I believe Christ was the Son of God, and I believe the Bible. Dear friends, faith is an inwrought principle in the heart — a live, veritable reality. There was no sentimentalism in Abraham's taking his son, binding him, putting him upon that altar, and stabbing him to the heart.

III. What's the connection between this kind of faith which justifies a man before God and these works that justify a man in the sight of men.

Gal. 5: 6. The connection between faith and works, rightly so called, is that faith produces works. Abraham had a genuine faith in God, and when God commanded him to offer Isaac he did it. A faith that won't work is no faith at all.

You might as well have sawdust in your head as to have brains that will not think. You might as well have a brickbat in your breast as to have a heart that won't pump the blood through your veins. You might as well have your head full of Ingersollism as to have a little milk and cider sentimentalism that says : "Oh, yes, I believe," and yet don't do anything.

Here is a man who has been to church for ten, twenty, thirty, forty years, but what has he got to show for it? Does he show more love, humility, zeal, self-denial, devotion? If not, such faith being alone is dead. It is a great slander on Christianity to say that a man can have such faith as Abraham's in his soul, and that it produces none of the fruits of the Spirit of God.

2. Faith is attested by works. Suppose Abraham had said: "No; I am not going to offer my only son." We would conclude that his faith was not genuine. As I go up and down in this field of evangelistic work I get sick clear down to the bottom of my soul. A good many of these church members are doing the same old tricks they did before they came into the church; have just as high a temper, are just as uppish and offish as ever, and it would take a constable and a search warrant to find the difference be-

tween them and a sinner that makes no profession. Such a faith as that will not keep a man out of hell. We prove our faith by our works when we do as Christ tells us.

3. Faith is *strengthened* by works. Abraham had a great deal of faith when he bade his wife Sarah good-bye, and went off up to the altar; but I believe he had a thousand times more when he came down from the mountain. He did just what God told him to do, and he got his faith strengthened. If you want your faith strengthened go to work for Jesus — do something.

This connection between faith and works is like that between a tree and its fruits. Rom. 6: 23: " Ye have your fruit unto holiness.

Phil. 2: 12: "Work out your own salvation," etc. I heard a preacher use that to preach to sinners to get them up to the mourners' bench. Paul is here writing to the church at Philippi, and he says: "Wherefore, my beloved!" Now Paul never talked to sinners that way. Where is the trouble? You have mistaken the verse.

When God regenerates a man He works salvation into him. If God does not work it in you can't work it out. When God made the fruit He injected into it the fruit-bearing element, and they are not to go into the fruit business, but are simply to work out what God has put in. Man's work is not to go into the saving business, but to let God put in salvation, and then he can prove it by his works, by working out what God has put in.

# The Baptism of the Holy Ghost.

By Rev. G. H. C. Macgregor, M.A.

---

### PART I. — MARK 1: 9-11.

In studying questions regarding the spiritual life, it is well to remember that in the experience of the Lord Jesus we have the norm of spiritual experience. In life, as well as in work, He left us an example that we should follow in His steps. In what He did we find the rule as to what we should do. In what He was we find the rule as to what we should be. This is strikingly true in regard to the relation of our Lord Jesus to the Holy Spirit. A study of what the baptism of the Holy Ghost meant for *Him* will be our best preparation for learning what the baptism of the Holy Ghost means for *us*.

From the Gospels we learn that ere His baptism —

1. Our Lord was *born of the Spirit*. The formation of the human nature of the Lord Jesus was in a unique sense the work of the Holy Ghost. The word to Mary was, "The Holy Ghost shall come upon thee, and the power of the Highest shall overshadow thee; therefore also that which is to be born shall be called holy, the Son of God."

Natural birth and spiritual birth in the case of our Lord were coincident. Though born "from above," He was never born "again." Though born in the flesh He was never of the flesh. He was from the beginning "the second man, the Lord from heaven." But we notice that in His case spiritual birth and the baptism of the Holy Ghost did not coincide. The one came long subsequent to the other.

2. Our Lord *lived in the Spirit*. His whole life was well pleas-

ing to God, and was kept thus well pleasing to God by the power of the Holy Ghost. The secret of the sinlessness of Jesus seems to be in this, that He was sanctified and kept continually by the Holy Spirit. The Holy Spirit dwelt in Him ungrieved, unhindered, ever honored, ever obeyed, and through the power of the Holy Spirit He repelled all temptation. But while this went on all through the thirty years, not until that memorable day at the Jordon was our Lord baptized with the Spirit.

3. *The Baptism of our Lord Jesus with the Holy Ghost* took place when He was entering upon His public work for God, and by this He was endued with the extraordinary powers and gifts which were necessary for the discharge of His work on earth.

From the fact that the baptism occurred at this stage, it has been argued that it had reference not to life, but to work, and it has been inferred that if this was the case with the Lord Jesus, it must also be the case with us. Hence by very many the baptism of the Holy Ghost is regarded as being an anointing for service, and that alone. They almost limit the ideas connected with the baptism of the Holy Ghost to ideas connected with work. And it cannot be denied that there is a good deal in scripture to support this way of thinking. The baptism of Jesus was at the outset of His ministry; the baptism of the Apostles was at the beginning of their world-wide ministry. Again and again the gift of the Spirit is spoken of in connection with service. But to limit the thought to service is to deal inadequately with the subject. We cannot separate life and work in this way, least of all in the case of the Lord Jesus. Our work must be the expression of our life. Work which is in the power of the Spirit is work which is the outcome of a life which has been made so full that it overflows in blessing to others.

No doubt there are unquestionable instances of men being wonderfully owned of God who were not themselves holy; men on whom the Spirit seemed to rest, but in whom He did not seem to dwell. But such cases are instinctively felt by the Christian consciousness to be anomalous. God is sovereign and may use such men, but their case is not one which we can argue from. Certainly no one has any right to expect to be used by God whose life is not right with God. Only when the life is full may we look for it to overflow. While, therefore, the baptism of the Holy Ghost is often spoken of in connection with service, we have no right to separate the thought of life from the thought of work. The two go together, but in order of thought life comes first.

This being so, I think we shall best understand what the baptism of the Holy Ghost meant in the case of Jesus, if we look on it as the outpouring of the Spirit on Him to give Him a deeper, fuller, richer spiritual life than even He had ever known. This event, I believe, marks a distinct stage in the personal spiritual history of our Lord.

Let no one be surprised at this language. Our Lord Jesus Christ was a perfect man, therefore He had a spiritual history. In His case there was no cleansing, but there was growth. "Jesus *increased in wisdom* . . . and in favor with God and man." He was always well pleasing to the Father, but I cannot read my New Testament without feeling that after this wonderful gift of the Spirit, His knowledge of the Father, His love to the Father, His sympathy with the Father's purpose, His trust in the Father, His delight in the Father's will were deeper and stronger than ever. There was, of course, no change in His character, but there was growth. And it was this that fitted Him for His work. It was in virtue of what He became through His anointing at His baptism that He was able to do what He did.

Were there time this might be worked out in detail.

What our Lord Jesus was, and what He did while on earth, He owed to the Holy Spirit resting on Him and dwelling in Him without measure. It was by the Holy Spirit that our Lord's miracles were wrought. It was by the Holy Spirit that He was guided, directed, comforted, supported in the whole course of His ministry, temptation, obedience, and sufferings.

It only remains to notice two deeply significant things regarding the baptism of Jesus:

1. The time when Jesus was baptized with the Holy Ghost was *a time of consecration.* It was after He had been baptized of John. But think of what that baptism of John meant. It was, as Mark tells us, the baptism of repentance for the remission of sins. But repentance Jesus needed not; remission of sins He

needed not. Therefore, when He presented Himself for baptism, John shrank back, saying, "I have need to be baptized of Thee, and cometh Thou to me?" It was only the word of Jesus, "Suffer it now, for thus it becometh us to fulfill all righteousness," that emboldened the Baptist to perform the rite.

But what did this submission to baptism mean on the part of Jesus. It meant the entire consecration of Himself to be the Sin-Bearer. In this act He gave Himself up without reserve to accomplish the Father's will. Here He deliberately took up the cross. The time was a time of consecration.

2. The time when Jesus was baptized with the Holy Ghost was *a time of prayer*. Luke expressly mentions that it was when Jesus was praying that the heavens were opened.

But what is the time of prayer? It is the time of *felt need*, of conscious helplessness in face of our work. It is the time of *desire*, when the cry goes out from the heart in passionate longing for the supply of our need. It is the time of *trust*, when we roll the burden of our need upon our heavenly Father and confidently look up to Him to deal with it. In a time like that our Lord was baptized with the Spirit.

Is not the whole story full of teaching and encouragement? If He needed the Holy Spirit, how much more do we! If He received Him, so also in His infinite mercy may we.

### PART II. — Mark 1: 8.

The principle laid down in the last paper for our guidance in studying spiritual experience, that the life of our Lord Jesus is the norm or standard of what our life is to be, I regard as a most important one. It shows us how closely our blessings are connected with Him. All our spiritual blessings are "in Christ." This is specially true of the crowning blessing of the Holy Spirit. This we receive, if we ever receive it, from the hand of the risen and ascended Lord. It is He who baptizes His people with the Spirit. This blessing must not be sought apart from Him, or thought of as something which is to carry us past Him. From the Lord Jesus the Holy Spirit in His fullness comes; and to glorify the Lord Jesus is His chief work.

With this in our mind, let us proceed to inquire what the baptism of the Holy Ghost means for the Lord's people. On a subject of such depth and difficulty it is inevitable that there should be a difference of opinion. I merely wish to state the view to which I have been led after prayerful study of the matter.

It may be well here to indicate the sense in which I use the word "baptism." I think there is a distinction between the baptism of the Holy Ghost and the fullness of the Holy Ghost. As will appear afterwards, I believe the fullness of the Holy Spirit is brought about by a special incoming of the blessed Spirit to our souls; and to His *first* incoming in this manner I apply the term "baptism." In my opinion, the baptism introduces the fullness. But while we may be filled and filled again, we are not re-baptized.

A series of propositions may now be made regarding this crowning blessing of Christian experience.

1. There is a blessing of spiritual experience, distinct from other blessings, which may be spoken of as "the fullness of the Holy Ghost."

The proof of this from the word of God is to my mind clear and full. In Luke 24:49, we read: "Behold I send the promise of My Father upon you; but tarry ye in the city of Jerusalem, until ye be endued with power from on high." This promise is repeated in Acts 1:5: "Ye shall be baptized with the Holy Ghost not many days hence." The fulfillment of the promise is recorded in Acts 2:1-4, where we are told that as the Apostles were gathered, "there appeared unto them cloven tongues like as of fire, and it sat upon each of them, and they were all filled with the Holy Ghost." What was experienced by the Apostles is promised to all believers in Acts 2:38, when Peter says: "Repent and be baptized every one of you unto the remission of sins, and ye shall receive the gift of the Holy Ghost. For the promise is to you and to your children, and to all that are afar off, even as many as the Lord our God shall call unto Him." The experience of Paul (Acts 9), of Cornelius (Acts 10), of the Samaritan and the Ephesian disciples (Acts 8 and 19), teach the same thing. The command addressed to believers in Eph. 5:18, "Be filled with the Spirit," points in the same direction. The word of God clearly indicates that there is a blessing of the fullness of the Spirit.

2. This blessing is distinct from regeneration.

This is proved by the fact that in the Bible we have instances when the one blessing was received long after the other. In the case of our Lord, the baptism of the Holy Ghost was long after His birth. But if anyone should say that this was before Pentecost, and cannot be used as a guide, then we may point to the cases in the Book of the Acts.

The most instructive for our purpose is that of the Samaritan Christians. In Acts 8:14, we read: "When the Apostles which were at Jerusalem heard that Samaria had received the word of God, they sent unto them Peter and John, who, when they were come down, prayed for them, that they might receive the Holy Ghost; for as yet He was fallen on none of them, only they had been baptized in the name of the Lord Jesus. Then laid they their hands on them, and they received the Holy Ghost." Here we have a band of baptized believers, who were regenerate, and who therefore had the Spirit of God, for "if anyone have not the Spirit of Christ he is none of His"; yet they had to receive the Spirit. In one sense they had the Spirit; in another, they had not.

The other cases in the Book of the Acts show the same thing. Only those who are born of the Spirit are baptized with the Spirit. But the spiritual birth and the spiritual baptism are not coincident. *Usually* an interval separates them, but as though to prevent us dogmatizing about the interval, one case is recorded in which the moment of receiving life seems to have been the moment of receiving the fullness of the Holy Ghost. (Acts 10.)

3. This blessing may also be distinguished from the ordinary presence of the Spirit in the believer's life.

All believers have the Spirit. As apart from the Spirit there is no life, so apart from the presence, the continued presence of the Spirit, the quickened life would die. So even of very unsanctified believers it may be said: "Know ye not that ye are a temple of God, and that the Spirit of God dwelleth in you?" (I Cor. 3:16.) It is due to the indwelling of the Spirit that we have any knowledge or love at all. It is due to Him that we are able in any measure to walk well pleasing to God.

But while all believers have the Spirit, *all are not full of the*

*Spirit.* There are many who are like the disciples before Pentecost. They need to be personally baptized with the Spirit, that in His fullness they may live and work.

4. This blessing becomes ours through a special incoming of the Holy Spirit into our souls.

When He so comes we are said to "Receive the Holy Ghost." It is to this incoming that I apply the term baptism. I believe the actual incoming of the Spirit in this sense may be sudden — is usually sudden — though the consciousness of it may dawn only gradually on the soul.

If I interpret the word of God aright, then this baptism of the Holy Ghost constitutes a crisis in the believer's life which is comparable to conversion itself. It is not a second conversion; there is no such thing. It is not a passing from death to life. But I believe it is a passing from life to fuller life. I would almost speak of it as a personal Pentecost. It marks in the individual case a point like what Pentecost was to the disciples. There is an historical Bethlehem where the word was made flesh, but there is a personal Bethlehem when Christ is formed in our hearts. So I think there is the historical Pentecost when the Spirit was poured out on the Church, but there is also the personal Pentecost when He is poured out on the individual believer.

5. This gift of the Holy Ghost we receive from the hand of the risen and glorified Lord.

He has received this from the Father and bestows Him on His people. He holds this blessed gift for all His people, and is willing to bestow Him on all His people. But I cannot think that all receive Him as a matter of course. I do not think that as believers all are baptized with the Spirit. In John 7: 39, we read: "The Spirit was not yet given, because Jesus was not yet glorified." This which was true of the church is, I believe, true of the individual. Until the Lord Jesus is glorified; until He is enthroned King in our hearts — this gift is not given to us. The coming of the Holy Ghost is intimately connected with the coronation of the Lord Jesus.

6. The baptism of the Holy Ghost is followed by marked results.

Among them we may note the following:

(*a*) An amazing enlargement of our knowledge. The Holy Spirit, when He comes, glorifies Jesus so to us, and so wonderfully reveals Him to our souls, that we seem to have found a new Christ. Knowledge of Divine things unattainable by years of study may be ours in a short space of time when taught by the Spirit.

(*b*) A manifest deepening of our love. The Holy Spirit deals with the heart as well as the head. All coldness disappears as that holy fire burns within us.

(*c*) An increase in our power to do the will of God. The Spirit, when He comes, performs a cleansing work, giving us deliverance from bonds that bound us. We become strong in the Lord, and are able to do His will.

(*d*) An increased boldness and power in our witness for God. This, in my view, is but one of the results of the baptism of the Spirit. But it is a result so important that in the minds of some it is the chief end of the whole matter. Some speak of the fullness of the Spirit for life, and the baptism of the Spirit for service. I have already indicated my dissent from this position. We should seek the fullness of the Spirit that we may be what God desires us to be; and leave it absolutely with Him to determine the use He will put us to. Then we shall find that if He calls us to witness, our witness will be in power, and many will be turned to the Lord.

7. The conditions on which this gift is received have been indicated when speaking regarding the baptisms of our Lord. They are, briefly, consecration and prayer. It is as we bow before God in utter surrender, and wait on God in earnest prayer, that He gives us His Holy Spirit, in whose strength we go forth to be all that God purposes, and to do all that God wills.

# Walking With God.

### By Rev. G. H. C. Macgregor, M. A.

---

"*And Enoch walked with God: and he was not; for God took him.*"—Gen. 5:24.

"Enoch walked with God." So shortly, so succinctly does the inspired historian describe the character and write the story of this Old Testament saint. Out of the dimness of those early times the figure of Enoch rises, towering like a spiritual giant above the men of his generation, and impressing the imagination of all time; but when we ask what is known of him the reply is, "Nothing, but that he walked with God." But that is everything. It is the highest praise that can be bestowed on any man. He of whom this can be said has mastered life. He has learned its secret, and has overcome it; and to him it is given to become a pillar in the temple of his God.

Of only three of the Old Testament saints — Enoch, Noah, and Levi — is it expressly said that they walked with God. But the experience described by these words is one which was not peculiar to them. Abraham knew it, and it was with God that he went forth from Ur of the Chaldees to take possession of a land which neither he nor his fathers knew. Moses knew it, and it was that which gave him strength and courage for the almost superhuman task to which he was called. David knew it, and it was with God beside him that he made his way from the sheepfolds of Bethlehem to the throne. And these were not men of heavenly mould. They were men of like passions with ourselves, and the experience that they knew is one which all God's children are meant to enjoy. If they in Old Testament times enjoyed it when revelation was still incomplete, how much more should we for whom Jesus Christ has fully declared God.

But what is meant by walking with God? It is not an act, nor yet a series of acts, but a condition of life consistently maintained through years. This is brought out by the mood of the verb used in describing the experience. Our English Bible tells us that "Enoch lived sixty and five years, and begat Methuselah: and Enoch walked with God after he begat Methuselah three hundred years;" but if the force of the verb were more fully given we should translate, "Enoch walked with God, and continued to walk with God for three hundred years." Walking with God, therefore, was no exceptional experience with Enoch; it was the normal condition of his life. So it should be with us. Our whole life, the daily life which is so apt to be uninteresting and monotonous, is meant to be lived in quiet, calm fellowship with God. Life is not made up of rapture. Our bodies are not so framed as to bear the strain of continuous rapture. Rapturous experiences in this life can only be occasional. Now and then at a communion time, at a convention time, at a revival time, we mount up on wings as eagles, and soar into the presence of God, leaving the world and its mist and darkness far below us. At other times of special activity we run without being weary. But there is a higher experience still, and it is that of walking and not fainting, of continuing day by day close to God, and having intimate fellowship with Him in the daily paths of life. He is closest to God to whom everything in life is a sacrament.

If you ask me what is the chief characteristic of the man who is walking with God, I reply: *His continual consciousness of God.* It is in this that the heart of the matter consists. Of the man who is truly walking with God it may be said that the thought of God is never out of his mind. He is always conscious of God, or I would prefer to say, sub-conscious. God lies below all his thinking, willing, desiring. He is as God-conscious as he is self-conscious. Let me illustrate what I mean. Suppose that you are in a room along with a large number of people strange to you. After a while there comes into that room one whom you passionately love. He may be far from you, and during the whole evening you may never have an opportunity of speaking to him; but you are conscious of his presence and rejoicing in it. Never for a moment do you forget that He is there. He is for you in a real sense the only one present. Even when you are speaking to others, at the bottom of your heart you are thinking of him. It is his eye you always seek to catch, his approval you seek to win. You walk with him the whole evening. Between you there is a sympathy of soul, heart beats answeringly to heart. So should it be between the soul of the believer and his God; so will it be with the believer who is walking with God. There may be nothing said; there may be no talking about religion. It is very interesting that in the only book of the Bible in which the name of God is not mentioned we come across a man whose whole life was controlled by the thought of God. Mordecai walked with God, and ordered his whole life to please God; yet in his whole history, as written by the pen of inspiration, the name of God is not mentioned. Walking with God does not necessarily imply articulate witnessing for God. Many a humble believer has walked with God for years who has never opened his mouth directly to speak for Him. But even though nothing be said, everything will be said. It is as impossible for a man to walk with God and keep it secret as it was to break the alabaster cruse and yet keep the odor from making its way through the house. For if we are walking with God, God will be in *all* our thoughts. We may be in business, or in public life, living a very full and hurried life with ten thousand things calling for our attention; yet not one of them will be settled without reference to God. Just as a loving wife is ever conscious of her husband, and does nothing into which he does not enter, so will it be between us and our God. We shall live in Him as in the air we breathe.

But if we are walking with God, what will be the character of our life? First, it will be a *joyful* life. The nearness of those we love is ever a source of joy. To walk with a dear friend is one of the highest of earthly pleasures. The sense of having him to yourself as your very own, and of being able to tell him everything, is an immeasurable joy. So the sense that God is with us in every detail of life, and that we are never alone, fills the soul with the bliss of heaven. He who walks with God may always know what the psalmist felt when he sang: "In Thy presence is fullness of joy; at thy right hand are pleasures for evermore."

But, further, the life of him who walks with God will be a *peaceful* life. What need of peace there is in the world! What a fearful factor care is in life!

> "Mostly men's many featured faces wear
> Looks of fixed gloom, or else of restless care;
> The very babes that in their cradles lie
> Out of the depths of unknown troubles cry."

But all worry and care in the life of the Christian arises from forgetfulness of God. God would have us without care. He tells us "to be careful for nothing." He tells us that His peace, which passes all understanding, shall keep our hearts and minds through Christ Jesus; and he asks us to remember this. A woman who knew that she had a rich friend who had promised to supply all her wants would not be worried lest she should not be able to pay her house rent. The remembrance of her friend would drive that fear away and give her peace. And the remembrance that God was in our life, and had made Himself responsible for us, would lead us to cast all our care on Him; the realization that He was ever by our side, ready to deal with any emergency, would bring rest to our souls.

Once more, the life of him who walks with God will be a *brave* life. Life is difficult, and to live requires courage. It is profoundly significant that light-heartedness is the attribute of youth, and that as men get older they get more grave. Unless a man is brave, the disappointments of life, the dangers of life, the difficulties of life, the losses and failures of life will take all the heart out of him. Life is difficult, and never was it more difficult than to-day. But the man who walks with God will be brave. He will sing like the Hebrew psalmist: "The Lord is on my side; I will not fear. What can man do unto me? The Lord is my strength and my song, and is become my salvation." Fear, like care, comes from forgetting God. If we walk with God we can face the worst that life can bring without fear. We know that in all things we shall be more than conquerors; for we are persuaded that nothing can separate us from the love of God which is in Christ Jesus, our Lord. How completely the remembrance of our God removes fear!

> "Great God! our littleness takes heart to play
> Beneath the shadow of Thy state;
> The only comfort of our littleness
> Is that Thou art so great.
> Thus doth Thy grandeur make us grand ourselves:
> 'Tis goodness makes us fear;
> Thy greatness makes us brave as children are
> When those they love are near."

Such, such-like are the blessings of him who, like Enoch, walks with God.

But now, passing on to the practical question implied in the text, let us ask, How is this life to be attained?

I need scarcely say that it can be lived only by the children of God. The unbeliever, the unconverted, have neither part nor lot in this matter. Walking with God is possible only to the children of the kingdom. Unless you have been in Christ reconciled to God, you cannot walk with Him. Reconciliation must precede communion. The walk with God starts from the cross of Christ; the first step toward this life is the acceptance of Jesus as our propitiation, and the committing of our souls entirely to Him. But though this life can only be attained by the children of God, I need scarcely say that all the children of God have not attained to it. God has many children who do not walk with Him; who do not even follow hard after Him, but are content to follow afar off. One is almost constrained to fear that this is the condition of the majority of professing Christians. How else is their coldness, their half-heartedness, their weakness to be explained?

Yet this life, though lived by few, *ought to be lived by all.* Let me emphasize this. All believers should walk with God; and to be content with anything short of this is to be guilty of sin. Now, how are we to attain this life? In answer to this I would say: 1. By a wise recollection of the fact that God has promised to walk with us. On our side, salvation is continually receiving what God gives, and advances in our spiritual life are made by our wakening up to see what God is offering us, and accepting it in faith. God is always offering more than we are wil'ing to receive. He ever takes the initiative, and often has to wait long ere we make a response. But our responses to his invitations would be much more frequent and much more complete did we only exercise a wise recollection. God often says to His children, "Remember!" If we would only remember the promises of God, if we would only remember that He is able and willing to fulfill every one of them to us, and then if we only went and claimed them, our advance in spiritual things would be almost incredibly rapid. Now look at this promise; it was made to God's people of old: "I will set My tabernacle among you; and My soul shall not abhor you. And I will walk among you, and will be your God, and ye shall be My people." And it was repeated to the spiritual Israel, the believers in New Testament times; for of them God has said: "I will dwell in them, and walk in them; and I will be their God, and they shall be my people." Therefore, if we would walk with God, let us remember this promise, and to our Father's loving invitation, "Children, will ye walk with me?" let us reply, "Blessed Lord, with Thee only will we walk."

2. If we would walk with God, there must be on our part a jealous care to keep out of our life things that offend God. This is perhaps the most practical thing one can say. It is striking that wherever in the Bible there is reference made to walking with God, there is reference also to human wickedness, and a call to separation from it. Enoch walked with God while prophesying in a wicked world of judgment about to fall on the ungodly. Noah walked with God in a world ripe for doom. And in the New Testament, God's promise to walk with His people is directly followed by these words: "Wherefore come out from among them, and be ye separate, and touch not the unclean thing; and I will receive you, and will be a Father to you, and ye shall be My sons and daughters, saith the Lord Almighty." This is the point that touches all of us, and reveals why so many are not walking with God. You know you are not walking with God. What is the reason? It is this: there is an offense, a stumbling-block, an unclean thing in your life which keeps God out. I do not know what it is; but you know, or may know if you care to examine yourself. It may be you have a quarrel with a friend.

He has wronged you, and you have not forgiven him; or you have wronged him and will not apologize. It may be an evil habit, an ungodly friend, a secret lust that you are not willing to forsake; and because you will walk with them, you cannot walk with God. God is a jealous God, and demands that they who walk with Him be separated unto Him. Therefore those who walk with God must be prepared to find it a lonely walk. Enoch found it so; Noah found it so; Jesus found it so. But they found that to be alone with God was to be in heaven. And one whom trouble and pain had driven to God could speak out his joy in this way: "Whom have I in heaven but Thee? and there is none on earth whom I desire beside Thee. My flesh and my heart faileth: but God is the strength of my heart, and my portion for ever."

3. The life of walking with God is to be attained by earnest waiting upon God. You cannot have that consciousness of the presence of a person in a crowd which, as I have already said, is the essence of what is meant by walking with a person, unless you have been often and long together alone. It is the friendship formed in secret, the understanding of one another which comes from frequent intercourse, the intimate knowledge gained in secret communion, that produces the love which makes the presence of a friend accompany us through life. And we cannot walk with God in the ordinary busy walks of life, among manifold pressing duties, unless we are often alone with Him. To be conscious of God's presence all through the day, it is especially needful that the morning watch be spent with Him. It is when He wakens us morning by morning that His voice rings in our ears all the day; it is when the first look of the wakened eye falls on the face of Jesus that all through the day our eyes are toward the Lord. Waiting on God is the great secret of walking with God. It is those who wait on the Lord that renew their strength, that mount up on wings as eagles, that run without being weary, and walk and do not faint.

One word more before we close; it is too important to be omitted: "Enoch walked with God: and was not; for God took him." What these words mean, the Apostle, writing to the Hebrews, teaches when he says: "By faith Enoch was translated, that he should not see death; and was not found, because God had translated him: for before his translation he had this testimony, that he pleased God." These words are to my mind of very great significance, and reveal to us one of the crowning characteristics of the life of which we have been speaking. It is a life ready, I do not say for death but for translation. "He was not; for God took him." What a thought for us who live so far down the stream of time, and for whom the words, "We shall not all die, but we shall all be changed," are so full of meaning. Are you walking with God? Then you also, like Enoch, are ready to be translated. Of how many is this true? How many of us are ready for the coming of the Lord? It is near us now, and coming nearer every day. The Jesus who rose from Olivet into the clouds shall so come in like manner. The second advent hurries on; are you ready for it? How near it is who can tell? Above there is a salvation ready to be revealed, like a statue finished awaiting its unveiling; and below there is a people waiting for that salvation. Are you one of them? Have you turned from idols to serve the living God and to wait for His Son from heaven? Then for you He will come. To them that look for Him will He appear the second time without sin unto salvation. May God help us all so to walk with Him that we shall look for and hasten unto the coming of our Lord; and to His promise, "Behold, I come quickly," answer with the prayer, "Even so, come, Lord Jesus."

# Humanity's Headlight.

By H. L. Hastings.

*Editor of " The Christian," Boston, U. S. A.*

Copyright, 1895, by H. L. Hastings

[The following is an abstract of a lecture by H. L. Hastings, on "Humanity's Headlight," which has been delivered five or six times by Mr. Moody's special request. The lecture was abridged in delivery, to bring it within the allotted hour, and its delivery being hurried, the report was imperfect. The author has only been able to give it a hasty revision, and permits its issue in its present form, hoping soon to revise and issue it complete as a number of his ANTI-INFIDEL LIBRARY, of which between forty and fifty numbers have already been issued, they having been printed by the hundred tons, and four or five millions of them having been circulated in nearly a score of languages on every continent. Nearly twenty tons of them were sent to Mr. Moody for distribution during the Columbian exhibition. They are furnished at five and ten cents singly; $2 per hundred; $15 per thousand, and may be ordered of H. L. Hastings, 47 Cornhill, Boston, Mass., U. S. A., and Marshall Bros., 5A Paternoster Row, London, England.]

Psalms 119: 130 : "The entrance of Thy word giveth light, it giveth understanding unto the simple." There is nothing, perhaps, that we are acquainted with that is more mysterious than light. It is the robe of deity. It flies with a swiftness beyond all our conception. If we take the wings of the morning we may go to the uttermost parts of the earth in an instant. Light is the source of beauty. A landscape does not change, but at night it is dark and dismal, gloomy and unpromising; but let the light come and flood the landscape with its splendor, and we have every variety of beauty, every variety of hue, every variety of color to inspire and cheer. Out of the light comes all the tints of the rainbow; out of light comes health; disease lurks in the shadows, and the pestilence walketh in darkness. "In Him was life, and the life was the light of men." And the Scripture tells us that "God is Light, and in Him is no darkness at all." Satan is "the prince of darkness," and the powers against which we wrestle are the rulers of the darkness of this world.

The Scriptures tell us that man is in darkness. "You were sometime in darkness, but now are ye light in the Lord." "The people that sat in darkness have seen a great light." "Darkness shall cover the earth and gross darkness the people." "Men love darkness rather than light, because their deeds are evil." They "became vain in their imaginations, and their foolish heart was darkened." "The dark places of the earth are full of the habitations of cruelty." The whole teaching of Scripture is that man without God is in a state and condition of darkness. To open the eyes of the blind is the first thing. Some people do not need light half so much as sight. The Epistle of the Hebrews bids men to "call to remembrance the former days, in which, after ye were illuminated, ye endured a great fight of afflictions."

Illumination makes a wonderful difference with a man. You look at some great cathedral in the shadows; it is dark and dingy, and you shudder almost as you pass it; but let the electric current touch each lamp, and what a stream of brightness gleams from every window and door, and the aspect of things is changed. So a man who is in the dark, and walking in the dark, when touched by the Light of the world becomes illuminated. Like the Israelites he has a light in his dwelling; even in the darkness of Egypt he becomes a marked man. He is a different man; no longer what he was. He was a child of darkness, but he is now a son of light. The Psalmist says: "Thy word is a lamp to my feet and a light to my path." God communicates His light by His word and by His Spirit. But there is a question in these days whether we have God's word; whether it is possible that we should have God's word. Men doubt it; men deny it. One thing is certain, we have a book which claims to be God's word. Hundreds of times we read: "Hear ye the word of the Lord,"

"God spake all these words." This is just what we would expect if we had a message from God. We would not expect it to come as an anonymous letter, we would suppose that it would have this signature. This is a plain indication as to its source. Then the question is, Does it prove itself to be the word of the Lord? How do you know? We know the difference between the words of a wise man and a fool. We know the difference between the words of a babbling child and the utterances of saints. There are certain things about this word which show for itself.

How do you know the difference between an electric light and a lightning bug? If you were as blind as a bat you could not see any difference between the two; but if you had eyes and could see out of one of them, you would know the difference without any argument. You know the difference between the sun and the tallow candles, and if you turn your eyes and look at this word you will find that never man spake as this man, Christ Jesus, has spoken. Our friends who do so much talking about God speaking to men, find no great difficulty in getting information from the unseen world. They can give you communications from the ghost of your grandmother or the spirit of your aunt or your uncle — all written out, signed, sealed, and delivered, at a price anywhere from fifty cents to five dollars each revelation, right from the unseen world. Now, if their spooks and hobgoblins and evil spirits can communicate, why cannot God Almighty communicate too. The devil can write to his children; you can write to your children. Why cannot God write to His?

But there are people who doubt whether we have any exactness about this matter. The Lord has given men a sort of inspiration in a general way, and impression, a concept, and they wrote it out the best way they knew how; sometimes they got it right and sometimes wrong, and we have the result. The Lord gives a man an idea and lets him tell it to suit himself. We have tried that plan in business, but it did not work. We have told clerks to write letters, and they have written what we did not want written, and we have had to tear the letters up and write them over again. There are thousands of men that sit down by their desks in this city, with a stenographer by their side, and *dictate, word for word*, the messages that they want sent all over the country in answer to other letters. We keep such persons at work to convey our exact words, so that men may have them and that we may know what we intend to say, and that they get just the message we have sent them. Now, the question is whether God Almighty, maker of heaven and earth, sending His messages throughout all the ages, takes as much pains to have them accurate and correct as a Chicago merchant does his letters when ordering a case of calico or a bale of cotton, or any such thing. Whether God Almighty takes as much interest in doing His business accurately as an ordinary Chicago business man does in doing his business accurately. If He does, then it would be very natural to have Him give us the words He wanted us to have.

There are people who do not believe in any written revelation. They have a kind of hazy, nebulous revelation, but not in black and white. Yet everything else they like to have in black and white. If they make a contract they want it in black and white; if they get married, they must have a certificate in black and white. Everything has to go down in black and white except what God says. If you make a bargain with a man he will say: "We had better make a minute of this." When God makes a covenant with man, do you suppose He does not put it in writing?

But there are a great many objections. For instance, there was Paul. And, says one, "Do you think Paul was inspired of God when he said: 'I speak as a fool'?" Yes, I think so; I will tell you why. I have heard so many people speak like fools but did not even know it, that when I find a man who is driven into the corner as Paul was, and has to speak as a fool and *knows it*, I think that gives evidence of divine inspiration.

There is no end to the objections of doubters. I read in an infidel book this objection: "The Lord said about Jacob and Esau, before they were born, 'Jacob have I loved, but Esau have I hated,'" and the writer went on to tell what a dreadful thing it was for the good God to hate a little child before it was born or had done good or evil. You say that is a great mystery, and we shall understand when we get to heaven. You will understand it before you get to heaven if you are not too lazy to read your Bibles. "Well, how do you explain it?" Supposing a boy came from the street and said he saw thirteen elephants out there standing on their heads? How would I explain it? I would say that *the boy lied.* And so, many of the objections of skeptics to-day are explained in the same way. The Bible does not say any such thing about Jacob and Esau. The circumstances were these: Two children were born twins. The ordinary usage was that the first born got the property and the youngest was subordinate. Before the children were born, it pleased the Lord to reverse this order and say that the elder should serve the younger. Paul refers to this and says: "As it is written, Jacob have I loved, but Esau have I hated." But when was this written? Instead of being written before they were born it was written in the first chapter of Malachi, a thousand years after they were both dead and buried—after Jacob's children had become servants of God, and Esau's children had become a band of robbers. But this blockhead churned the whole thing together, and concluded that what Malachi wrote a thousand years after they were dead was what God said a thousand years before they were born.

### PART II.

You know critics are no new thing. There was a critic in the Garden of Eden. He said God had not said any such thing. The last king on the throne of Judah was a critic. The prophet of God told him that he would be taken captive, and taken to Babylon and die there; and another prophet told him he would never see Babylon. The king put the two statements together and did not believe either. But when he was taken captive, and his children brought before him and slaughtered, and his own eyes were put out and he was taken to Babylon, what the prophet told him, that he would go to Babylon and die there and yet *not see Babylon*, proved to be true. The trouble was he did not know how, like the colored preacher that Dr. Gordon tells of. The deacon found fault with his preaching, and said he wanted him to expound the Scriptures and not spend all his time telling "antidotes." He said: "Our minister can take the Scripture apart equal to any man I ever saw, but he does not know how to get them together again." This reminds me of an old man in Massachusetts. His clock needed cleaning, and he thought he would save fifty cents by cleaning it himself; so he took it to pieces, cleaned it up and got it together all right, but he had wheels enough left to start another clock. There is the trouble with these critics, they do not know what to do with half of the wheels in the clock, and they wonder why the clock does not go.

Says one: "What about your theory of inspiration?" I do not know whether we need any "theory of inspiration." We read that " God, who at sundry times and in *divers manners* spake in time past unto the fathers by the prophets, hath in these last days spoken unto us by His Son." Sometimes by dreams, sometimes by visions, sometimes by voice, sometimes by impressions, sometimes by writing on tables of stone, sometimes by the power of inspiration which makes Balaam talk, and which instructs and teaches Nebuchadnezzar and the great men of earth; sometimes by words which are closed up and sealed, and never understood by men who heard them, and which must be accurately recorded or no one else could have understood them. So we read in I Peter 1:11 that the prophets searched, etc. What were these prophets studying? They were studying their own prophecies. Why did they study their own prophecies? Because they did not understand them. "Oh," says one, "the Lord gives a man an idea and lets him work it out." But they did not get the idea to work it out themselves. If you should dictate a letter to me and I should write it out, I might very well study it out. So here we have words conveyed by men who did not understand them, and who sealed them up for future generations; and so we have the truth in accurate words exactly as spoken. But what does the Saviour say of the Holy Spirit as you find it in John, 14th and 16th chapters? "When He, the Comforter, is come, He shall bring all things to your remembrance." He brings to remembrance the words of Christ, He teaches, He shall guide you into all truth. He shall take the things of God and show them unto you. He shall show you things to come.

There we have an inspiration of recollections, the inspiration of instruction, the inspiration of guidance, the inspiration of suggestion — all forms of inspiration. Then we have an instance where it is said: Speak what I command thee, "diminish not a word." "Add not to His words lest He reprove thee."

Taking it then as a fact that we have the word of God, the Psalmist says: "The entrance of Thy word giveth light." Dull people are brightened by intercourse with brighter minds. You put a dull, heavy-faced child into a family where there is sunshine and brightness, wit and intelligence, and how soon he begins to brighten up. He gets ideas; he begins to think, and in a little while you find that he is a new sort of a person. It is just so with men dealing with men. There are men whose ideas have illuminated a nation; there are men whose songs control generations. The Psalmist says: "A man's wisdom maketh his face to shine." You know we have some people who spend considerable money on cosmetics. The best cosmetic you can find is the wisdom of God, the word of God in your soul. Just see how much better a person looks when he gets illuminated with the word of God; and we are told that "The fear of the Lord is the beginning of knowledge."

There is this foundation principle in wisdom, that what it does not have at the bottom is intellect. What is the use of a man knowing how to read Greek when he gets so drunk that he cannot read English? What is the use of a man having the pencil of a Landseer when it is held in the trembling hand of a sot? What is the use of a man having intelligence if there is sin and ruin at the bottom of it all?

The Scriptures represent Christian men as called out of darkness, as illuminated, brightened, lighted up, everything made over, by the presence of this word of God. I heard of a man who, after he was converted, went home and lighted his house up from cellar to garret—every window was ablaze with light. What was the matter? There was a good deal the matter. In war when they gain a great victory they illuminate the cities and towns and this man had gained a great victory. We celebrate emancipation, and he was emancipated. He wanted people to know that something had happened, and he lighted the house from cellar to garret. A lawyer went home to his wife and said: "Wife, I have found the Lord; and now let us have family prayers." "Well," she said, "husband, there are three lawyers in the parlor, and perhaps we had better go into the kitchen." "Wife," he said, "I never invited the Lord Jesus to my house before, and I will not take Him into the kitchen." So he went into the parlor and told what the Lord had done for him, and kneeled down and prayed, and for many, many years that lawyer occupied the highest seat of justice in that land. It was Judge McLean of the United States Supreme Court. He was illuminated — lighted up with the word of God. There is a great difference between men who are lit up by the word of God and men who are not. There is a great difference between a lighthouse and a smokestack. The smokestack may be the tallest, the costliest, and the biggest, but while the lighthouse sends its gleams across the waves the smokestack vomits out smoke. We need a few illuminated men in this nation to show people the way, and I think some would be very useful in Washington in these days. We have a great many smokestacks pouring out smoke, and tobacco smoke at that. What we want is men full of the light of God — men that can see, and men that you can see in the darkness of the night. Latimer said: "Be of good cheer, we shall this day light a candle which shall never go out."

God has been lighting up men and men have been lighting up nations and shedding abroad the brightness of God's glory far and near. And not only is all moral light from the word of God, but all intellectual light. That which is really valuable is dependent upon this same illumination. The intelligence of the world bears witness to this fact. People say: "Do you suppose that God gave a revelation to a few Jews, a little people on the shores of the Mediterranean?" Why did He not give it to the Chinese? There are four hundred million of them. Supposing He had given it to the Chinese, how would you read it? You would have had forty thousand different characters to learn before you could read it straight. Why did He not give it to the Assyrians? Sure enough. Why didn't He? For more than a thousand years there has not been a man on the face of the earth that could read the Assyrian language; and then there are from five hundred to eight hundred different characters in it. Why did He not give it to the Egyptians? For more than a thousand years not a man on the face of the earth could read a line of their literature, though there are acres of it scribbled on the walls and palaces of Egypt to-day. But God gave His revelation to the

Hebrews with twenty-two letters in their alphabet that a child could learn in an hour, and there has never been a day when that language or that alphabet has been forgotten. God sent the revelation of His will down through the only channel in which He could send it, and the light of God shines every day, while the wisdom of the world goes out in darkness.

People say sometimes that the Bible is not a scientific book — that it is opposed to science; but how comes it that they have no science except where they have the Bible? There is not a scientific book worth two cents a pound at the paper mill, except where the Bible has gone. What makes such a difference? Go to the Hindu and he will tell you that what makes it rain, is a big elephant, squirting water through his trunk; that the earth rests on the backs of elephants, and when there is an earthquake it is the elephants jostling around. Go to the Chinese and they will tell you an eclipse is caused by a big dragon swelling the waves, so they play on tom-toms to scare him away and save the moon. There is science for you; plenty of it. But what is the good of it? Buddha — I have every respect for the old gentleman — killed himself eating pork. If he had read Moses he might have lived longer.

I heard a man in Chicago say that the progress of the age was not due to the Bible, but that it was due to the steam engine and the printing press. Well, I would like to know what progress there is in the printing press if you use it to print column after column about Sullivan's fights and that kind of stuff. What is the printing press good for unless you have something to print? What Hottentot was it that made the first steam engine? What Fiji Islander was it that invented the telegraph? From what island of Kamtchatka was it that the first telephone came? What African invented and gave us the first sewing machine and the first reaping machine? Where did all these things come from? There have been within the past century more than 443,000 patents issued in this country. Seven-eights of the business of this nation is done by the use of these inventions; destroy them and we would be in danger of starving to death in less than a week. Business would be paralyzed, and everything would be dead and done for. These inventions are only found in the light of God's word. How many inventions have they in China? How many patents have they issued in India? They do not know enough to invent a milking stool there. How many inventions come to us from Italy, with all its magnificent history of the past? How many inventions have come over to us from Spain? Where did all the jimcracks come from that gave us machines by which one man could do the work of ten? Where did they come from? You can no more get inventive genius where they have not got God's word, than you can raise cabbages in the bottom of a well. You have got to have light, and "The entrance of thy word giveth light; it giveth understanding unto the simple."

### PART III.

People tell us how things move on in an orderly process, of progression and evolution, by which we start as monkeys and progress and get along up to where we are now. We do not know exactly, sometimes we are not going up but down towards the monkey again. Well, forty years ago you could buy men in the Fiji Islands. You could buy a man for seven dollars, and they had just as long a time to progress as we have had. It is just as long since they were monkeys as it is since we were. You could buy a man for seven dollars and you could work him just as long and just as hard as you had a mind to, and then you could kill him and eat him, unless he was soaked with tobacco. You go to Fiji now and you cannot buy a man for seven dollars, nor seventy dollars, nor seven hundred dollars, nor seven thousand dollars, nor seven million dollars. What has raised the price? Twelve hundred Wesleyan chapels scattered over the Islands, make the difference; and the men who half a century ago could tear human flesh into pieces and devour it are now preaching the Gospel of the Son of God. Evolution, long ages of progression, that does not do it. It is not evolution, it is regeneration; it is the new creation by the power of God, and it does not take a thousand million years to do it when He gets hold of the job.

The great trouble with these gentlemen is questioning. One writer says that the bird began with the egg; but where did you get your egg to begin with? I think there would be two hens before you had the egg. There you are again; you have not found any beginning. "In the beginning God," and that answers all questions.

I heard a skeptic say that all this progress springs from free thinking, from free thought, and all that. You have sometimes seen a little monkey in a store window turning a crank around and around, you think that is an uncommonly smart monkey, but when you look a little closer you find that instead of the monkey turning the crank it is the crank turning the monkey. That is what is the matter with our free thinkers. They think they are turning the crank, but the crank is turning them. God's Word gives light; it gives light on ourselves, it gives light on the world, it gives light on the church, it gives light on duty, it gives light on destiny, it shames men into decency, it elevates civilization, it regulates, it improves man in a great many ways and the skeptics of the day who are fighting against God's Word are kicking down the ladder on which they climb up. But for that Word they might have been cannibals, or naked savages. People talk about certain things that happened "in the dark ages." When were the dark ages? When you get outside the light of God's Word the ages are just as dark to day as they were two thousand years ago. You go into central Africa; you go into any country where God's Word does not shed its light, and you will find it just as dismal and just as devilish as it ever was in the ages that have gone by. You go to China, and opposite the rich man's fish pond you will read on a board: "Please do not drown girls here." They drown a girl like a blind pup in spite of all Confucius teaches, and it was only in the year 1889 that the first law was passed forbidding a man killing his own daughter. You go anywhere outside of the light of God's Word and you will find this same darkness and cruelty and sin.

I was in London a good while ago and saw the most scandalous infidel newspaper, and it issued a "Christmas number." What under heaven had that paper to do with Christmas! Well, we have got an infidel club in New York and its name is "The Nineteenth Century Club." Nineteen centuries of what? They have an infidel paper there and the title of it is "The Twentieth Century." A little ahead of time. Twentieth century of what? When the sultan of Turkey issued bonds he could not sell them until he put Anno Domini on them. And in New York if you take up a Jewish newspaper you will find 1896 has to be on it or they will think it is a back number.

When the Word of God touches men it changes them. I have photographs of people in heathen lands taken before they were converted, and others taken of people after they were converted. It is positively startling to see how their faces changed under the illumination of God's Word and the power of the Holy Ghost. And not only did they change in aspect but in intelligence. A few months ago in Japan they were having the scholars examined with a view to promoting them to a higher grade. And there was one school that had missionary teachers, and before they were to be examined they all got down and prayed that the Lord would help them through the examination. Well, the heathen around said they would not pass, but they did pass, every mother's son of them. They all went through and the examiners said: "What school is this that *all* the children passed." The answer was: "This is the Jesus Christ school." "Take My yoke upon you and learn of Me" if you want intelligence, if you want intellectual development, and you will find that "the entrance of God's Word giveth light."

And young men and maidens entering upon life, what you are to be in this world depends upon your attitude towards God's Word and the power of God's Word in you. You may have all wisdom and be nothing, says the apostle. Look at the men whose names have gone down through the ages. They are men whom God has touched. If God had not called Abraham he might have been an idol worshiper and an idol maker to the day of his death. If God had not sent his Word to Moses he might have been a shepherd in the land of Midian all his life, or worse than that, in the Court of Pharaoh all his days. If God had not touched David he might have lived and died among the shepherds of Bethlehem. If God had not touched Simon Peter he would have lived and died a boatman on the sea of Galilee, and the world never known him. If God had not touched Paul with the power of His Word he might have lived and died persecuting the saints. If God had not touched Timothy with His Word and His power his name would have never come to us, but would have been lost among the myriads of his country. If God had not stirred the heart of Luther by His Word he would have lived and died a monk like thousands of others, and no one would have known him. If God had not touched John Bunyan by his Word he might have mended old pots and kettles to the day of his death; but when God touched him and filled him and sent him forth to do His will, he becomes a power not yet spent in the earth. Sometimes in the back yards of old machine shops we see a gear well cut, perfect in all its parts, but it is not attached to anything, it has no shaft; it is worth a cent a pound for old iron, that is all there is of it. But if you only knew the machine it belonged to, put it upon the shaft and put the power upon it, that gear would start every spindle in the factory moving; that gear would be worth its weight in gold. Many a man today is in just that condition — broken off; he is not connected anywhere, he has no hold on God, he has no power and is worth a cent a pound as old iron. Oh, get belted onto the main shaft and then you will know what God made you for. Everywhere in our cities are the electric light wires. When the current is off it is a dead wire, then it is just so much old iron or old copper, but when the current is on it is chain lightning. Now, the question is whether you will be a dead wire or whether you will be chain lightning! whether you will be old iron or whether full of the power and energy of the Holy Ghost.

We have a great idea of numbers. We have the world against us, but Gideon with his three hundred is more than a match for all Midian. You cannot settle great moral questions by counting noses, especially if the noses are red ones; you have something else behind, and a man with the power of God counts for more than a myriad without it. Let your light shine, do your work. You go out into a world full of unbelief, skepticism, doubt, and uncertainty. Most of it is the doubt of men who do not know God. Do men who doubt God know whether they are saved? Their neighbors do not know, their wives do not know, their friends do not know. The first thing is to be saved and then it is easy to know. The first thing is to have the Word of Christ dwelling in his heart with divine power, and then it is not difficult to know. And when we see what God can do by our instrumentalities we have reason to be of good courage.

How do men deal with doubt?

Men write big books; they look well on the shelf, and stay there, too, most of the time. The common people never read them. Do you think God inspired a man to write a big book. The biggest book Paul ever wrote was a ten-page tract. A man said that if Paul was here he would be editing a newspaper. One thing I do think if Paul was here, he would *be writing tracts*. He wrote fourteen while he was on earth. He seemed to have a knack for that business. It did not take him long to write what he had to say, because he knew what he was talking about. Many men do not. In the Chinese Cyclopedia, there are six thousand volumes, and eighteen volumes of index. It would take you twenty years to learn to read, and when you have read these six thousand volumes you are prepared to worship your grandmother. Paul's little ten page tract would run all over it. In the British Museum is an Encyclopedia of Thibetian Buddhism. There are two hundred and twenty-five volumes of it, and each volume is two feet long and six inches thick. But God has given us a Bible made up of *little books* that can be read through in an hour or ten minutes and yet they have in them the words of the Eternal We read in Jeremiah of a higher critic that whittled away at the Bible, and managed to burn it, but there was still enough left, and what he whittled came back again enlarged. But suppose they managed to get away wtth three-fourths of the Bible, I wonder if they would leave us John 3: 16. Maybe they would leave us John 14; maybe they would leave us the twenty-third Psalm — a few such verses here and there. If they would, there is power enough to save a soul. Do not worry overmuch about that. Hold fast the faithful Word. "The entrance of Thy Word giveth light; it giveth understanding to the simple."

# Jesus as Our Example in Preaching.

### MAJOR D. W. WHITTLE.

---

[Stenographic Report.]

### JESUS AS A PREACHER.

Heb. 2:3: "First began to be spoken by the Lord." I make a great deal of that. Jesus Christ was the first preacher of the Gospel. The authority we have for preaching is because it began to be spoken by the Lord. What we believe we believe on His authority. What we preach we preach on His authority. Mark 1:14; Mark 2:2; Luke 4:18-19.

### WHERE HE PREACHED.

1. In the synagogues. Lake 4:16.
2. By the lake. Luke 5:3; Matt. 13:1.
3. In Matthew's house. Luke 5:29.
4. On the mountain. Matt. 5:1.
5. In the temple. Luke 21:37.
6. On the Mount of Olives. Matt. 24:3.
7. On the well. John 4:6.
8. By night. John 3:2.

He preached everywhere; He was always preaching. That should be the case with us. It is a wrong conception of the preaching of the Gospel that we are simply to go to the pulpit. It is our example in the house, in the mountain, in the temple, and on the streets, as living the Gospel, and our personal testimony to individuals, that will make our words in public effective. A godly life, is the powder behind the bullet, that carries the word to the mark. Christ was ever proclaiming the Gospel. To many the preaching of the Gospel means going on Sunday and standing in a pulpit and preaching. I heard it said of a man that he would be a splendid preacher if he could be kept in a tunnel through the week and only let out on Sundays. That was not Christ's way. We should be living and giving the Gospel out through the week, and if we are not improving our opportunities as we should we will not be in condition to preach on Sunday. Everywhere Jesus went He preached the Gospel. I remember in England of a gentleman who said his mother, who was about 110 years of age, told him how John Wesley would preach the Gospel at four o'clock in the morning and crowds would get out to hear him. When the Spirit of God is upon us we will be ready as the Master was, early in the morning or late at night, sitting beside the seaside or in the temple. We won't depend upon our surroundings for an inspiration, for the Holy Spirit will be our inspiration.

### WHAT HE PREACHED.

1. He magnified God's word. Matt. 5:17-19.
2. He applied God's law to the conscience. Matt. 5:44.
3. Atonement for sin. John 3:14-16.
4. Repentance. Matt. 4:17.
5. Personal trust in Himself. Matt. 11:28.
6. Regeneration by the Holy Spirit. John 3:3-6.
7. Holiness by the indwelling of the Holy Spirit. John 14:15-16.

How beautiful these verses are! If you can get your attention upon Himself; if your heart goes out in love to Christ, an obedient life will follow.

8. Resurrection. John 11:25.
9. Judgment. John 5:27.
10. Eternal punishment. Matt. 25:46.
11. The rejection of Israel and the calling of the Gentiles. Matt. 21:43.
12. His second coming in glory to be revealed to Israel and set up His kingdom on the earth. Matt. 25:31; Matt. 24:30.

This is not all that He preached, but in these twelve truths we have that from which the truths that He preached radiated, and in which all the truths He taught might be concentrated, and our preaching should be along their line. We should find authority for all we say in God's word. Preach as He preached; preach what He preached; preach where He preached, is our safe guide. We don't want to go outside the word of God. How wonderful are His words? How they sweep from the morning of creation to the culmination of all things; Jesus the central figure in every one of these truths.

#### HOW HE PREACHED.

1. With authority. Matt. 7: 28-29. We have Paul, in writing to Timothy, saying: "Let no man despise your youth," and, "these things command and teach;" and how frequently we have Paul requesting prayers for himself that he might speak boldly as he ought to speak. So when we go out into the work we are to have the sense of authority. If we are called of God we will have it. As some one has said, "We are not to prop up the cross, but point to it." He that is sent of God will speak with authority. There will be boldness to what he says, just the same as when a young officer on the battlefield is carrying an order from the general. How he goes with the order to the different divisions of the army in the name of the general. It does not make any difference how little he may be, he is recognized as from the commander. So, as we go out, we have our orders, our commission, from Jesus Christ, with the Holy Ghost making use of us, simply to give His message.

2. With power. Luke 4:32, 14. The power of the Holy Spirit, not the power of the flesh. Power in the pulpit is not making a noise or getting excited. With what calmness did Jesus teach, and what power there was with His word. It was not what man looks at, but the power that comes from the Spirit of God. We have this power through fellowship with Jesus Christ, and it is only given by the Holy Spirit.

3. With grace. Luke 4:22. (Rev. Ver.) They were words of grace because Jesus was so occupied with what He was talking about and was lost to Himself. He was talking about the love of the Father, and if you and I want to have grace in our ministry we must be occupied in our own hearts with what we are talking

about. Talk about the love of God the Father, and the love manifested in Christ, and have your own heart occupied with it and your words will be of grace. In the words that fell from Christ's lips from the fourteenth to the seventeenth chapters of John, over fifty times you will read the word "Father." That is the meaning of His prayer, "I have manifested Thy name." What name? The name of the Father. Jesus was so filled with love for and occupied with the Father, in trying to show forth the kindness of the Father, that "words of grace" ever fell from His lips.

4. With compassion. Matt. 14:14. If we are following our Master, and are in touch with Him and filled with His Spirit, we will have compassion. It is easy to lose the burden for souls, but you will not be much used if you do not have it.

There are three stages in our prayers. First, we pray for ourselves. Second, for our wives and children, etc. Third, for all the world; and we pray that God will bless the world through us.

5. With simplicity. Luke 20:24. Christ used the simplest things in preaching. Takes a penny from the pocket of the man standing near Him and uses it as an illustration. He employed the humblest things to teach truths. This is a great lesson for us. We are in constant danger because we are aiming too high. We are not simple enough. We try to get up some big, profound sermon instead of just standing up and talking in the simplest way possible. Simplicity is the power of Moody, and it was the power of Charles Finney and Spurgeon. There will always be results from it. I remember a friend of mine coming home and saying that he wished their minister would talk in language that they could understand. He quoted a sentence that had been used in his sermon, and asked me what it meant. It was: "The radical will strike downward and the primitial go upward." I did not know what it meant myself until I looked in the dictionary, and I found out that "radical" meant "root" and "primitial" meant "stem." It is a great drawback to cultivate anything but a natural instead of an artificial tone in the voice. Let us be simple and present the Gospel in a simple way. God keep us from ambition for distinction, or of being admired for anything we may say.

## ON JESUS AS OUR EXAMPLE IN PREACHING.   125

6. With humility. Matt. 11 : 29. Oh to be humble as Jesus! True humility is being humble without talking about it. As Dr. Bonar says: "You can get into a state of mind that you will be proud of lying in the dust." You must keep your eyes on the Lord Jesus if you would be humble. If there is real work of the Spirit of God in my heart I cannot speak about it without being humbled. There's where you get rid of your self-consciousness and self-conceit. You have to look away to Jesus. If you talk about yourself being humble you cease to be humble. I heard a good story over in Ireland. The Bishop of Waterford had asked a young man, a university man, to preach for him. As they were going up the steps he asked the young man what he was going to preach about. The young man replied that he would settle that when he rose. He had not yet decided, but that as he was just from college he had plenty of resources. When he arose he uttered two or three sentences, and became so confused and muddled that he was forced to sit down and the bishop had to continue the service. When the young man came back to the study he groaned and wept, so mortified was he. The old bishop said to him: "If you had only gone up as you came down you would have come down as you went up." It's a great thing to have our humiliation before we go up.

7. With joy. Luke 10:21. I remember Mr. MacPherson of Scotland telling me about the great cotton famine there, and going out and feeding the people. He said he would buy a whole milk wagon and go down among the people, crying, "Free milk!" and how they would come flocking around him and he would give them milk. It is something like that to preach the Gospel. To give out "the milk of the word" and rejoice as it feeds the multitude. Our Saviour rejoiced in spirit. Let us be joyful in our work. If you lose your joy you will lose your power.

# Christ in the Old Testament.

By Major D. W. Whittle.
Bible Institute, Chicago.

---

(Stenographic Report.)

---

## Lecture 1.

---

**ADAM AND EVE, TYPE OF CHRIST AND THE CHURCH.**

Eph. 5: 22-33. There is no type in the Old Testament that we have so much New Testament authority for using as a type of the church, as the relation of the woman to the man brought out in the creation story, and for this reason every devout Christian should refuse to accept any theory of Scripture teaching that explains away the facts of that narrative. Too much of the teaching of Christ, and too many of the fundamental doctrines of redemption, are built upon these facts to allow of their being tampered with.

1. Adam created in the image of God: Gen. 1: 26-27. So Christ, Col. 1: 15; Heb. 1: 3; II Cor. 4: 4. Genesis is the seed book of the Bible; and the first three chapters of Genesis is the seed book of Genesis. We have here Adam, the first man that is put upon this earth as the representative of God, created in the image of God, and his failure, and Christ as the second man, coming to take his place, brought out in these passages. He is on the earth as the manifestation of God, the representation of God. There are a great many who consider that Christ, the eternal Son of God, was in form as a man before the formation of the first Adam, and I am inclined to think that that is the meaning of it. Jesus Christ had some form before the creation of the first

Adam upon the earth. What is Adam? He was created in the image of God. I believe we might go into it and find it to bear out that view.

2. Man placed in dominion over all lower creation as God's representative. Gen. 1: 28. So it is said of Christ. Col. 1: 16-19. Jesus Christ stands as the head of the new creation. He is the second Adam. I Cor. 15: 45-49. "The first Adam was made a living soul, and the second Adam a quickening spirit." This brings out the contrast between the two Adams.

3. The woman created for the man and from the man. Gen. 2: 20-25. So Christ. Eph. 5: 29-32. Everything connected with the first pair and their surroundings is connected with redemption. We wonder so many times at the number of things round about us that illustrate spiritual truths. They were created for that purpose. The man created, the woman a creation to manifest that purpose that Jesus has concerning us. Canaan was created by God to be a place for the Jews to illustrate spiritual truths. So the church is created for Christ. The man existed before the woman. Christ was in glory but there was no helpmeet for Him. It is for the glory of God and the glory of Christ that He is to have a people for His name through whom He manifests His glory. We have Christ existing before the foundation of the world, and God choosing the bride before creation; and so man existed in the Garden, and the woman is chosen from the man to be a helpmeet for the man. Cf. Prov. 8: 29-31; John 1: 1. A deep sleep fell upon Adam, and in the deep sleep there was taken from him that which was builded into a woman. The same expression as is used in regard to the church. "We are builded together." In the sleep that came upon Jesus Christ, from His death to His resurrection, there comes this that is builded into the bride, the helpmeet for Him. She shall share the throne, fulfilling all the purposes of God. Eph. 2: 4-7. Raised together, seated together, is the position of the Church of Christ; the whole completed body as to the purpose and decree of Almighty God. Jesus Christ when He hung upon the cross, was there bearing the sin of the whole body of believers, paying the price of their redemption. When He rose from the grave and ascended into heaven, He took with Him the whole body of believers that shall

be gathered by the Holy Ghost and united to Him. The thing is accomplished. He entered in as the representative head of all His people, and they are seated with Him in the heavenly places. Cf. Rom. 6: 3-5. From this you see we are united with Him in His death; united with Him in His resurrection and in His glory.

The woman was made, or taken, from the side of the man. Not made of his head, to bear rule over him; or from his feet, to be under him; but from his side, that she might be with him. As John Tripp says, "Ever since the Garden of Eden man has been always seeking for his missing rib." This is so, and back of it is something deeper. There is nothing nearer heaven than a Christian home. It brings out the spiritual truth of union with Christ, and the man who apprehends that will be the most loyal, chivalrous man on earth. Those who say mean things about Paul, especially women, have not got into the spiritual things taught by Paul.

4. Man in the transgression for the sake of the woman. Gen. 3: 1-6, 12. We read in the Bible very plainly that the man was not in the transgression in the sense that the woman was. The woman was away from the man. She was away by herself when she fell into temptation. The conversation was carried on between the woman and Satan. An old negro preacher, in speaking to his congregation, said: "That's the reason she got into trouble. What business had she 'round that tree? If she had only been home taking care of the house she would not have got into trouble." Maybe he had a lesson for his own good wife. But there is a point there as to why the conversation was carried on alone by the woman. "The woman that Thou gavest me." It is not, however, as though the man is excused. He ought to have been there to take care of the woman. What use do we make of all this? Cf. II Cor. 11: 2-3. "The serpent beguiled Eve." He deceived her, and the implication is that the man was not deceived; that the man knew what he was doing; he knew what the consequences would be. He went into this transgression with his eyes open for the sake of the woman. This is the spiritual application of it. I Tim. 2: 13-15. Here we have it very plainly stated that the woman was deceived, and the implication is that Adam knew and believed that the penalty would come

just as God had said. Read the fifteenth verse in the Revised Version. "She shall be saved in the child-bearing." I think this looked forward to the Messiah and His birth. "The seed of the woman shall bruise the serpent's head;" and when the first child was born Eve said: "I have gotten a man from the Lord." This was her cry as she held the first wailing infant in her arms, as though she expected that to be the fulfillment of the promise. The seed of the woman shall deliver her from sin. That's the meaning in Timothy. "She shall be saved through child-bearing." Not simply the generation of the race on the earth, but in the birth of the Lord. Now refer to Rom. 5: 14, and Eph. 5: 25: "Gave Himself for it." We know the eyes of the *Lord* were open, and *He* knew what it meant when He came down here and He became man to die. He did not come to be a teacher, or example, but He became man to die. Heb. 10: 7-12. He knew what was before Him; and in the Old Testament we see how man in Adam, for the sake of the woman, not releasing him from responsibility, but for her sake, entered into the transgression; and if you will dwell upon it you will see that if the woman had entered into the transgression, and the man had not, there could have been no deliverance. Gal. 4: 4-6. Made under the law voluntarily, coming under the curse of the law for our redemption. This was done that we might be put back into the son's place, through Jesus Christ taking the curse. And through Adam coming under the curse with the woman, a seed is prepared by which the woman is delivered from the curse. Rom. 7: 2-4. "Dead to the law by the body of Christ." No hope for you until you are dead to the law, and no hope for the woman. "Raised from the dead." The deep sleep fell upon Adam, and when he awoke with new life here was the woman who had also been brought into life. This is a type of our resurrection life. We are married to Jesus Christ in resurrection life. But this could not be until in His death we died as under the curse of the law. After the third day He awoke from His sleep, raised from the dead, His Church united by the Holy Ghost receiving life from Him that they may bring forth fruit unto God.

5. The woman fell through being separated from man. Gen. 2: 15-18; Gen. 3: 1-2. The commandment was given *before* the

woman was created, and she received this commandment and the knowledge of the will of God through her husband. The word was not given to her directly, but through her husband; and the first wrong step seems to have been in doubting her husband. She wanted to pursue an independent investigation of this subject. She might have said: "*You* say so, but God never told me anything about it." Just so all we receive from God is through our husband, the Lord Jesus Christ. When we pursue independent investigation, thinking His own word does not satisfy, wanting to speculate and reason like the woman, saying, "I don't see *why* I should be kept from using my reason; I don't know *why* I should take my husband's word;" the result will be that the devil will come in. If we depart from simple confidence in Jesus Christ, from receiving the knowledge of God's will through Him, we will be on the same line or falling that Eve was on. Cf. also I Cor. 14: 33-35. Our husband will never leave us to meet Satan alone as Adam left Eve. Our standing is secure in Christ. Rom. 3: 19-26; Rom. 6: 7-12; Rom. 8: 29-39; John 10: 27-29.

6. All that God purposed of blessing to man lost in Adam was regained in Christ. Heb. 2: 5-16; I Pet. 1: 3-5.

7. To man and woman united, the promises were made of dominion. Gen. 1: 28. So Christ waits in glory for the completion of His bride before He comes to reign. Eph. 1: 17-23; I Cor. 12: 12. It was one name given to Adam and Eve. The woman never had a separate name until she went off by herself investigating on her own hook. It was Mr. and Mrs. Adam. When she went off she became Eve. So we bear Jesus' name. We are united to Him. The true Christian has one soul between Jesus Christ and himself.

## Lecture 2.

### GENESIS, THIRD CHAPTER, AS DEVELOPED IN ROMANS.

1. The origin of sin. Cf. verse 13 with Rom. 16: 20. This is the promise here in this chapter, "Thou shalt bruise his head," as in Gen. 3: 15. He said to the woman: "It shall bruise thy heel and thou shalt bruise his head." It is the only time Paul men-

tions the devil, Satan, in Romans. He was writing to the Romans, looking on the world as it is, and in his treatment of sin in the first three chapters you cannot but see that he must have had in his mind the narrative of Genesis. Cf. I John 3:8. That is the origin of sin according to the Bible. That is the only answer we have from the Scripture to give to anybody.

2. Nature of sin. Cf. verse 11 and Rom. 1:21. The latter is a perfect description of verse 11. By their failing to obey they glorify Him not as God. This is the nature of sin, disobedience to God. Cf. I John 3:4; Jas. 1:13-15. I use the last verses a great deal in talking with inquirers and answering cavilers. We have here God's dealings with everyone. There will be no change. Taking the thirteenth verse this is the question for every man,—What have you done? "I told you that if you struck that machine with a hammer you would break it. Well, why have you done what I told you not to do?"

"You have destroyed the machine." God deals with man on that basis. No matter what led you, you have done it. You have disobeyed My command. Did you not know it was My word? We knew it was His word and we knew the result, and we must meet it. I sometimes use the illustration of the man who was being tried for stealing a sheep, and he took the position that he did not steal it; he had a horror of stealing; he was an honest man. It was not him, it was his flesh. The judge said: "I will send your flesh to prison and you can go where you like." There is no entering into discussion as to why the devil was permitted to come there, or how did the devil become a devil, or was he the devil. They were held to the one point just as the judge holds the criminal to one point, "What is this that thou hast done? Don't you know I told you not to? Well, I must deal with you." So we have to deal with inquirers in the same way. It is part of the fact of sin trying to excuse, like the man who said—"He didn't do it but something else in him."

3. The effect of sin.

(a) A condemning conscience, as in verse 10. So in Rom. 2:15. Conscience works in men everywhere. John G. Paton, in the story of his life, tells of an incident. He had been forced to take refuge in a tree, and he saw a man asleep on the ground.

While there he saw a form creeping toward the sleeping man. He did not dare to cry out, and he saw this man's enemy take his hatchet and kill him while he was asleep. He watched that man the next day, and he said he could see the working of conscience in him — the memory of the deed done. Conscience works among the heathen, accusing or excusing them. The effect of sin is a condemning conscience.

(b) Afraid of God, as in verse 8. So Rom. 1:28 — "They hid themselves"; "Did not like to retain God in their minds." There was something in their minds not in harmony with God. They did not like to go to the light just as I might not like to hold up my hands before the light because my hands are unclean. "Did not like to retain God in their knowledge." Cf. Rom. 8:7, 8. Just think what being afraid of and hiding from God involves. Insubordination, hatred, rebellion, defilement — all are connected with it. The very moment I wander away from God I become afraid of God, and don't like to retain Him in my knowledge as a holy God.

(c) Seeking to justify himself, as in verse 12. If there is a woman within a hundred miles of a man when he does wrong he will seek to lay the blame on her. If a man tips over a cup of tea on the table he will blame his wife. It seems to be in man. If you stub your toe you will look around to see whom you can blame. My little girl came to me one day and said: "Brother says he don't love God." On questioning the boy he said he did not say that. "What did you say?" I asked. "I was pounding tacks with the big hammer and I hit my thumb, and I said I did not like God to make me hit my thumb with a big hammer." So right here we see Adam saying to God: "The woman Thou gavest me, she made me to do it."

Rom. 2:1-3. I was riding on a street car the other day and I saw a very ungodly looking man reading a newspaper. He was reading about a murderer, and when he had finished he exclaimed: "That man deserves no mercy." He condemned him. How many there are who condemn right and left, and they show by the very power to condemn the faculty to discriminate between right and wrong. They admit that men who do wrong ought to be punished. "Oh man that judgest," you are in an awful position yourself. By judging another it is an awful condemnation of ourselves. We have got to come under judgment.

(*d*) Knowledge of good and evil. Verse 22. How good God was. He just kept man from living in his present condition forever. He kept man from that which would perpetuate his existence in a state of rebellion against God. Cf. also Rom. 1:32. They have a knowledge of God. He has said, "Thou shalt not," yet they do the same. Rom. 2:14, 17, 18; Rom. 7:18-24. They know the good but have not the power to do it; they know the evil but have no power to keep from it. Satan knew that; but he did not tell Eve what the full condition was, that knowing the good they would not have the power to do it, and knowing evil would not have the power to keep from it. I think in Romans there are nine places where Paul speaks of "good and evil." It runs through the epistle, showing a connection in his mind with the narrative over in Genesis, especially when he is making his wonderful analysis of sin.

(*e*) Labor and sorrow in this present world. Verse 19. So in Rom. 8:22, 23. We see here how the sentence upon the first man is carried forward: "The whole creation groaneth," etc.

(*f*) Under sentence of death. Verse 19, and chapter 2:17. So in Rom. 5:12. The great law of propagation which transmits to man's offspring. Chapter 5:1-3. There is great help in studying to think of the word "generations" as that which has been generated. It is that which links us together. It is the generation of Adam. "Adam lived an hundred and thirty years, and begat a son in his own image." That is very striking to my mind. Adam was created in the likeness of God. When he begat a son the son was in his own likeness, not in the likeness of God. The first man corrupted the nature, and ever since the nature corrupts the man. We, here, to-day, are just as bad as we can be in this old nature. We are in this family, and are no better than anyone else. We belong to the fallen family of Adam. I Cor. 15:47-49 is a very direct application of the New Testament.

4. God calling the sinner.

Verses 8, 9. "Jehovah"—that is the name of the covenant-keeping God, the God of grace. The Jehovah of the Old Testament is the Jesus of the New Testament. Satan in this narrative never speaks of God as Jehovah. "Where art thou?" That is the first message of grace. If God had intended to leave man to the consequences of sin He would never have sought him. The very fact that the Gospel is preached, that the Holy Ghost is here, is a token of the grace of God. If God were going to leave you to the consequences of sin you would have no message sent. Now this lies all through the Bible, — God coming out after man; God appearing unto Abraham, Moses, and others, right down to the revelation of God in Jesus Christ (John 3:16, 17; Luke 19:10; Mark 16:15); and just so far as we are filled with the Spirit of God and in fellowship with Jesus Christ we shall "go." We cannot stay home. "Where art thou?" Those who are hiding from God, those who are ruined by sin, "Go," still calling, "Where art thou?" Go and preach the Gospel to them.

Rom. 1:1-7. "Apostle," "one sent." Paul, an Apostle, sent out to preach God's message, "Where art thou?"

5. "God dealing in judgment. Verses 17-19. There is always judgment before grace. Grace comes on the ground of judgment satisfied. This is our Gospel. Rom. 3:19-20. There is no grace for you until you take the place of judgment and come out from your hiding-place. God is merciful, full of love and pity, but He will have no sham, hypocrisy, or pride of man. When we have to come to the place of judgment God meets us as the father met the prodigal.

6. God dealing in grace. Verse 21. After He had shown to them that they had no clothing, and brought them before His presence in the confession of what they had done and in their nakedness, God clothed them. Just so, as we come to the sinner's place — lost, ruined, undone — why God has a Saviour for us. Here is man needing clothing, and here was death passed upon innocent animals to clothe guilty man. Rom. 3:21-26. What an application this is. Man has to come out from his hiding-place and make manifest before God his nakedness, and then God provides for him. There is no possibility of offering any excuse to God; the law condemns us. "All our righteousness is as filthy rags in His sight." Phil. 3:9. He wants God's

clothing and stands before God in that which He provides. How sure man can be of acceptance when he stands before God in what He has provided. If you stand before God in anything which you have provided yourself, God will not deal with you in grace. I Cor. 1:30. I think this is one of the most beautiful passages as to what Christ is to the sinner.

7. God dealing in discipline with the subjects of His grace and heirs of His glory. Verse 19; so in Rom. 8:22-28. Here upon the earth the whole creation travaileth and groaneth, and we who have the first fruits of the Spirit groan within ourselves, etc. This is all discipline for us.

8. Prophecy of Paradise to be regained for man. Verses 22-24. And so the paradise has been kept. Cf. I Peter 1:4, 5. God has kept us, and He has kept the inheritance. The cherubims with flaming sword are guarding the Garden of Eden, but when we have our resurrection bodies we will enter in again. Rom. 8:16-21. If we have the Spirit we are heirs of God and joint heirs with Jesus Christ, heirs to all Christ is heir to. Christ is heir to every promise that God ever made to man. Christ is heir to the Garden of Eden and Paradise. All that God purposed in man He is going to give to Christ and we will share with Him. Rom. 16:20. When Satan is bruised under foot the cherubims will sheathe their swords and the way will be opened. Cf. Rev. 2:7.

## Lecture 3.

### THE FOURTH CHAPTER OF GENESIS.

The putting of men before us in pairs, with their lives running parallel, showing our characteristics and illustrating great aspects of truth runs through the Bible. Here we have Cain and Abel; farther on Shem and Ham; Lot and Abraham; Ishmael and Isaac; Esau and Jacob; Eli and Samuel; Saul and David, — seven pairs of men in the Old Testament. Then in the New Testament (Luke 18:10), "Two men went up into the temple to pray;" and (Luke 23:32-33) two men divided by the cross. Cain and Abel represent flesh and spirit. Gal. 4:22-24, 28, 29. Cain, the firstborn of man in this world, was set aside as not acceptable to God; so it was also with Abraham's first born, Ishmael; Isaac's firstborn, Esau; Jacob's firstborn, Reuben; Joseph's firstborn, Manasseh; and in the Kingdom of Judah, Jesse's firstborn set aside for David; and Absalom, son of David, is also set aside; all this showing forth the setting aside of the flesh. That which is born of the flesh is not accepted by God. Noah's firstborn, Shem, is an exception; but he is a type of the resurrection and the new earth, with the curse done away.

Points as to Cain and Abel:

1. Both born outside of Eden after the fall. Both with sinful natures, and both under the curse of the law. Gen. 4:1-2. Both of these men were born under sin and both were under penalty according to this word. Cf. Rom. 5:12-14. Paul is showing that sin and the curse had been upon man from the time of Adam. Sin was in the world before the law was given. They had not committed the same sin as Adam did, but death was passed upon them. Because death reigned from generation to generation, it is a proof that sin was in the world and that there was a violation of law. Sin is not imputed before there is a law. It was impossible for death to have been visited if there were no sin. Sin was imputed to Abel and to those living before the law. The argument of Scripture is that from the time of Adam's sin death reigned. Rom. 3:18, 19. We have become subject to the judgment of God. There is no exception.

2. A way of coming to God through sacrifice had been instituted. This universal guilt and condemnation, and being under the penalty of broken law, had shut man off from coming to God except in some way that God would provide, and the way of coming to God by sacrifice was instituted. Verses 3-4, marginal reading, reads, "At the end of days," or week. A day they were in the habit of observing—a Sabbath. So in Gen. 8:20, and Gen. 12:7, we have reference to Noah's and Abraham's altars. This shows that sacrifice was instituted by God before the time of Moses. Noah had his altar, Abraham had his altar, and Cain and Abel had their altar. So atonement by blood was instituted before the time of Moses, and the truth in Lev. 17:11, if it were a truth for those after the time of Moses it is a truth for those before the time of Moses; it is a universal truth, and a truth for

all time. The word "life," according to the Hebrew, is "soul." "The soul of the flesh is in the blood." It is not the blood in its material aspect that is accepted, but the soul in the blood, for the soul of the offerer. I think it makes it stronger to remember that the Hebrew word "life" is translated "soul." We believe atonement by blood was revealed to Adam, and is co-extensive with the fall; and the analogy of Scripture requires this. The clothing of the guilty pair, Adam and Eve, was from animals slain for sacrifice and not for food. From Gen. 9:3, 4, we are warranted in the inference that flesh was not given for food until after that time. The first word of primitive man was a prayer, and the first act of fallen man is a sacrifice. That which prevented God's immediate judgment, and held back the execution of the sentence, "In the day that thou eatest thou shalt die" (Gen. 2:17), was substitution. History tells us that sacrifices for sin were made by all the peoples of the known world before the time of Christ. Every nation had their sacrifices. Julius Cæsar made an offering of two men on the altar to the gods, and Augustus Cæsar sacrificed four hundred men on the altar of Cæsar as late as 43 B. C. This simply shows what has sprung out from this truth in the Bible,—sacrifices for sin, substitution.

3. As Adam shows the nature of sin in the transgression of the law, Cain shows the nature of sin in the rejection of grace. Verse 3; so Heb. 10:26-29. Remember Paul was writing to the Hebrews who were apostatizing from Christ, returning to Judaism, to sacrifices. If after the knowledge of the provision God has made you go back to Judaism, there remaineth no more sacrifices. God has provided one sacrifice and He won't accept any other. This is exactly Cain's sin. There was a knowledge of God's will, how God should be approached, and he turned from it; he would not accept it; and this is the sin of to-day. It is not the sin question, it is the Son question. God has provided a substitute in Christ, by which the sentence of the broken law is met. Cain deliberately turned away from the provision God had made. This is the sin of unbelief, the same as those who reject Christ. I Cor. 1:18. Original thinking led to both these sins; *original thinking* on the part of the woman, and on the part of Cain not willing to take God's provision. We want to beware of original thinking. Cf. Psalms 119:113.

For you and I to set up our ideas against the infinite, all-wise omnipresent God! *we*, poor, ignorant, miserably fallen creatures; original thinking, departing from what God says, — can there be anything more absurd?

Cain and Abel distinguished from each other, not by difference in the nature of the flesh, but by the difference in the attitude of their hearts toward God, shown in their offerings. Verse 4; so Heb. 11:4. Abel's was a more acceptable offering than Cain's, and by this offering he found acceptance with God. There was not any difference as to being under the curse of the law, or as to being a sinner in the flesh, but he came in the way appointed.

Abel's offering indicated:
1. Confession of sin.
2. Acceptance of judgment due.
3. Acceptance of God's word that the judgment due was death.
4. The bringing of a substitute to take death in his behalf.

That is exactly what it means to believe on Jesus Christ. I Cor. 15:1-4. That is the Gospel, that Christ died for our sins, and was raised the third day. He is the substitute. In the acceptance of Christ on my behalf I made a confession of sin, that the judgment due was death, and show repentance toward God.

Cain's offering indicated:
1. No true confession of sin.
2. No honest confession of judgment due.
3. A rejection of God's word as to what judgment required, death.
4. A bringing of what he thought was better than that which God provided. What a sin that is — a bringing before God what *I think* is better! Yet a great many people sympathize with Cain. It was beautiful, and he had worked hard to cultivate it, and, as compared with what Abel brought it was far more acceptable to the natural heart. How many there are to-day who deny the atonement, the blood, and put man's philosophy in place of it. They are Cain worshipers.

So Luke 18:9-14. Probably there are a great many of you here to-day on the Cain line, groaning around and trying to satisfy God with yourself, and yourself with yourself. Get your eyes on the blood. The Pharisee is Cain bringing in the fruit of the ground, talking about himself. The publican is Abel. It is the exaltation of self. If we are full of self we are Pharisees, Cain worshipers. If we are on the Abel line we will be satisfied with the Lamb. The publican made the prayer before the altar, and a lamb was on the altar being offered for a sacrifice. Just the sinner's attitude standing before the cross. Abel confessed: "I deserve death, and I accept the death of the lamb as being the death due to me as a sinner." This is the meaning of our standing before God in the name of Jesus.

The altar and the bleeding lamb separated Cain and Abel. This is a foreshadowing of the cross of Jesus Christ that separated the two men at Calvary, one on either side, and it separates the race. We have two streams begun right here. Abel on one side believed, and was saved. On the other side Cain rejected, and was lost. And so in the preaching of Christ to-day. "To one it is the savor of life unto life and to another of death unto death." From the time of Cain the world has been divided into two classes, Cain worshipers and Abel worshipers. All who reject Christ as the Son of God and the one sacrifice for sins are of the former class. All who accept Him are of the latter. We must trust in His blood for the remission of our sins or share with Cain in the condemnation of being murderers; the blood of Christ testifying against us as did the blood of Abel against Cain. Cf. Heb. 12:22-24.

5. All that has ever been developed in the race of sin was here in germ in this first born man. Gal. 5:19-21.

(a) Willfulness and conceit. This is shown in his bringing of what he had cultivated, as in verse 3. The idea of thinking we can please God in bringing to Him something different than what He has provided.

(b) Pride. Offended that His offering was not accepted. If you are ever on the line of believing you are perfect, that you have got rid of the evil of the flesh, and that you will never be troubled with the flesh, I think this will be of value to you. The flesh is unchangeably evil in its nature. Being regenerated does not mean a change of flesh, but bringing in a new nature with power from the Spirit of God, so that I can keep my flesh under and die daily. If I get out of touch with Jesus Christ, if I get lifted up or careless, if I get so that I think I can live a single hour without Christ, I will fall. Some of the meanest things done on this earth have been done by children of God while out of fellowship with Christ.

(c) Envy. He was displeased with Abel, his younger brother, because he had been preferred before him. That envy is in us.

(d) Hatred. This was in his heart and grew out of his envy before any overt act.

(e) Wrath. A desire to hurt in some way the one whom he hated took possession of him.

(f) Evil speaking. Verse 8. He called his brother names. "He went out and talked with his brother" and showed by his tongue what was in his heart. "The tongue set on fire of hell" no man can tame it. It is a wonderful thing to have control of the tongue.

(g) Murder. The solemn thing about this is that if he had never killed his brother, murder was in his heart. This was the only possible ending of the passions that possessed him, and would always be the ending in you and me but for the restraining providence of God. When you allow pride, envy, to come into your life, and you are holding bitter feelings against another brother, you are a murderer; you have that within you which would lead to murder. That is the meaning of Christ's words. Matt. 5:21-24.

(h) Impenitence. Shown in three ways. Verses 9-15.

1. Refusing to confess.
2. Defiance of God.
3. No faith for forgiveness. When God faced him He said: "What hast thou done? Don't you know you have disobeyed Me? you knew My will. What hast thou done?" He had to face this question just as Eve and Adam had been forced to. "Where is Abel, thy brother?" "I know not." He lied; he had killed him and hid him away. He defied God. "Am I my brother's keeper? You preferred Abel, why did you not take care of him? What did you let me kill him for?" When he received his sentence his cry was: "My punishment is greater than I can bear." The same unbelief that led to the pride that rejected the atone-

ment by blood, leads now to blindness of mind as to the value of the atonement. Verse 13 is very solemn in its application to the rejector of the blood.

Note that Cain came under the power of the devil and killed Abel after the Lord's reasoning with him as to the offering (verses 6, 7), and he still hardened his heart in refusing the lamb. So Acts 3 : 14 ; I Thess. 2 : 14-16.

## Lecture 4.

### GENESIS, FIFTH CHAPTER. ENOCH.

There are two Enochs. One of Cain (Gen. 4 : 16-22), and one of Seth (Gen. 5 : 18-24). It is very interesting to see how these two are set before us. One illustrates the flesh, its development and end, and the other illustrates the spirit, its development and end. One belongs to a family gone out from the presence of the Lord to the land of Nod (vagabond), who spend their time in building cities which are called by their name, multiplying wives, and in making harps and instruments of brass. It is interesting to note that the seventh from Adam through Cain is Jabal, with Jubal and Tubal-cain as brothers, and the picture of them closes with murder. That is the flesh and its development. On the other side Enoch, the man of God, is brought out in the biography as given in chapter 5 : 18-24. He walks with God for three hundred and sixty-five years, and as we part from him he disappears in glory, taken to be with God. There are two lessons connected with Enoch's brief biography:

1. Dispensational, for our learning as to things to come.
2. Practical, for our profit in marking out the life of faith, in its method, hope and reward.

1. Dispensational.

(a) He occupies a dispensational position, — "seventh" from Adam. For the meaning of this see Heb. 4 : 4-9 (Rev. Ver.) When Joshua brought the children of Israel into the land of Canaan it was not a fulfillment of all the promises. It was a type but not a fulfillment. If Joshua had given rest he would not have spoken afterwards of a rest : " Therefore there remaineth a Sabbath rest for the people of God." The meaning of "seven" in Scripture is a period of completed time. II Peter 3:8. Among the early fathers, those that lived right after the Apostles, they thought that this dispensation would last six thousand years, and the seventh thousand year would be the millennial period (Sabbath period of rest). We have not any Scripture for it, but Polycarp, living contemporary with John, taught this in connection with these words of Peter. We cannot avoid seeing the significance.

Note what "seventh" meant to a Jew. Gen. 8:4; Lev. 23:39; Josh. 6:4; II Chron. 7:10. Now this does not begin to exhaust the use made of "seven," but to show that it was a very significant number. We have in the Bible seven distinct dispensations in the revelation of God to man. The seventh dispensation is the one which we are now in, which will close like the taking away of Enoch. They are,—1, Eden; 2, Patriarchal; 3, Mosaic or priestly; 4, Judges; 5, Kings; 6, Prophets; 7, Son of God and the church. Heb. 1:1, 2.

(*b*) The wickedness of Enoch's time a type of the last days. We have here in seed first development of the flesh, "multiplying wives, committing murder, making of harps and organs, real estate speculations, building twenty-story-high buildings, and so forth." Gen. 6:11, 12, and Jude 14-19. Enoch knew and prophesied of these. Who are the "these." See verses 8, 10, 12, 16, 19. Well, this condition of things that Enoch was surrounded by and from which he was taken away is an example; it is a type of what the last days shall be. In the third verse of Jude Enoch is introduced as an example of faithfulness, to emphasize exhortation to us. Cf. I John 2:15-18; I John 4:3; II Peter 3:3, 4; II Tim. 3:1-4. So Peter, John, and Paul, the three great Apostles, in their last words to the church, in their old age, all write in their testimony as to the state of evil on the earth just before the church is caught away, and the Lord comes in judgment to purify the earth and set up His kingdom. It is a very solemn thing to teach that which denies their testimony, or to substitute any other hope for these dark days than the scriptural one of the coming of the Lord. The state of things before Enoch was caught away is to be reproduced in the last days.

(*c*) Enoch walking with God, a type of the attitude of the believer in this present world. Rev. 3:20. It is an individual attitude. As we get into the last days we are not to look at the state of the church or amongst Christians, but it is to be a matter of individual communion with the Lord; and walk in fellowship with Jesus Christ like Enoch did, even if you have to walk alone.

Some points about Enoch.

1. Reconciled by blood. He kept in the presence of the Lord by worshiping at Abel's altar from which Cain turned away. Eph. 1:7; Eph. 2:13. There is not a step to be taken in walking with God except the blood is on us. We don't walk with God in order to be redeemed, but we walk with God after we are redeemed. Because we are redeemed we walk with God in sanctification and holiness.

2. Separated himself from the evil around him. II Cor. 6: 14-18. Many are not walking with God because they do not separate themselves from the evil around them; they are linked up with evil. I don't believe Enoch was connected with any secret society in the sense of associating with those who did not recognize God. Enoch came right out from the world with its pleasures and godlessness. In these last days there is great need of those who are filled with the Spirit of God, who have taken the place of separation, and, Enoch like, will walk with God never minding what the world says. They laughed at Enoch and scoffed at him, but he lived a separated man.

3. Found his delight in God. Heb. 11:5. He had been well pleasing unto God. What a beautiful thing it is to be well pleasing in the sight of God, and Enoch had this testimony. John 14:16-21. How little everything on earth is compared with the experience as described in these verses, to be kept in communion with God, in all God's love, and have my heart returning that love to God. To have the love of God and be in fellowship with His Spirit is better than His gifts. If we make our delight in God that will be on the line of Enoch. It only grows out of this separation; not separation in the spirit of legality, but from my heart, and then I cannot enjoy that which God has not a part in. If our hearts are fixed on God we will not have delight in things where God is left out.

4. Set his affections on things to come. Col. 3:14. When

Christ comes back to be manifested on the earth then you will have a part in the glory; and Paul, writing to the Corinthians, says: "Now ye are rich, ye have reigned as kings without us," etc., while he was an object of contempt, being hungered and as the filth and offscouring of the earth; but their reigning was an earthly one. The real time of reigning will not come until the manifestation of Jesus Christ.

5. Jude 14. Enoch believed the Lord was coming to right things. That is our hope, the coming of the Lord. No matter how dark it is the Lord is coming and with His coming things will turn. I Thess. 1:9, 10; Titus 2:11-15.

(d) Enoch caught away from the surrounding wickedness and impending judgment, is a type of the church of Christ taken out of the world, escaping the judgment, while Noah and his family left on the earth and preserved through the judgment are a type of the Jews, who are to pass through the coming tribulations and be preserved as God's people, to take possession of and rule over the new earth in the name of Christ. I Thess. 4:13-18. This we call the rapture of the church typified by Enoch's translation. Zech. 14:1-9. This is the coming tribulation of the Jewish people and their conversion to Christ. You find coming out in the Old Testament similar testimony as to the gathering of the Jews to their own land in connection with the wickedness of the earth, and with all their rejection of Christ the Jewish people refuse to depart from God. They refuse to bow down to idols or anti-christ. They pass through a terrible persecution from which they emerge when Jesus Christ is revealed to them. Acts 15:14-17. Blessings shall flow to all the earth through Israel after their return. Rom. 11:1. The argument is, "Has God forsaken Israel?" Paul says: "No; God forbid, for I am an Israelite," and the mercy of God to me shows that some are going to be brought to Christ right along to show that God has not cast them off, that He still looks down on these Jews that murdered His Son in mercy, and brings in the argument from the prophecies that God has not cast them off.

Verses 25-29, same chapter. All these verses deal with the dispensation of blessing to the world by Christ through Israel.

## Lecture 5.

#### NOAH.

Genesis, sixth to ninth chapters inclusive; and Scripture references to Noah, Isa. 54 : 9; Ezek. 14 : 14-20; Matt. 24 : 37; Luke 17 : 26; Luke 3 : 36; Heb. 11 : 7; I Pet. 3 : 20; II Pet. 2 : 5. Here are six different writers that allude to Noah, so you see how the Bible is linked together. We cannot accept any of these ideas about the story of the flood not being true. Those who do this dishonor the testimony of the Saviour, and make Him a false witness; and also dishonor the testimony of the prophets and the Apostles, and make them false witnesses.

#### POINTS IN CONNECTION WITH THE STORY.

1. Man in his nature unchangeably evil. Failure before the flood type of every succeeding failure and of final failure. How foolish it is to think otherwise. Back there in the early history man arose. There were just a few families and they had every advantage, example, and lesson given them; and if they fell how can we hope for the world now with all the evil and immense population in darkness? What can we hope for if man were a failure back there; if flesh is so corrupt that it just sank right down, generation after generation, lower and lower. Man in his nature is unchangeably evil.

Gen. 6: 1, 2, 5, 11. Understand that Scripture means that the daughters of men were Cain's descendants. It refers to the family of Cain, and as we have had in the preceding chapter sons of God descendants of Seth. I think it is a fanciful interpretation to say that "the sons of God" refer to angels. There is nothing so productive of mischief as the union of a believing man with an ungodly woman. No power on earth so hurtful as an ungodly woman ; and no power on earth brings greater blessing than a good woman.

Psalms 53 : 1-3; John 2 : 24, 25; John 7 : 7; Rev. 9 : 20, 21. Under the judgments men are not regenerated and reformed by punishment of God. "They repented not." We must strike at the heart of things. His nature is evil. "He must be born again." Bring them to the Son of God that they may be regenerated. No help for them in the government or in reformation.

2. Judgment pronounced. Gen. 6: 7-13. I believe that this is the key to the Bible right here at the commencement. God will have nothing to do with what man is in the flesh; he may be a giant in his works and beautiful but "the end of all flesh is come before me," "set aside." God will have nothing to do with any son or daughter of Adam except in Christ. If you want to be accepted by God you must be in Christ. We read in Matt. 3: 7, that judgment is upon this present world. Acts 17: 31; Rom. 3: 19; Rev. 6: 16, 17. This gives the same line of testimony of judgment to come over this world; where they say to the mountains, "fall on us, etc." In the day of judgment God will arise once more to shake not only heaven but earth. It runs right through the Bible that this world, is in judgment, and we are just to draw men out of it and get them into Christ as Noah tried to get them into the ark. II Pet. 3: 3-7.

3. A period of grace before judgment. Gen. 6: 3. Most writers understand that this was a period of warning. During that period of one hundred and twenty years the ark was building and Noah was preaching. It was a period of grace. Grace always comes before judgment. II Peter 3: 9, 10.

4. The ark as a type of Christ. Gen. 6: 14; I Pet. 3: 18-22. I suppose there are no verses in the Bible over which there are greater differences of opinion in regard to what it means as to Christ speaking in prison. The Roman Catholic church teaches that these verses refer to purgatory, where Christ went after His death; and a great many persons accept this; but it seems to be a forced interpretation. The time is fixed. The preaching is unto the people then under judgment, and the preaching was by the Spirit of God through Noah. This is in harmony with Scripture and does not introduce an element that brings in false doctrine like this idea of purgatory, or salvation after death, which is so mischievous. I believe this is in harmony with Scripture that it was Christ's Spirit preaching in the days of Noah. It is that which was a figure of the Gospel. The ark is a type of Christ, a like figure. As they had the ark we have Christ; as they in the ark pass safely through judgment, so we in Christ are delivered under judgment.

The ark as a type of Christ. Gen. 16: 4; I Pet. 3: 18-21.

*a.* Provided by God. II Cor. 5 : 18, 19 ; I Cor. 1 : 29-31. God gives; we take. God builds the ark; we enter in. It is not we giving anything — we take, eat; everything is provided for us.

*b.* A refuge from judgment. So Gal. 3 : 10, 13. The curse is universal for the disobedience is universal. Our refuge from judgment of Christ is in I Thess. 1:10. "A refuge from the wrath." A refuge from the storm as the ark was the only refuge from the flood. Rom. 8 : 1.

*c.* Death and resurrection typified. Gen. 8 : 4. This is the same day that Christ was raised from the dead — the seventh month of the civil year which corresponds with the first month of the religious. His death was on the fourteenth day of the month at the time of the Passover, and the third day was the seventeenth; thus this corresponds with the resurrection day. It is wonderful the harmony of Scripture in connection with that which is fulfilled in Christ. They came out on the new earth — resurrection ground. The ark rested on the new earth — resurrection ground. Rom. 6: 3-5. Death and resurrection, that is the Gospel. Acts 5: 31; I Cor. 15: 1-4. And so the Gospel as it is delivered up to the church is His death and His resurrection. His death as the sinner's substitute, to make atonement for sin; His resurrection for the sinner's justification. Just as sure as the ark rested on the ground the occupants rested too. In our resurrected head, Jesus Christ, we are carried over death and resurrection; accepted in the Beloved. This is a wonderful figure. The very judgment that destroyed this world lifted up the ark, and the flood that drowned all outside of the ark lifted up the ark over in a new earth into a new relationship with God; similarly we in Jesus Christ pass over into a new kingdom, covenant, family, entirely, just as it was here in the ark. Verse 21. How? By baptism? Nothing of the kind. By the resurrection of Jesus Christ from the dead. The only answer of a good conscience, the only thing that can keep us in assurance of acceptance with God is to keep your eyes upon the resurrected Saviour, "accepted in the Beloved," in His resurrected life. Josh. 4: 8-9. The twelve stones buried typified the death, and man entering into a new relationship; and the twelve stones taken out of the river, resurrection.

*d.* Root word for atonement, "kaphar," Gen. 6:14. This is a word that runs all through the Bible. It is one of the important words of the Bible, and is carried over into the New Testament and there applied to Jesus Christ. It is translated here "pitch." It is translated, "ransomed, purged, purified, reconciled, atonement." You will find a great many words of which this word is the root. Its meaning is, "to be covered over." Thus we are guarded from the Unitarian view of the atonement, explaining it away as "at-one-ment." You have got to take Christ as an atonement before you can take Him as "at-one-ment." If you will study that word "kaphar" as to the use of the word atonement you will see this. I am a sinner. I need atonement; I need that which satisfies the Lord God; I need that which covers the sinner from the righteousness of God and in Christ I have it. Lev. 1:4. "Make 'kaphar' for him," that he might be covered before God from the condemnation of God due to the sinner. Luke 18:14. The word "merciful" is the Greek word "hilaskomai" which comes from the same root, "kaphar." Meaning of the phrase here is, "May God have respect for the sacrifice for my sin." Rom. 3:24, 25. "Hilaskomai" the same root here. Rom. 5:11. "Reconciliation" in the margin. The same word, "kaphar," that which makes reconciliation. Heb. 2:17. Reconciliation. I John 2:2. "Propitiation" word is again used here.

### SOME POINTS ABOUT NOAH.

1. Noah found grace. Why was Noah saved? He was corrupt, that is, in his flesh he was a sinner. What is grace? It is kindness, pardon, shown or provided for the unworthy. He is saved out of all this world not because he was righteous under the law, not because he was not a sinner. We are not saved out of this world because we are righteous, "not our righteousness." We are subjects of God's sovereign grace. He has drawn us out of this world and put us in Christ. No matter if it does storm and thunder and rain, we are in the ark, and we are going to enter into eternal rest.

Gen. 6:8; Titus 2:11; Eph. 2:8. Noah was seen righteous because he found grace, and when God bestows grace upon any man He makes him righteous. He looks upon him as righteous because of His grace. Gen. 7: 1; Phil. 3: 9; Rom. 3: 21-24. Many of us want a righteousness under the law. We want to be satisfied with ourselves, and we get to looking at ourselves. We have no righteousness under the law. It is the righteousness which is without the law.

2. Made obedient. Gen. 7: 5.

3. Kept by the Lord. Gen. 7: 16; I Pet. 1: 5. The Lord shut him in and he could not have got out. We are kept by the power of God.

4. He was remembered by the Lord. Gen. 8: 1; Isa. 50: 10; John 3: 36.

5. Came out on the new earth. Gen. 8: 15-20; John 6: 37-40; Col. 3: 1-4; Rev. 21: 14.

# Public Reading of the Word of God.

By Rev. Arthur T. Pierson, D.D.

Bible Institute, Chicago.

---

I begin by a few hints about the public and private reading of the Word of God. It is a remarkable fact that the reading of the Word of God was enjoined and practiced in the synagogues. While speaking or exhorting was a matter of choice, the reading of the Word of God was a matter of divine injunction and habit. No church keeps up spiritual power if the reading of the Word of God is neglected. I am sorry to say that I observe as one of the marks of decline in the modern church, that very frequently the Word of God is being neglected entirely. I have been present at services of worship where not a word of the Bible was read.

Thomas Cartwright gives seven reasons why the Word of God should always be made prominent.

1. The Scriptures are holy in and by themselves.
2. They are in themselves perfect and profitable.
3. They have in themselves perfect concord and harmony.
4. They have in themselves admirable force and power.
5. Great plainness and easiness of style distinguish them.
6. Our Lord always spoke in language adapted to the people.
7. The Word of God deals in the sublimest mysteries and in the simplest truths.

It is the child's book and the book of the poor, the world over; and wherever the book has not been translated into the language of the people, children and the common people have no literature. There is a gracious simplicity and impartiality in all Bible narratives unknown to other literature.

My hints on Bible reading cover such points as these: selection of passages and determining the limits of such reading; laws of emphasis and inflection; the economy of voice and nerve and vital force; the laws of expression.

We have now to do with the Bible as a literary book for public use, and for use in the family and at the sick bed. In II Tim. 3:16, 17, Paul lays down a fundamental law to Timothy. Let Neh. 8:8 be your motto in the use of the Holy Scriptures. I once put this latter sentence on the walls of a Sunday-school building, and some Sunday-school teachers asked me where I got that sentence.

We have great reason to rejoice in King James' version. Forty-seven scholars gave an unspeakable boon to the English race in this noble monument of Anglo-Saxon simplicity. The Revised Version has never taken its place and never will. The Book of Ruth has in it twenty-seven times as many Saxon words as it has words of foreign derivation. This English Bible has been the book of the English speaking people since 1611, and has done more than all other causes combined to shape whatever is good in the English and American people. It is held in such reverence in England that it is sometimes inscribed on the walls of great public buildings. This is beautiful to see. "The earth is the Lord's and the fullness thereof" is inscribed on the front of the Royal Exchange.

The great bottom principle in the reading of the Scriptures is naturalness as against artificiality. This naturalness is not easily acquired. Dr. Edward M. Kirk, of Boston, was very anxious to be a good reader of the Scriptures, and used to go to the market place and study the ways in which people sold their merchandise, and how they haggled over prices. He studied their vocal sounds, inflections, and intonations. He became the most perfect reader of the Bible I ever knew, and when I heard him read once I could scarcely believe that he had read correctly. He made everything stand out remarkably. A great many people got an inspiration from hearing him read that they never got from his preaching.

Never imitate anything but nature. Observe what tones carry power in the use of the voice. Cultivate the colloquial; that is the style of ordinary conversation; but avoid all that is affected or dramatic in the reading of the Scripture. The actor and the preacher are as far apart as the east is from the west.

Reading Scripture is interpreting Scripture, and emphasis is exposition. Many of you will perhaps think this has little to do with you. There is not one of you that can afford to spend your life in Christian labor without making a great deal of Scripture reading. It is not necessary to understand the Hebrew and Greek tongue in order to understand the ways of reading and rendering the Scriptures. You are probably all aware that Hebrew poetry does not depend upon rhyme or rhythm of words, but on rhyme and rhythm of thoughts; that is, upon the thoughts corresponding and following along in a certain method and order. This is what is called parallelism. There are three or four kinds of such parallelism.

The idioms of speech, belonging to the genius of the language, enter into its very structure, and hence it is important to study the stern majesty of the Hebrew and the elastic and discriminating Greek. Catch the spirit of these tongues. Get to understand the force of peculiar words. It will pay you to study every word, as to its roots. Do not pass over a word in the English Bible the original meaning of which you do not know. It may take you a long time to study in this way, but it will make the Bible a living source of light and power to you.

Take for instance the word "conversation." It does not mean in the original "talk," but course of life. If you do not understand the meaning of words you cannot read the Scripture correctly nor enjoy it to the fullest extent.

Pauses help in the reading of the Scripture. A pause is made where the continuity of reading is interrupted. Pauses can be used with great power in public reading of the Scripture. Take the grand poem of creation in the first chapter of Genesis: "In the beginning God created," etc. Here you have an interval of time between the first sentence and the second — "And the earth was without form." If you read the first verse and then make a pause, you suggest the idea that there might have been a great period of time between the creation of the earth and its final preparation for man, but if you hurry on you convey the impression that the two events occurred very close in time. A pause must, however, be very carefully used. A theological student read: "Christ sent me not to baptize but to preach the Gospel," conveying the strange impression that he might have been sent to *baptize the Gospel* as well as preach it.

Note I Corinthians, twelfth chapter, last verse: "But covet earnestly the best gifts." Here occurs one of the most pernicious divisions in the English Bible. The division of the Bible into chapters and verses is not part of its inspiration. It was for the most part done by Robert Stephens while riding on horseback from Marseilles to Lyons, and it looks as though it had been jolted together in some such way. The pause at the end of the chapter here is unhappy. The "more excellent way" is the cultivation of love. Therefore there should be no pause. Do not hesitate to mark in your Bible that there should be no chapter division here; connect the last verse of chapter twelve with the first verse of chapter thirteen.

There is a good deal of force and power dependent on the *rate of reading*. Where the events described occurred rapidly, hurry your reading, and where the events were slow and interrupted, retard the rate of your reading. In the Ephesian demonstration, where Demetrius and his associates produced a panic, there is a rush to the theatre, and the town clerk representing the government calms the agitation of the assembly and dismisses it. Read the first portion of this with increased rapidity, and when you come to the speech of the town clerk diminish your rate. In Acts 14:14, where we read about the proposed sacrifice to Paul and his companions, we are told that Paul ran in among the people. The reading here should be accelerated. In the case of Jacob's petulent and impatient rebuke, try and put yourself in Jacob's place and read it as he would have spoken. It grieves me to hear people misrepresent the Scriptures by careless and slovenly reading. You will remember that the prodigal in a far country, having decided to go home, prepared a speech to deliver to his father, but his father interrupted him before he could utter the last sentence of his speech — "make me as one of thy hired servants." If this story is read as it was interrupted, it will give great effect to the reading.

It is a grand thing to enter into the *personnel* of the narrative, in a kind of impersonation. Be reverent, but put yourself in the place of these persons. When reading Job, enter into the circumstances of the dialogue and get the spirit of the dialogue in your own heart. So in the thirteenth of John, where Jesus washes the disciples' feet and a dialogue occurs between Peter and Jesus. I never heard but one man read it properly. In reading Peter's words: "Thou shalt never wash my feet," many emphasize the word "never," while it is the word "thou" that should be emphasized. It was not that Peter did not wish his feet washed, but he could not allow *his Lord* to do it. In Peter's words: "Why cannot I follow thee?" the words "why" and "now" should be emphasized. This gives new life to the passage.

I believe there is a power in the proper reading of the Holy Scriptures which is not transcended by any of the most eloquent sermons. A passage of Holy Scripture properly read or quoted moves an audience more than any words of ours.

You will always relieve the Scripture of monotony by proper *emphasis*. Take the refrain in the forty-sixth Psalm: "The Lord of Hosts is with us, the God of Jacob is our refuge." The first time you read it you might emphasize "Lord" and "hosts" and "Jacob"; the second time emphasize "us" and "refuge." The words are the same, but you bring out a new idea. Sometimes there ought to be measured utterance where solemn declarations are made. I always read the passage: "Ye must be born again," slowly. Mrs. Siddons, the noted actress, who was a fine woman morally, spent hours trying to find the proper emphasis for two words — "we fail" — in the case where Lady Macbeth is contemplating murder. Returning again to the Gospel of John, where we have the story of the feeding of the multitude upon the lake, Christ interprets the whole of this wonderful parable and discourse following when He says: "The WORDS that I speak unto you THEY are spirit and THEY are life." So Peter, on the day of Pentecost, when they were accused of being drunken, said: "These are not drunken, as ye suppose; but THIS IS THAT which was spoken by the prophet Joel."

Monotony in reading reduces even the thoughts of Holy Scripture to a dead level. A kind of churchly tone is becoming common which probably comes from the ritualists of our day.

The human voice is the most musical of all instruments. It has the delicacy of the flute or the lute, the peculiar nasal tone of reed instruments, all the staccato power of the piano. What a pity not to use the human voice as God would have it used. It ranges from sixteen and a half vibrations per second of the deepest bass to thirty-two thousand vibrations per second of the highest soprano. A great singer practiced three months on one trill until she got it. Many read the Word of God in public as if they never thought of the musical instrument that God has given them wherewith to make the word musical. If you do not agree with me, the pity is yours; you ought to feel the importance of these things. In passing from one passage of Scripture to another the voice should change to express the sentiment of the verse or passage. Take the words, "There is therefore now no condemnation to them which are in Christ Jesus." This should be read with an air of jubilation. You would think to hear some read this that there was a terrible condemnation upon those in Christ Jesus.

In reading the Word of God one should use the inflections of nature. As, for instance, in calling a person who is some distance off, the first time you call the inflection is upward, and the last time downward. Compare "Lord, Lord, open to us."

Do not anticipate in your reading a change of words which can only be understood as the reading progresses.

In reading the Scriptures make them alive, make the sense stand out, compel attention. It will become a new book to you and to others. Familiarize yourself with the history. Get into the sense yourself. Get all the side lights from geography, history, science, and the customs and manners of the people. Study the argument of a passage. Several chapters in the Epistle to the Romans I have very little doubt are reported addresses, because they have all the vitality of a forensic advocate.

Study the Scriptures prayerfully. Remember that a spiritual character is absolutely indispensable to rightful interpretation of Holy Scripture. Heart culture is the greatest secret of all. No professor or elocution teacher can ever do this for you.

# Methods of Studying the Word of God.

By Rev. Arthur T. Pierson, D.D.

Bible Institute, Chicago.

## Lecture 1.

### LAWS OF BIBLE STUDY.

The first law of Bible study is, *have your own Bible*. Get the very best, and one that will last you a lifetime. Use the same Bible in private study, in family worship, and in preaching the Word of God. If you need to have more than one Bible, let them all be alike; that is, with the corresponding chapters and verses of each book located on the same part of the page.

The locality of texts on the page is one of the principal helps in the practical use of the Word of God. I use the Bagster Bible. It is the best for me. What I mean by the locality of texts is that it is much easier to remember the location of a certain passage of Scripture on the page it is than to remember the chapter and verse.

*Master the Bible* as nearly as possible. What would you think of a physician that did not master medical science, or of a lawyer that did not master law? You ought to know more about your Bible than anybody else in your congregation.

Second suggestion, *emphasize leading texts*. A very simple method of doing this is to take a fine pointed pen and broaden out each letter of the word to be emphasized, making it stand out like heavy-faced type, or like some object in the foreground of a picture. There are what I call "seven little Gospels" in the New Testament—short verses that contain the substance of the whole Gospel, and which I have marked or emphasized. I will give them to you: John 3:16; Rom. 10:8, 9; Titus 2:11-14; I Peter 2:24; Heb. 2:14, 15; I Cor. 1:30; Eph. 2:4-9.

Third, *use connection marking;* that is, noting the connecting links in the argument. In Romans, fifth chapter, the words "much more" occur five times. They are the outlines of an argument and should be linked together. Man's ruin is great, but his rescue is greater. Whenever you look at your Bible you should see these five "much mores" standing out, and they will be marked in your mind as well as in your Bible. Take the words in the First Epistle of John: "Light, life, love," which you will find scattered through the Epistle. They are keys to the Epistle. Draw lines from one word to the other. Do not be afraid to mark your Bible; make it as practically useful to you as possible.

In John 15:1-10, you will find three words — "abide," "remain," "continue." They are from the same Greek word and ought to be translated the same. Put the Greek word "*Meno*" in the margin of the Bible and draw lines from these words to it, indicating that they are all from the same original word and mean the same thing.

Fourth, *division marking.* The divisions in our English Bible are, of course, arbitrary. Make your own divisions. Where a new paragraph, a new thought, or a new line of argument begins, indicate it in the margin with the printer's sign for a paragraph (¶). Even if such paragraph division comes in the middle of a verse mark it.

Another helpful mark is one which printers use for a section— "§." There are five books in the Book of Psalms. Learn where the books begin and end. All are marked by a doxology. At the beginning of each book put your sectional sign.

Note critical points or turning points in the history, teaching, or argument. The sixteenth chapter of Acts is a good illustration of this, where Paul first carries the Gospel into Europe.

Fifth, *symbolic marking.* You want a few simple symbols so that you will not have to use prolonged markings on the margin. My system is this: Wherever there is a reference to the atoning work of Jesus Christ, I draw a cross in the margin. Wherever there is a reference to the blessed hope, I draw an anchor; wherever there is a reference to the Holy Spirit, I make a Greek letter, which stands for a body with wings. Be sure that you understand your signs yourself. Wherever there is threatening I make a rough indication of a lightning flash. Wherever there is reference to the altar of burnt offering I mark a square; wherever reference to the ark or cherubim I add two wings. Wherever the Lord's Supper is referred to I outline a table. Reference to the crown, or reward, I represent by the circle. When such symbols become fixed in your mind, the truths they represent will at once be more easily kept track of and indicated.

Sixth, *marginal notes*. (a) In the first place, you should write your own "introduction" to each book of the Bible on the blank part of the page preceding. In the Bagster Bible there is a blank space that can be used for this purpose. I have a short analysis of the Book of Acts in my Bible. I do not need to go to my library. Let the introductions cover five P's *Place* where written; *Person* by whom written; *People* to whom written; *Purpose* for which it was written; *Period* in which it was written. Follow this by your analysis of the contents of the book.

(b) Find the *key to the book* if possible; some verse in the book, or better still, some word, and put that at the head of the book. Take the Epistle to the Romans. At the head of the book put your key word, which is "Righteousness," and that you may understand what righteousness means, put under it "Justification," and refer to the verse which authorizes you in taking this as a key—Rom. 3:23-25. You will usually find some hint as to what the book means near the beginning, often in the first verse. In Romans it is chapter 1:17. Mark the key word or key verse in the margin. I have written a little book called "Keys to the Word," the result of such studies.

(c) Trace these *key notes through the book*, noting the different variations to find the relation of each part to the whole. For instance, take the Epistle of Peter in which the key word is "precious," and occurs seven times. Mark the words, link them, and then on the margin make a list of them, or a summary. Put them in the order in which they ought to stand; build them up around the precious corner-stone, which is Jesus Christ, like the spokes of a wheel. Be sure and understand the key to each book and then trace it out through the book.

(*d*)· Note the *history;* that is, the circumstances which suggest and explain the various facts. For instance, in I Corinthians, third chapter, you have reference to gold and silver; wood, hay, and stubble. Paul wrote from Ephesus where the great Temple of Diana was situated. It was built in the midst of a marsh, and all around it were the hovels of the poor built of wood, hay, and stubble, and when the fire tried the work the temple stood and the hovels were destroyed. Paul, looking at this temple, says: Build not of wood, hay, and stubble, but gold and silver and precious stones. It helps you to understand Corinthians if you understand where written and the circumstances and surroundings. In reading the Epistle to the Philippians read also the parallel passages in Acts, sixteenth chapter. When you read about the Apostle being in prison with Silas, with their feet fast in the stocks, it will help you to understand the words: "Rejoice in the Lord always; and again I say, rejoice."

(*e*) Keep on the margin of your Bible all *useful analyses* of Scripture texts, and brief and helpful comments. For instance, write on the margin opposite Isa. 45: 22 the following:

Greatest good: Salvation.
Simplest way: Look.
Greatest breadth: All
Farthest reach: Ends of the earth.
Strongest assurance: For I am the Lord.

Put on the margin of Gen. 42: 21 the following three elements in "man's natural retribution":

*aa.* Memory: "We saw the anguish of his soul."
*bb.* Conscience: "We are verily guilty."
*cc.* Reason: "Therefore is this distress come upon us."

(*f*) Note the *results of your own discoveries*. Where you find a parallel text that illustrates another text, and where in study you experience the Spirit's illumination, put on the margin of your Bible what is sacred to you because it is what the Lord taught you.

(*g*) Put the *meaning of names* in the margin of your Bible. It will be interesting to you to know that the meaning of the name "Barabbas" is "Son of Abba," so that the Jews accepted the false and rejected the true Son of Abba.

There are what may be called degrees of inspiration of the Bible, and people are often at loggerheads because they do not understand this. There is no doubt about there being *three degrees* of inspiration.

In some cases inspiration covers nothing but the accuracy of the record. Gen. 3:4: "Ye shall not surely die," is an instance of this. Inspiration here covers nothing but the fact that Satan said this.

In other cases, inspiration covers the breathings of piety on the part of God's people, but does not necessarily sanction all their utterances. II Sam. 7:2 is an instance of this.

The highest degree of inspiration is where there are direct communications from God, or where it is declared that He spake by prophets, apostles, or evangelists. This is the highest possible form of inspiration. Everything about that is guaranteed — the accuracy of the statement and the authority for the statement.

(*h*) Use the *fly leaves* of your Bible, on which make, for example, a careful list of the parables of Jesus Christ. The division which I believe to be the best is, first, *didactic* or *perceptive;* second, *prophetic* or *predictive.*

1. Didactic, — those teaching moral truth, like that of the prodigal son. 2. Predictive, — like the wise and foolish virgins, intended to illustrate truth regarding the coming of the Lord. In every case where the parable is predictive it is largely couched in allegorical language, but where simply didactic, it is in historical language.

2. With regard to miracles. The miracles may be divided into three divisions. (*a*) Those showing power over nature, like the winds and the waves; (*b*) miracles showing power over diseases. (*c*) Miracles showing power over demons. I have arranged the miracles in this way with great benefit to myself.

It is interesting to notice that there are seven classes of miracles under the division of diseases, which ascend toward a climax.

(*a*) Miracles reaching common sickness.

(*b*) Power over malignant diseases, like leprosy, palsy, etc.

(*c*) Power over disease incurable in its nature, like blindness.

(*d*) Power over diseases that imply deformity, like the woman that "could in nowise lift herself up," or the man lame from birth.

(*e*) Power in regard to people maimed, like as if a lost arm were spoken into existence. None but the Creator could do this.

(*f*) Power over death.

In dealing with people who doubt the power of Christ show them how His miracles thus ascend toward a climax of power.

Even under the head of death there are three divisions of miracles.

(*a*) The raising of a person *just dead*, like the daughter of Jairus.

(*b*) Of a person being *carried out to burial*, like the widow's son.

(*c*) Of a person *four days dead* and buried, like Lazarus.

It is a great thing to make new discoveries in God's book. It is amazing that people will spend so much time on other books when here is the greatest book of the ages. I have made no inventions; what I have given you are simple discoveries.

7. Rules for the *study of the Bible generally*.

(*a*) Study systematically. Study the whole Bible from Genesis to Revelation; neglect no part of it. Find out the relation which each book bears to the whole.

(*b*) Study chronologically; that is, with reference to the chronology of the Bible. For instance, Job belongs between the tenth and eleventh chapters of Genesis. Make a note on the margin of your Bible that here is the place for the Book of Job. Arrange the books of the Bible according to their chronological order, and when you come to where any book belongs, read that book. Paul's first Epistle was the First Epistle to the Thessalonians, and in reading the Acts of the Apostles when you come to the time of the writing of this Epistle read it, and so you will get the Epistle connected with the history.

(*c*) Study microscopically; have an eye on the exact words — moods, forms, tenses, numbers, etc. Much is said in these days about the verbal inspiration of the Bible. I am confident that

God not only directed the thoughts of these men of old, but directed their utterances. There could be no inspired Bible without this. I would want to look over my addresses before they were published, no matter how intelligent and honest the man was who reported them. A single word would turn a sentence about in such a fashion as to convey an entirely different thought from that intended. And if I could not trust the most honest reporter to report my words, how do you think Almighty God could trust men to give words to His thoughts. I asked Dr. Hall what he thought of Dr. Briggs. He replied that Dr. Briggs was himself the principal argument against his own theory; that in regard to his inaugural address, about which such a disturbance was made, his defense was that his concept was all right but that people did not understand his language. If he could not express his own thoughts so as to be understood, how was a man to express God's thoughts so as to convey God's meaning.

I insist that the Bible is not inspired at all if the words are not inspired.

Heb. 12:27 illustrates that you cannot change a *clause* of the Bible without interfering with its completeness.

John 19:36, 37, and John 10:34, 35, and Micah 7:20, show that a *word* is significant and cannot be altered.

Gal. 4:9 is an illustration of the fact that you must not meddle with the *voice of a verb*. "That ye have known" God, or rather "are known of God." The great thing is not that I have known God, but that He has known me. You cannot change the voice without breaking the Scripture.

John 8:58; all depends on the words, "I am." It is the everlasting I am that Christ asserted for Himself. Here the *tense* is important.

Gal. 3:16 illustrates the fact that you cannot change the *number of the noun*, "seed" not "seeds."

Luke 15:3: "He spake *this parable* unto them." People are every day teaching that there are three parables in Luke 15, but it is really three parts to one, representing the various sides of redemption.

Matt. 2:23: "Spoken by the prophets." The word is *plural* for a reason, showing that you cannot change the number of a noun. Matthew referred not to any one prophet but to a general testimony of prophecy.

The voice or tense of a verb, or a noun, or even the number of a noun, cannot be changed without breaking the Holy Scripture, and if that is not *verbal* inspiration, I do not know what is.

(*d*) Study the Bible teachably. Never go to the Bible with a prejudice, to get authority for it, for if you do you will find what you are after. If you want to find Universalism or Unitarianism, if you want to find any heretical theory, you will find it; it is because it is in you, not in the Scripture, however.

Do not stumble at the Word of God because there are mysteries in it. There is an ocean of truth in the Bible and do not expect to take it all in. There are a great many mysteries in the Bible, but they do not touch practical duty. All practical duty is just as plain as the sun in the heavens.

(*e*) Study prayerfully. If you do not have light, wait until light comes and you will never be disappointed. The Spirit of the Lord that inspired the Bible illuminates the reader of the Bible, and if you claim the guidance of that Spirit, He will open the word to your eyes to behold the wonders of the Holy Scripture.

# The Unity of the Word of God.

By Rev. Arthur T. Pierson, D.D.

## Lecture 1.

The unity of the Word of God, especially in connection with the Old and New Testaments, will now engage us. I have two reasons for presenting this subject: First, I want to enable you to see *the connection* between the two great parts of the Word of God; but my higher purpose is to give you what I consider the greatest argument for the *divine origin* of the Holy Scripture.

The two books were given to mankind about four hundred years apart, and yet the second book lies latent or hidden in the first, as in germ. Unity could not be expected from the human point of view. Here is a book, a volume which is a library of books all in one, where all the conditions are against unity. You have sixty-six books in the Bible by forty different authors; and one thousand six hundred years during which they were in preparation, written in three different languages — Hebrew, Chaldaic, and Greek. Now tell me what points of unity would there be in any human work, if it were written during a period reaching from Herodotus, the father of history, to Abelard, and contributed to by people scattered all through the ages, having no connection with each other? Notwithstanding all this, the Bible is a marvel of unity, and this implies that some mind, spanning the ages from Moses to John, controlled and guided all these men so that each man, coming successively forward to take his part, was guided. Just as in an orchestra, where all the members take up their different musical parts, each one does not compose the music as he goes along; some mind had already composed the music and the musicians are presided over by one person. It is like the temple on Mount Moriah, each stone was prepared at the quarry for its place in the temple, and the temple was built without the sound of a hammer; but it was all planned by one master mind, and he saw that each stone was made ready for its place. The Scripture is like the completed temple on Mount Moriah. Each part has come to its place prepared beforehand, because God planned the whole. The unity of the Scripture is not always apparent, just as when you look into a stereoscope there often appear to be two pictures; but if you keep on looking until you find the focal center the pictures will come together.

First there is the unity of *structure*. The two Testaments are like two buildings of different dimensions made on one general plan. There are three main divisions in each of the two Testaments. First, historic; second, didactic, or that which has to do with the teaching of moral and spiritual truth; third, prophetic; and curiously enough they are in this order in both Testaments. For instance, Genesis, Exodus, etc., compose the historic part; and then you come to the parts which are mainly didactic; then the purely prophetic forms the last portion of the Old Testament. In Isaiah, the first thirty-nine chapters are almost entirely historic, while the rest of the book is almost exclusively prophetic, In the New Testament the Gospels and Acts are historic, the Epistles are didactic, and Revelation is prophetic. You will find some prophecy in connection with the Epistles, but they deal mainly with "doctrine and practice." Titus 2: 11-13 outlines the whole Old and New Testament. "The grace of God that bringeth salvation,"—that is the Gospel. "Teaching that denying ungodliness," etc.,—the Epistles—didactic; "Looking for that blessed hope,"—the Apocalypse—prophetic. Both Testaments are thus built on one plan : history, teaching, and prophecy. This shows the working of the divine mind.

There is a difference between a building and an organism. You all know what organic unity is. It is unity of a body, not a building. For instance, if you were to take out part of the materials of this building and replace them by others, you do not destroy the unity of the building. You might take a number of leaves out of a book and put others in, but you do not destroy the unity of the book. But if I lose the least joint of my little finger the unity of my body is gone; it could never be replaced. The Bible is a *body* of truth, and you cannot drop anything out of the Bible without distroying its unity.

Cuvier, the great comparative anatomist, had three laws of organism. First, that all parts are needful to a complete body; second, that each part is the complement of every other part; third, that all parts must be pervaded by vital power — there must be life in every part. As an application of these principles, take that one of the lion's teeth, which corresponds to the eye-tooth of the human jaw. That tooth has a peculiar form and is curved outward. It implies a jaw strong enough to hold that kind of a tooth; such a jaw implies that the head must be so constructed as to work such a jaw; that implies that the neck must be short and very muscular in order to sustain such a head; that implies that the shoulder blades must be compactly built with the muscles of the head and neck in order that the neck and shoulder blades shall co-operate with the head; and all this implies that the forepaw at the bottom of that body shall have curved claws, and that the paw shall rotate so as to work the curved claws in the opposite direction from the curved tooth, so that the flesh held by the tooth and claws may be torn apart. So that from one tooth the skillful anatomist can construct a model of a whole animal. Each part is necessary to the whole. One part implies every other part as it is the complement of every other part, and life must pervade the whole. There must be life in the tooth as well as in the brain. What has this to do with the Bible? Much every way. Do not let anybody convince you that any book of the Bible can be dropped out and you can still have a whole Bible. A book taken out of the Bible maims the body of truth. The Bible is one complete whole; nothing can be omitted from Genesis to Revelation. Genesis, as the name implies, is the book of beginnings; Exodus is the book of departure; Leviticus the book of sacrifice; Numbers the book of pilgrimage; Deuteronomy the book of obedience; Joshua the book of conflict and conquest. Some say that Ruth is nothing but a love story; but it is the only book in the Old Testament that sets before us the twofold nature of the person of the Redeemer. The word *Goël*, or "Redeemer," occurs four times in two verses. What is a redeemer? It is a man who belongs to the family that is in poverty and trouble, so that he has the *right to redeem*, but who belongs to a higher branch of the family not involved in the trouble, so that he has the *power to redeem*. What a hint of Christ's twofold nature as both man and God!

Some say the Book of Esther is of no use because the word "God" is not in it. But that is the one book that is devoted to the demonstration of the *providence of God* in human affairs. There are seven lessons on providence in the book. First, that God overrules all history; second, that he gives to the good their reward and to the evil their retribution; third, that evil sometimes appears to triumph, and the good sometimes appears to be defeated; fourth, that the smallest events enter into the purposes of God's providence, as, for instance, the sleeplessness of the king; fifth, we must judge providence by the final issue; sixth, there is no fatalism in providence; last, the providence of God does not appear obviously, but it is a hidden secret. The name of God is not found, but the activity of God is. That is why God's name is not there. What I am trying to prove is that every part of the Bible is needed. The New Testament sets forth the facts of Christ's life and the supervising activities of the Holy Ghost. The Epistles are like the garden of the Lord. Some think the Epistle to Philemon valueless. Philemon was a runaway slave and was converted by the Apostle Paul, and Paul sends him back; nothing, some say, but the story of a servant returned to his master. But it contains the finest unfolding of the *philosophy of redemption*. Here is the idea: What is the sinner but a runaway slave who has robbed God besides, and who has no hope in the law, just as a slave had no hope in the Roman code? But, as Roman law permitted the slave to go to the friend of his master and get the intercession of this friend with his master, so Paul writes to Philemon who had been wronged and says, Put it to my account. What does Christ do? We have wronged God and He says to God, Put his sin to my account, I will pay the whole debt myself; inasmuch as this sinner is my friend, receive him as myself, and take him right into thy family, not as a slave, but as a brother.

Each part of the Bible is needful to the whole. Each part is the complement of every other part. Take the four Gospels. Why four instead of one. If you were to draw a picture of a house, what idea can you get from it with only a front view? You must have a view of the four sides. The Gospels present Christ not as a picture, but as a fourfold personality, as in Ezekiel you have the one great living being with four heads — the face of a man, the face of an ox, the face of an eagle, the face of a lion. So in Matthew you have Judah's lion, in Mark the ox for sacrifice, in Luke the Man among men, and in John the eagle soaring far above us, and looking into the face of the sun itself.

There were five writers of the Epistles — Peter, John, James, Jude, and Paul. Why five epistolary writers? There are three graces which need treatment — faith, hope, love; then we need to be taught as to good works, and the risks of apostasy.

John is the apostle of love, Paul of faith, Peter of hope, James of good works, Jude of apostasy.

Take the relation of the two Testaments. Suppose you want to understand John, compare it with Genesis. If you want to understand Exodus, the book of separation, you must read the Epistle to the Corinthians. If you want to understand Leviticus, the book of sacrifice, you must read Hebrews. To understand Deuteronomy, the book of law, you must read James, the epistle of outward conduct. To understand Joshua, the book of the wars of the Lord, you must read the Acts of the Apostles. To understand Ruth and Canticles you must read Ephesians and Colossians. The point is that each book in the New Testament has a counterpart in the Old Testament, and to understand them you must compare them.

## Lecture 2.

The third principle of Cuvier is that all the parts of the body must be pervaded by the life. This is the only book in the world that is a living book. The Word of God "is quick," that is, living. For instance, you go to the Bible as a mirror. There is but one living mirror in the world, and that is the eye. It mirrors or reflects all life. Just so the Bible is a living mirror. It shows me myself as I am, and as I ought to be.

The Word of God is called a counselor. I speak into a living ear and a living tongue responds; so the Bible will talk back, it will counsel. If you treat the Bible as a living friend, and go to it as a counselor, you will commune with God through the Bible.

II. The second thought is that the Bible is a unit *in its history*. It is the history of the kingdom of God. When Adam was created, dominion was given him. God said: "Let us make man." Why this consultation in the Godhead? If you had a farm and was going to buy some pigs, you would not think it necessary to have a very serious consultation. You would go and get the very best pigs you could find. But if you were going to put a man in charge of an empire you would want to be pretty sure of your man. God was not making animals to stock the world, but He was going to give man an imperial sceptre, and after a consultation Adam was made, the world-prince. But Satan took the sceptre out of Adam's hand and has been the prince of this world ever since. When Jesus met Satan in the wilderness He regained the sceptre out of his hand, but Satan acts as the usurper of the kingdom; and so Satan remains the prince of this world until Christ comes again, although having no right to the world's dominion.

Now notice that the history of the Bible is not a history of the nations, peoples and tongues and languages, but a history of the kingdom of God as given first to Adam and lost in his fall and usurped by Satan. God raised up a people, Israel, "prince of God," and He erected a theocracy. All centers around about Israel. Do you know where in the Bible the true history begins? Not in the first chapter of Genesis, but in Gen. 10:26, with the first man who was called out, after Adam's fall, to be the representative of the kingdom of God. With the history of Israel the Old Testament closes. With the apostasy and dispersion of the Israelites Old Testament history stops, and is never resumed. Events of great interest were occurring in the world, but God's kingdom was not among men. It is the same in the New Testament. When the Jews were finally abandoned, history stops. There are prophetic intimations of history to come, but only when the Jews are restored will history begin again.

The "Times of the Gentiles" represent long intervals between

Nebuchadnezzar and the coming Christ. There is no history of the "Times of the Gentiles" in the Bible, you must look for that in Gibbon, Macaulay, and other secular historians. Only the times of Israel's fidelity are reckoned in the time-tables of God. This is a most marvelous fact. There are three periods of 490 years each, from the Exodus to the coming of Christ. I Kings 6: 1, reads 480 years from the Exodus to the building of Solomon's temple; but add ten years for the completion of the temple and the time is 490 years. From the completion of the temple to the captivity 490 years; and from the captivity to the coming of Christ 490 years. These numbers are not according to the calendars of men, but by the calendar of God. Here is something for the critics to notice. God counts this sacred 490 *only during the time of Israel's fidelity*. The real time from the Exodus to the completion of Solomon's temple was 620, but during that period there were 130 years of captivity which are not counted. The next 490 is reckoned in the same way. The real time was 560, but there were seventy years of captivity. God counts nothing on His calendar for the time we do not spend in fellowship with Him. Think how some of the self-constituted critics would open their eyes if they could see these things. How God must smile at their follies. All the years of Israel's bondage in Egypt have no history whatever, because they were not in fellowship with God. Neither has the captivity any history.

III. The next unity is that of *dispensations*. Dispensation is the method of God's dealing. Dispensations are always marked by seven features. The seven marks are these:

1. There is an advance in revelation.
2. Then there is a decline in godliness. This shows the depravity of humanity. More light from God and more shadow and darkness among men.
3. Then the sons of God wed the daughters of men. That is, the world and the church join hands, or there is an amalgamation.
4. Out of this unnatural wedlock there comes a gigantic civilization, but of a worldly type. We have a good sample of it here in Chicago to-day. The church scarcely preserves a relic of apostolic purity, and how proud the people are of their "civilization"!

5. Evil and good develop side by side, like the tares and the wheat—a parallel growth of good and evil.

6. Apostasy, especially among those who profess to be teachers of truth.

7. And at last comes catastrophy. That is, judgment on the one hand and the bringing out of God's true people from the mass on the other. All along through history these seven marks have distinguished every dispensation.

There have been at least seven dispensations, each ending with a crisis, or catastrophy, or judgment.

First, from the creation to the fall, ending with judgment and catastrophy.

Second, from the fall to the deluge, ending with a catastrophy.

Third, from the flood to Abraham, the catastrophy being the judgment of the cities of the plain.

Fourth, from Abraham to Moses, ending with a catastrophy in Egypt.

Fifth, from Moses to Christ's ascension, the catastrophy being the destruction of Jerusalem.

Sixth, from Christ's ascension to His second coming, the catastrophy being the destruction of the man of sin.

Seventh, to the close of the millennial reign, ending with the destruction of Gog and Magog. We are now in the period of the CHURCH, which did not exist before Christ's coming and will be withdrawn when He comes again.

IV. Unity of *teaching*. There is no inconsistency in the teaching of the Word of God, and no adulteration in the truth of God. It is winnowed wheat. We hear a great deal in these days about natural religion, about the fatherhood of God and the brotherhood of man, and some have been a little troubled; but I think I can give you a key which will help you out of the difficulty. There is indeed some truth in the "universal fatherhood of God" and the "universal brotherhood of man." That was man's original condition, and if man had continued as he originally was, this is all the religion there would have been on earth; the Holy Spirit would not have been required to foster such bonds; but sin overthrew that original condition and man turned against God and denied his relation to his own Father. He denied also the brotherhood of man, hence there came slavery and caste. At last there comes in the spiritual religion when the fatherhood of God and the brotherhood of man will be restored in Jesus Christ by the Holy Ghost, creating the new bond of fellowship. Sin destroyed the original condition of the fatherhood of God and the brotherhood of man, and hence there must come in the work of the Holy Spirit based upon the vicarious atonement of Jesus Christ.

## Lecture 3.

V. The next center of unity is *Prophecy*. All here also revolves around one center, and that center is the kingdom of God. Consequently, the person of the King will naturally be prominent. Prophecy revolves about two comings of the King. The first coming was nearly two thousand years ago, to lay the foundation of the kingdom and make possible the reign of Christ in and over man. Let us understand that we could have had no kingdom if He had not come and if the Spirit had not come when He went away. During this period the kingdom is invisible, it is not to be identified with the external organization called the visible church. There is much in the church that is not in the kingdom, and something in the kingdom not in the church. Prophecy in the Old Testament has very largely to do with the kingdom.

Christ comes again to set up the empire in fact, in visible form and in glory, and to carry on that empire under His own personal reign until He has subdued all enemies under His feet —I Corinthians, fifteenth chapter—then when all things are subdued He will deliver up the kingdom to the Father. Let us fix in our minds that prophecy revolves about the two comings of the King.

The first prophecy is Gen. 3:15. Notice, "the SEED of the serpent." "Ye are of your father, the devil," Christ says. Again He says: "Oh generation of vipers,"—brood of the serpent. Wicked men are in this world, the SEED of the devil. Now here in Genesis is the germ of all prophecy. First, a war, to extend to the very end between the children of God and the children of the devil; secondly, the final victory of the Messianic seed crushing the head of the serpent; thirdly, victory, but at the cost of the wounding of the heel or lower nature of the Messianic seed. Just think of this. Here is a brief prophecy that outlines the whole Scripture. We have to be wounded in the heel if we are to crush the enemy — the loss of the lower in order to gain the higher.

Prophecy touches other subjects, but only as related to the kingdom of God. For instance, the Gentiles are touched upon in the Old Testament, but only as related to Israel. In the New Testament hostile powers are touched upon in prophecy — the beast, the false prophet, the scarlet woman, and the devil. The beast represents world kingdom; the scarlet woman represents the apostate church which is bolstered up by, and carried on the back of, the world kingdom. Notice how the Bible anticipates the evil results of the identification of church and state. Whenever the state has carried the church, the latter has become corrupt. The false prophet represents false teachers outside the church, and the devil the great adversary of God and men.

VI. The next center of unity is the *ages*. In the Epistle to the Ephesians you will find all the ages outlined. There are five ages indicated in the Epistle.

As long as I have studied the Bible I never discovered or noticed this until a few weeks ago.

First, the past eternity, indicated by the phrase: "Before the foundation of the world."

Second, the past age, which includes all the past periods from the foundation of the world to the ascension of Christ. In the first age the kingdom was united, and in this, the second, it was fallen and become apostate. And when Jesus Christ came He offered the kingdom once more to the Jews, but they refused it.

The next age is the present, which is always called the evil age, because evil is to be dominant and prominent in this age from the beginning to the end. This age ends with the second coming of our Lord Jesus Christ. During this time the King is in heaven, hence the expression in Matthew, "the kingdom of the heaven," which covers this entire period from the ascension of Christ to His second coming, during which time the King is in heaven and the laws are promulgated from heaven. During this time the kingdom is invisible like the presiding Spirit. He dwells with individuals and with the church of Jesus Christ — He dwells in the invisible church. We make a mistake in saying that the Spirit necessarily resides in the *organized* body. You who are going out to be pastors, try and start a church that shall be as far as possible one in which the Holy Ghost dwells as an organized body. Fifty years ago George Muller said that he could not longer remain in connection with the organized body. He found two or three other persons that felt as he did and they started a little church, Since then that church has come to have a membership of 1,760, and there is not a dancing, a card playing, an opera going, a theatre going, a drinking or horse racing Christian among them. I was in that church in Bristol and preached in it. I never saw such a gathering of believers. Nobody presided over the meeting but the Holy Ghost. There was no one in the pulpit. One man got up and read the Scripture, another led in prayer, another gave out a hymn. I had to speak as the Spirit moved me. The whole meeting seemed presided over only by the Spirit of God. They had twenty missionaries in the foreign field, they had not a paid servant of any kind, nor a rented pew, nor a fair or festival. Everything was done in the Spirit of the New Testament, and nothing to interfere with the Holy Ghost. I am grieved every day at the way things are done in the modern church. Would to God that we had an apostolic church! You brethren going out into the world, can you not insist upon an apostolic style of church where people can worship God according to the Scripture pattern?

This is the present age — the evil age. Do not be deceived by worldly civilization; do not talk about the millennium having come because of a World's Fair that beats everything ever known. Satan is the usurper and holds the keys of this world and its civilization.

He said to Christ: "All these things are mine, and to whomsoever I will I give them — worldly power and patronage." Do you suppose he would have said that if it were not true? Evil is predominant in this age.

The coming age. Then the kingdom is to be visible, not invisible; collective, not elective; general, not partial; destined to move on to universal supremacy. At the end there will be universal triumph when the last enemy will be destroyed and the King reigns over the redeemed earth.

The final age is the future eternal, when the kingdom is to be established, as it was in the former eternal age, undivided, undisputed, and universal. This will be the age of the Father, not the age of the Son.

VII. The next unity is the harmony of *science and the Word*. Science is general secular knowledge or information with reference to secular truths. Science means simply knowledge.

There are three consistent laws in regard to science observed in the Bible.

1. It never makes a direct statement in regard to scientific fact, because the Bible is not a scientific book. Supposing the Bible had directly and definitely stated that the sun was the center of the solar system and the planets revolved around it, and told the number of the planets and the number of the satellites of the earth and other planets. Do you not see that science would have been announced in advance of the preparation of the race to receive it? God never tells you anything you can find out for yourself. You can find out the elements of the soil and He does not tell you. You would not know what constitutes man, so He tells you — body, soul, and spirit. You would not know how far man was different from other animals if God had not told you that He breathed into his nostrils the breath of life. You might know that there was a God, and so He never tells you that in the Scripture. "The fool hath said in his heart there is no God," but the Bible was not written for fools. He does not tell you that God has power, that He is wise, that He is just. These things were already revealed, and God takes it for granted that you know these things already. But you would not know that God was gracious and forgiving until He told you, so the Bible tells of the grace of God.

2. There is never a contradiction of science or a misstatement of scientific fact. There is not a single place in the Bible that I have ever found where a directly and plainly wrong statement is

made, as to scientific fact. There are forms of expression which may be misconstrued, as when we read that the dew descended upon the mountains of Zion. We all know that dew does not come down from heaven. The air becomes full of moisture during the day, and when night comes on the earth becomes colder, and a distillation of the moisture takes place and the dew is formed. The expression in the Bible is simply a form of language to suit ordinary styles of speaking. We still speak of the sun's rising and setting. In the most advanced state of scientific knowledge we still make use of the same forms of statement as found in the Bible, though not scientifically correct.

3. The Bible uses language which expands itself to meet the growing knowledge of the race. In the first chapter of Genesis there is a word translated "firmament." The meaning of the word is "expanse." The ancients held that the firmament was a solid metallic sphere — firm-ament. When the translators came to that word in the Hebrew they translated it "firmament." The higher critic says there is a blunder, Moses speaks of the firmament as if the heavens above were solid metal. But the word simply means space. If the most modern scientist had tried to find a word to express the idea, he could not have found a word better adapted than the very word Moses used. You have heard a great deal in these days about the inharmonious or irreconcilable hostility of the Bible to modern science. I will give you a few samples of the mistakes that Moses did *not* make, and that there was every reason to believe that he would have made. Remember that the Bible is the oldest book in the world, and that the sacred books of other nations contain huge blunders.

The Hindoo cosmogony teaches that millions and millions of ages since, this world began to be; a flat, triangular plain, built in three stories. This plain was held up on the backs of elephants with their tails turned out; the elephants stood upon the back of a huge tortoise; the tortoise stood on the coil of a huge serpent which held his tail in his mouth. What the serpent rests upon nobody has yet found out. This is the Hindoo story of creation; and they tell us that what makes an earthquake is that the elephants shake themselves. Supposing such nonsense was found in the first chapter of Genesis? You and I would have flung the Bible to the winds. What does geology teach? A watery abyss. The appearance of continents. Three forms of vegetable life—plant, herb, and tree. Animal life, beginning with the lowest forms and advancing to the higher, until man came upon the earth. This is exactly Moses' order of creation.

Two hundred and fifty years ago comparative anatomy became a science, and it was discovered that there were grades in the animal kingdom, and the way the grades were regulated was this: comparing the brain with the spinal column was the great criterian. Now, for instance, in the fish it was found that the brain sustained the relation to the spinal cord of two to one; in the reptile two and one-half to one, in the bird, three to one; in the mammal, four to one, and in man, thirty-three to one. This is exactly Moses' order. Two thousand years before comparative anatomy began to be a science Moses classed animal life in this order—fish, reptile, bird, mammal, man. This is one of the mistakes that Moses did not make. It is very remarkable that he should not have made it.

## Lecture 4.

In Jer. 33: 22 we read that the hosts of heaven cannot be numbered, and they are compared to the sand of the seashore which cannot be measured. At the time that this was written nobody had any idea that there was a countless host of stars. Catalogues of the stars have been made in one hemisphere of the heavens, and they numbered one thousand six hundred and thirty. Ptolemy made a catalogue of the whole sphere of the heavens, and he made the stars three thousand three hundred and fifty, and gave them names and numbers. Anyone could count three thousand three hundred and fifty. It seemed absurd to talk about stars being as countless as sands. But how wise the God was that guided Jeremiah. When Galileo turned his telescope on the heavens he found stars that never had been seen by the naked eye. It was amusing to see how he was confronted by the higher critics of his day. One professor at Pisa said: "It is utterly impossible that there are more than seven planets, for there are but seven days in the week, seven openings in a man's head, seven colors," etc. It is a pity there had not been one more opening in his head so as to get an idea in! When Lord Rosse turned his great reflector to the heavens he found that there must be not less than four hundred millions of stars that could be seen by his telescope alone. When Herschel turned his telescope to the skies, and began to dissolve that cloudy mist known as the Milky Way, he discovered that it was composed of myriads of stars which were absolutely as countless as the sands of the seashore. He further discovered that the Milky Way that we see is but the narrow edge of a plain of stars beyond which stretches a universe of orbs of which we have not the slightest conception. In regard to our own solar system: If you take one dimension — length — drawing a straight line from our solar system to the nearest fixed star, there is space enough to put in thirteen thousand systems as large as our own, placing them all on this straight line. If you take two dimensions — breadth and length — you can put in one hundred and thirty millions of systems like our own in this empty space. If you take length and breadth and depth, you can put thirteen billions of systems like our own in the space, and this will occupy but one little portion of the empty space of the heavens! It is literally true that the hosts of the heavens can no more be numbered than the sands of the seashore. How did Jeremiah come to use such an expression without omniscient guidance?

Another illustration. In the twelfth chapter of Ecclesiastes we have an account of the various methods of death. "Then shall the dust return to the earth." There is no doubt that it refers to dying. There are four ways in which death is represented as coming to us. Life is a table with four legs. One leg is the brain, another is the lungs, another is the heart, and another is the nervous system. If death comes by the brain we call it coma; if it comes by the lungs we call it asphyxia; if by the heart, syncope; if by the nerves, paralysis or apoplexy. Solomon described in figure the four ways of death. "Or ever the silver cord be loosed." If you saw a dead body dissected you would find inside the backbone a silver cord, the spinal marrow. If this cord is loosed, paralysis and other forms of disorder occur. If you take a surgeon's saw and cut through the human skull you have a golden bowl. When the skull is shattered death ensues. If you open the chest you will find something like a pitcher — the lungs, which take in and pour out the air like water. Shatter that pitcher and death occurs. Near the pitcher the lungs, the heart. One lobe receives the blood from the veins, the other lobe throws out the blood. Here is a 'cistern' into which the blood comes, but here also is a 'fountain' that pulses the blood out through the arteries. This is the wheel at the cistern. In Syria you see a wheel at the well which draws up the water on one side and pours it out on the other as it revolves. So the heart draws up the blood from the veins and pours it forth through the arteries. Many centuries before Harvey discovered the circulation of the blood Solomon gives a description of it. How do you account for that?

Another illustration. One of the latest discoveries of science is that light is a form of motion. I have compared thirty sciences and have never found a single disagreement between an established fact of science and the Word of God. Has there been any modern discovery that is more marvelous than the nature of light? It has always been a question as to what light is. Light is a form of motion and motion causes sound or music. Music ranges from sixteen and one-half vibrations per second to thirty-two thousand vibrations per second. Supposing you continue the vibrations beyond this point, you go through an octave of color just as previously through an octave of sound, so that when you increase the vibrations you get color instead of sound. That is, the ear cannot any longer detect the motion, but the eye detects it as color. Music is motion; so is light and color. If our nerves were sufficiently delicate they would detect color as sound. We know just how many vibrations produce blue, yellow, green, red, etc. All colors are lost in a white light. In the Scripture light, music, and sound are mixed up. Psalm 19: "Their line has gone out through all the earth, and their words to the end of the world." The rising of the sun is as rejoicing, its light is music. Job 38: 7: "The morning stars sang together"— vibrated. The Hebrew was right, and God inspired men to write it as they did, for light is a form of motion.

VIII. A few words on the unity of symbols. In the Old and

New Testaments you will find a corresponding use of symbols in three distinct departments. First, *form;* second, *color;* third, *number.* The main forms that are symbolic in the Scriptures are the square, the circle, and the cube. For instance, the cube is length, breadth, and height, all of which are equal. The holy place in the tabernacle was a cube, it was ten cubits every way. It was an expression of perfection. The heavenly Jerusalem mentioned in Revelation was a cube — length, breadth, and height were equal. It represents absolute perfection. The different colors are symbolical. White stands for purity; red stands for two things, guilt and atonement; blue stands for truth and fidelity. Blue also stands for the promises of God, a very sweet symbol, because blue is the color of the heavens. Green, which is the union of yellow and blue, represents fertility, yellow represents glory. Purple, which is the compound of red and blue, is the symbol of royalty, the color of the king. Glistening white always represents heavenly purity, as when Christ was transfigured. Livid green represents death, hence the pale horse; and black refers to terror and disaster.

Take the numerical system of the Bible. 1, 2, 3, 4, 5, 6, 7, 8, 10, 12, 24, 40, 70, 100 — what do these mean? I would not suppose they mean anything but for the fact that these numbers are constantly recurring. How many times the number seven recurs! One stands for unity; two stands for comparison and contrast; three stands for trinity; four, the number of this age — the world is four square, four points to the compass, etc. Seven is the number of completeness because three and four make seven, which is the number of the world added to the number of God. Twelve, — three multiplied by four makes twelve — twelve apostles, twelve tribes. Suppose you divide seven, the number of completeness, by two, you get three and one-half, you break completeness into incompleteness and you get three and one-half, the years of anti-Christ. Six hundred and sixty-six is the number of perpetual unrest; seven is the number of rest; eight is the number of victory; eight hundred and eighty-eight is the numerical equivalent for Jesus. Whenever you find recurring types in Scripture do not dare to say that they mean nothing, and when you find numbers constantly recurring, do not dare to say that there is nothing in them. Take the number 144,000. I do not suppose that is a literal number, but a typical. Of what do you find it composed? Twelve times twelve, and ten multiplied by ten multiplied by ten. Take another number of completeness: 1, 2, 3, 4, added together make ten; 10 in the Bible is the number of time and 12 the number of place. Supposing God wanted a typical number to represent the full number of redeemed through all time and space? Take the square of 12 and the cube of 10—144,000.

I told you that 7 and 10 were numbers of completeness.

Suppose we find a lesser completeness represented by 7 and a greater represented by 10. I can point you to many instances where we have the 7 and 10 together, and where they are enumerations of blessings or privileges. Take two instances, one in the eighth of Romans, where Paul comes to a climax and says: "What shall separate us from the love of Christ?" 1, "Tribulation;" 2, "Anguish;" 3, "Distress;" 4, "Persecution;" 5, "Nakedness;" 6, "Peril;" 7, "Sword." The next is: 1 "Death;" 2, "Life;" 3, "Angels;" 4, "Principalities;" 5, "Powers;" 6, "Things present;" 7, "Things to come;" 8, "Height;" 9, "Depth;" 10, "Any other creature."

The lower number of completeness first and the higher afterward. Note again in Heb. 12: 22-24.

Dr. Bullinger has gotten out a book on the numerical structure of Scripture. He said the first occurrence of the number 13 was in connection with revolt, and that it stands for revolt and apostasy from that time forward. He found that when you take the numerical equivalent of the kings of Israel they all amounted to 13, and the numerical equivalent of the kings of Judah they amounted to 8.

In the Book of Esther, if you take the adversaries of God, the numerical equivalents make 13. When you come to the sons of Haman you will find their names in the Hebrew, placed one under another, looking, as one has said, as if they were strung up. The numerical sum of the sons of Haman amounts to a multiple of 13. Dr. Bullinger found the name Jehovah written as it were right in the pages of the book of Esther in the form of acrostics. Every page of the Word has His signature.

# The Spirit and His Work.

By Rev. Arthur T. Pierson, D.D.

## Lecture 1.

There is no possibility of overrating the importance of understanding the Holy Spirit and His work. We are now in the dispensation of the Holy Spirit. Before Christ came the Father was Himself conspicuous among the persons of the Godhead, filling the horizon. Then when Christ came there was a brief dispensation in which He filled the horizon; then He went away and sent the Spirit of God to be His substitute, and that Spirit is now filling the horizon. In the believer's heart He governs, and in the true church of believers He governs, and He will preside in Christ's stead until Christ comes to take the kingdom for Himself. Inasmuch as we are in the dispensation of the Spirit it is immensely important to understand the Spirit and come in contact and fellowship with Him.

We need to understand the personality of the Spirit. A prominent clergyman in Brooklyn said that the Holy Spirit of God was a "thin, shadowy effluence from the Father." But you will notice that the Spirit is treated as a *person* in the New Testament. Think of Him bound up with the Father and Son in the apostolic benediction. Think of Him bound up with the Father and Son in the baptismal formula: "I baptize thee in the name of the Father and the Son and the Holy Ghost." He is just as much a person as the Father and the Son. He is treated as a person and addressed as a person.

There are two fundamental teachings in the New Testament. First, the atoning work of Christ, and, second, the renewing work of the Holy Spirit. If you do not understand both of these truths there is a radical deficiency. Notice that there are two forms of substitution. Christ is the substitute for sinners and the Holy Spirit is the substitute for Christ. See how these things are intimately associated and linked together.

There are three departments in the work of the Spirit. I will call your attention to them. First, the relation of the Spirit to truth as "the Spirit of truth." And this again may include three subordinate heads. First, inspiration, which virtually means the choosing of his own channels for the conveyance of truth. Second, revelation, which implies the unfolding of truth hitherto unknown. Third, illumination, which is the bestowal of inward light for the understanding of outward truth. This latter is a most important distinction. Revelation and illumination are not the same.

Second department of the Spirit's work: The relation of the Spirit of God to the life of God in the human soul. He is the Spirit of life. This again may be divided into three separate heads. First, conviction or demonstration. In I Corinthians, second chapter, we read: "Demonstration of the Spirit." The Spirit demonstrates by a flash of light. The word "conviction" is used in John, sixteenth chapter. He shall convince or convict the world. Second, regeneration. Regeneration of the nature. Third, sanctification, which is the carrying forward of the life of God in relation to its maturity and perfection.

Third, the relation of the Spirit to the church as a body. First, organization. It is not the church that man organizes that God necessarily recognizes. There are many churches that have been organized by man which God does not recognize. In Germany at one time were ten thousand students studying for the ministry, and not five of them knew anything about what regeneration was. It was the Lord who added to the body of spiritual believers. See how the Lord opened the mind of Lydia to attend to the things of Paul. All through the Acts it is the Spirit's divine work convicting and adding to the body of Christ. Second, administration, which includes all the gifts and graces of the Spirit and all the spheres and works in the department of service. Read I Corinthians, twelfth chapter. Third, qualification. In order that all may have efficiency in service the Spirit bestows unction. This is that power which the Spirit of God gives. It is a peculiar anointing for testimony.

I want to call your attention to your dependence for spiritual dynamics on the Holy Ghost. Dynamics is power in operation. In the spiritual field it is spiritual power in exercise. Power does not do anything without application. If you have a proper application of power you can have results. Spiritual dynamics is the application of the power of the Holy Ghost to the work of God on earth. There is but one pulley, one wheel, one lever, known in the Word of God, and that is the Holy Spirit. He is the motive power in all Christian work. And if you do not get this drilled into your minds and grounded in your experience, I would not give a farthing for your work as Christians. I believe I worked for ten or fifteen years in my ministry and knew little about that motive power. God gave more souls in sixteen months than in the entire sixteen years before I received that illumination in 1876. Nothing on earth would induce me to go back to where I was then. Acts 1:8: "Ye shall receive power after that the Holy Ghost is come upon you." A better reading is: "Ye shall receive the power of the Holy Ghost coming upon you." It is not power *after* the Holy Ghost comes, but the Holy Ghost *is* the power. "And ye shall be witnesses unto me." He told them to tarry in Jerusalem until endued, no matter how long it took. We are in these days multiplying our labors and forgetting the quality of our labor in quantity. I would rather spend three hours in getting ready for one hour's work than to spend one hour getting ready for three hours' work; for by being prepared you can do in five days what you could not otherwise do in five years. In these days the temptation is to perpetual activity. We do not allow time for prayer and spiritual meditation. You have no time to be alone with God and get the unction which is to make you a power. I decline all invitations that interfere with proper preparation for duty. In London they would hurry a man off in a hansom cab to a meeting at six o'clock, another at seven, another at eight, and another at nine o'clock. They do not seem to think it is necessary to be much alone with God. The Lord is not in a hurry. You may be. God sent Moses forty years into the desert to get prepared, when he was already forty years old. He sent Paul into Arabia for three years to get ready for his evangelistic career, when the world was waiting for the Gospel. Jesus Christ spent thirty years getting ready for the work of three and a half years; and if Jesus Christ needed such a preparation, what do you think of poor mortals like you and me? I want you to be done with the idea of hurrying to your work without proper prayerful preparation.

The sole secret of all success in work for God is this, that I have got God back of me in the power of the Spirit of God; and I can afford to wait any length of time to get in league with the Holy Ghost.

Let us take this one text of Scripture and study it carefully. Luke 18:27: "The things which are impossible with men are possible with God." Think of it; with God ALL THINGS are possible.

## Lecture 2.

One of the most harmful apostasies of our day is the apostasy of naturalism. It means the denial of any real power that is above nature and above humanity. Every event, every occurrence, every development, every causation, every result, must be within the domain of what is called "natural laws," or the "forces of nature." Hence come the denial of inspiration which is resolved into the inspiration of genius; and the denial of all proper prophecy, which is resolved into a shrewd guesswork. A man in Scotland issued a book on prophecy. He is an evangelical minister. Here is what he says — I think I can quote the substance of his words.

He says: "We clearly see what is the nature of inspiration under the old covenant. Isaiah had received from God, or thought he had received from God, a communication of the two great principles of God's moral government; first, that iniquity must be punished; and, second, that Israel as God's witnesses must be preserved. On the basis of these two great moral principles, together with a shrewd observation of the tendency of his times, Isaiah was enabled to predict the future of his people. He says further, that we see something very like this in the scientific world. Men study the laws of nature, and then, having obtained an accurate knowledge of the fundamental laws of nature's working, they add to it an accurate and careful observation and comparison of phenomena, and so are enabled to predict eclipses, and in the signal service to foretell storms. If there ever were a definition of inspiration that let the supernatural out, then this is it. According to this naturalistic notion, there would be no miracles, and of course the resurrection of Christ is a logical absurdity. There is no such thing as regeneration and sanctification; they are simply names for the forms and grades of spiritual and moral culture. The praying man may have hold of the arm that moves the world, but the arm is moving him instead of his moving the arm. It is like the man in a small boat on the ocean. Somebody throws a rope from the shore into his boat and then he pulls on the rope until he pulls himself ashore. He fancies the shore is moving toward him when the boat is only moving toward the shore. Prayer is only a man pulling on his boot-straps to lift himself from the earth, or blowing on the sails of his own boat to propel himself along; but it is good work for the muscles and for the lungs! Everything is thus accounted for by natural causation; hence it is dependent upon human endeavor and human environment, and the thing is to make more endeavor and get better environment. "To the law and to the testimony; if they speak not according to this word, it is because there is no light in them."

I want to refer you to the witness of God. Jer. 32:17: "There is nothing too hard for the Lord." Not only hard things but impossible things to men are easy and possible to God.

Mark 10:23-27. Jesus Christ utters these words in regard to the rich man whom he told to sell all he had and give to the poor. He said: "How hardly shall they that trust in riches enter into the kingdom of God; it is easier for the camel to go through the eye of a needle than for a rich man to enter the kingdom of God." There is a tendency in these days to explain away this scripture. Some say that in the east there are large gates to the cities, and small gates, which are called "the needle's eye," and that when the camel comes to a large gate that is shut, he goes to a small gate, his load is removed, then he crouches down and goes through the smaller gate on his knees. I do not know of any such gate; I never knew a man that found one of these gates in any city. Thomson, the author of "The Land and the Book," does not know anything about them. What does our Lord say?—The things that are impossible with men are possible with God. What does that mean? For the camel to squeeze through a small gate is not impossible. But the Scripture reads: "They were astonished beyond measure and said, Who then can be saved." The things which are impossible with men are possible with God. It is impossible, humanly speaking, for a camel to go through the eye of a needle; but it is not impossible when God takes hold of the camel and the needle's eye. This general position is abundantly exemplified in the Holy Scripture.

What do men hold of most value and depend upon? These seven things. 1st, numbers; 2d, riches; 3d, time, to do a thing; 4th, worldly wisdom; 5th, human power; 6th, natural law, I use their own term; 7th, ordinary means, especially the more abundant the means are. These are the seven sources of men's confidence. It is a remarkable fact that God has always acted with absolute independence of every one of these, and often in real defiance of them. I want to illustrate this from the Scripture alone.

1. Independence of numbers. Lev. 26:8. Now compare this with Deut. 32:30. The first statement is, one shall repel twenty-fold his own number, and even one hundred-fold his own number. On the contrary, when the children of God are forsaken by Him one of the foes chases a thousand, and two put ten thousand of the believers to flight.

Judges 7:4-7. This is the great lesson of Gideon's remnant. God said, these people are too many for me. He first eliminated the unbelieving—those not trustful or fearful, and told them to go home to their mothers, and the thirty-two thousand was reduced to ten thousand. God said again, the people are still too many, and then there was a further elimination. People have been trying to find out why these men lapped after the fashion of a dog. I have been reading what one man said, who explained that this implied dexterity. I think all these explanations are unsatisfactory. I think that this was simply a mark that God had chosen to point out the men He wished to use. He reduced that thirty-two thousand to three hundred. Did you ever notice the proportion between the number used and the original number? It is less than *one in one hundred and seven*. One man out of every one hundred and seven of the original number was used. I wonder whether God finds any more than this proportion in the church to-day ready for service. How many Christians of to-day does God really use? What an amazing reduction and yet God did the whole work with the three hundred.

I Sam. 14:6. Jonathan and his armor-bearer, just two men. "These uncircumcised." They were not consecrated to God's service and God did not abide with them. "It may be that the Lord will work for us." Let us go to the garrison of the uncircumcised for there is no restraint to the Lord. And Jonathan went boldly into the midst of those people, and what a great victory he won. The two men moved by prayer and moved with prayer, and they waited upon God for a sign. They prayed and they watched, and having prayed and watched they boldly assaulted the stronghold. Jonathan said to his armor-bearer: "Come after me." He did not send him first. This brave and holy man said, Come after me, for the Lord hath delivered them into the hand of Israel. See how the Lord is with him all the way through. What was the result? First, they slaughtered twenty men, then God assisted the two brave fellows by a panic and by an earthquake. Contempt again of numbers.

II Kings 7:3-7. Four men who were lepers lifted the siege of the city of Samaria.

II Chron. 14:11. Zerah came out with a million followers and three hundred chariots. Asa had but three hundred thousand, but notwithstanding his large army, which was not half as large as the army of the enemy, he had no dependence on his host. I would to God that there was not a day of the evangelistic work of this campaign in Chicago that was not begun by a repetition before God, on our knees, of the words of Asa. It is one of the most remarkable prayers in the Old Testament. What an inspiration in going against the multitudes of the enemy. No lesson is more needed. I affirm that there is a definitely unspiritual and unscriptural tendency prevailing among modern Christians to emphasize numbers, to pride ourselves on crowds, to do superficial work and to be discouraged if we have only a small following. The whole thing is of the devil and offensive to the Holy Ghost. There are two great lessons to those believing in the Holy Ghost. David numbered the people. II Sam. 24: 1-25. The translation of the first verse is corrupt. It should read, "And one moved David," not the "Lord" nor "he." This one that moved David was the great adversary of God and man—Satan. David took nine months and twenty days to complete this numerical estimate; then God gave David his choice between seven years of famine, three months of flight, or three days of pestilence. These mean about the same thing in the end. Seventy thousand perished in that awful slaughter of the angel of God.

Deut. 32: 36. That is the way God feels when you come to conscious weakness. If you pride yourself on your numbers then comes pestilence and famine, but when God sees that you are consciously poor and shut up to Him, and that there is no resource left, He repents Himself. God reveals Himself in the crisis of conscious weakness.

## Lecture 3.

Luke 18: 7; also II Cor. 12: 8-10. "My strength is made perfect in weakness." Did you ever think what that means? What does it mean but *at the very point of weakness?* Here was Paul's thorn or stake in the flesh. My strength shall touch you at the point of weakness. I cannot but think again of the lesson taught me on this subject on the 24th of March, 1876. I had long been worshiping worldly fame and reputation, and the Lord had shown me six months before that the only way to be a winner of souls was to give up my idols, and I gave them up. As the time passed the impression took possession of me that I was close to the verge of the period of new service. That night I had a prayer meeting with my people in Detroit and I unfolded my heart to them. It was a very bad night; there were three inches of sleet and snow and only about sixty people present. In previous years I should have been dreadfully discouraged, for I had a church of eight hundred and fifty members, but the Lord prevented my feeling any discouragement. So I unfolded my heart to the people and said, let us get down here and pray that the Lord will take out of the way anything that hinders our reaching the multitudes; and *while we were praying the church took fire.* This threw us into the opera house on Sunday, and there I began to preach to thousands of those that were not attending any place of worship, and in those sixteen months God gave us more souls than in all the previous years of my ministry. I always remember that the one meeting in which God did more for me in my ministry than in all other meetings, and the meeting that transformed that whole church and moved that whole city, had only about sixty people present on one of the worst nights I have known. So long as you are discouraged by small numbers, or exulting over large numbers, God will never use you. You may have more blessing with six souls than with six thousand. The great lesson is that I am not responsible for the numbers that wait upon my ministry. The only thing I am responsible for is to give the message uncorrupted from my Master to the people that come to hear me, and leave all the rest with God. My business is to preach the Gospel with the power of God sent down from heaven, and leave to my Master all other responsibility. It is sin for you to go home and toss on your bed because you did not have half as many as the church would hold. Your business is to take the message from your Master and give it over to the people. Do all you can legitimately to bring the people to hear your message, but not by sensational advertisements, not by concerts, nor by magnificent furniture and garniture in the house. Look at Saul of Tarsus when Stephen was stoned. I do not suppose that Stephen had a very large or a very attractive audience, but one stood by and held the clothes who received impressions that were never lost. He could never forget, and I have no doubt that that testimony of Stephen to that stoner was the means in God's hands of raising up the greatest apostle the world has ever seen; and you can afford to be stoned if your testimony brings one to Christ who becomes an Apostle Paul. Lydia was among the women that Paul met at Philippi and she was turned to God by the first sermon ever preached in Europe. Out of this conversion all churches in Europe and America have grown.

Second, the independence of God as to money. Notice the terms we apply to coins. We call the English pound a "sovereign"; the largest French piece of money "a Napoleon"; the German, "a Kaiser"; the American coin, "the almighty dollar." What a commentary on human nature? These are the "sovereigns" and "Napoleons" and "Cæsars" and "almighty dollars" that rule. But see God's independence of it all. Read the fiftieth Psalm. You think you are bestowing an obligation upon God when you bring your offerings. It is you that need to bring, not He that needs the gift. Even God's poor could be provided for in some other way if giving was not for your own good. You would otherwise be like the snail carrying its shell around on its back. It never comes out except to pick up a dainty bit, then creeping back to enjoy it. Any dainty morsel that some people get they take back into their shell to enjoy it all by themselves. The poor ye have always with you, not for the benefit of the poor only, but for your benefit, that whenever you will ye may do them good. Doing good and giving are for the purpose of cultivating benevolence in us.

I Kings 17:12. God said: "I have commanded a widow woman there to sustain thee." If we are commanded of God to sustain another we can do it, and though we have but a morsel, the meal will never waste nor the oil give out.

Luke 7:5. The elders of the Jews came to Christ to urge his kind offices in behalf of a rich man because "He loveth our nation, and he hath built us a synagogue." This is the way men of modern times do. They think they put God under obligation by gifts.

Ex. 36:6. Here is a remarkable example of giving. The people brought more than enough for the service, so "the people were restrained from bringing." This is the only time in history when people had to be told not to bring any more.

II Cor. 8:2-4. This is a marvelous passage. The Macedonian church, though "in a great trial of affliction, the abundance of their joy and their deep poverty abounded unto the riches of their liberality." I have heard of people, out of their riches abounding to liberality, but I have never heard elsewhere of the abundance of poverty abounding unto liberality. God loves a cheerful giver. Dr. Gordon says the word "cheerful" means hilarious. God loves a hilarious giver; there are not many of them. These people entreated Paul to receive the gift; and when Paul said you are too poor, they earnestly entreated him to receive their gifts and permit them to have fellowship in the ministry to the saints. In these days we have to entreat people to give. Did you ever know anybody that has entreated you to receive his gifts? I would like to see a few of such saints.

Mark 12: 42-44. The widow cast in more than they all; not because of the smallness but because it was all that she had. You would think by the collections that people give that the virtue was in the smallness of the mite. Christ honored this woman for her gift because it was her all. A rich man said to Mr. Moody: "I will give you the widow's mite." "All right," said Mr. Moody, "give me all you have; that is what she gave."

Third, God is independent of time. II Peter 3: 8. This is a remarkable statement. "That one day is with the Lord as a thousand years and a thousand years as one day." What indifference to time — shortness or length. Compare II Kings 7: 1. There was a terrible famine and the prophet said: "To-morrow about this time." In twenty-four hours the famine was broken up. Solomon was thirteen years building his house, but God only took twenty-four hours to break up a famine. Amos 9: 13. Christian workers, notice this promise: "The plowman shall overtake the reaper"—a quick succession of seed time and harvest. "And the treader of grapes him that soweth seed." You have here the sower overtaking the reaper and the reaper overtaking the sower, one coming immediately after the other. God defies all ordinary lapses of time. The plowshare is often on the heels of the reaper, there is scarcely any breathing spell.

Psalm 126: 6. Did you ever examine the Hebrew of this scripture? "He that *goeth out* weeping, bearing precious seed, shall *come home again* bringing sheaves." He went out bearing the seed and returns the same day with an armful of sheaves. What a promise of direct fertility.

In Isa. 66: 8 we have the same thought. But one day elapses between seed time and harvest. A nation is not only born in a day but born at once — born like a flash, without lingering pains of travail.

Mal. 3:1. "Shall suddenly come to his temple."—Come in an instant.

Fourth, God is independent of the wisdom of this world. I Cor. 1:20. The whole teaching of this part of I Corinthians is that God hath made foolish the teaching of this world and that the wisdom of this world comes to naught.

# God's Independence of Man's Wisdom.

By Rev. Arthur T. Pierson, D. D.

## Lecture 1.

The whole teaching of I Corinthians, second chapter, is to show us that God disdains human wisdom. He counts it foolishness because in its highest reach it never has found God. I have sometimes thought that human wisdom can be compared to a great arch that rises very high but always returns back to the earth. But true wisdom, though starting from the earth, like the Gothic arch, at whatever height it reaches, it points still upward to God. All human wisdom goes back to earth. It is not sent of God and hence God counts it foolishness. He has made foolish the wisdom of this world. You have all noticed what is said in that second chapter of I Corinthians about the princes of this world—the princes of human wisdom. They come to naught. What is naught? It is zero—0. They think they are something, but God thinks they are nothing—0. They think they are units, but God thinks they are zero—0. The Bible tells us that God hath chosen the nothings (0), of this world to bring to naught the somethings. That is the literal translation—the nothings to bring to naught the somethings. We are told that God by the foolishness of preaching saves those that believe. Not preaching foolishness, of course, but what man counted foolish—the preaching of the cross. And He also tells us that we make the cross of none effect by introducing the enticing words of man's wisdom. Carry out this idea of zero—0. You can see now how the zero becomes valuable, and how it adds value to a unit. By putting the unit before it thus—put zero after unit—10, it in creases the value of the unit tenfold; put another zero (0) after the unit and it increases it one hundred-fold. But suppose you put the zero (0) in front of the unit, thus — 01, it reduces its value tenfold. Put another zero in front of the unit and it reduces it to a one hundredth part, thus — .001. The more you introduce your human wisdom the more you crowd out the wisdom of the Spirit of God, from which all human wisdom gets its value. If you make the cross of Christ the unit, standing first, then you are the zero, or nothing, that adds to its value. All this poetry and logic and human wisdom and skill which men use to make up for the attractiveness of the Gospel is crowding the unit back and making the cross of none effect.

Gen. 40:8, and 41:16. When Joseph was called upon to tell the dreams, he said: "Do not interpretations belong to God?" Then again he says to Pharaoh: "It is not in me; God shall give Pharaoh an answer." Then again, in chapter 41:25, he says: "God hath showed Pharaoh what He is about to do." See the humility! He attributes all to God. And so Daniel in Babylon, Dan. 2:20-22, when he was required to make an interpretation of Nebuchadnezzar's dream, he goes to the other three holy children and asks them to join him in prayer to God, and then, when before Nebuchadnezzar, he does not take any glory to himself, but turns the king's attention to Jehovah.

II Tim. 3:15. "From a child thou hast known the Holy Scriptures which are able to make thee wise unto salvation." You may not know any other book, but if you know the Scripture you have the secret of all wisdom.

Psalms 25:9. "The meek will he guide in judgment; and the meek will he teach his way." The meek and unselfish souls look directly to God for His guidance, and are taught.

II Sam. 15:31. "Turn the counsel of Ahithophel into foolishness." What a prayer this was. When some man in our congregation is controlling and upsetting the spiritual work of God by his worldly policy, go and ask God to turn his worldly counsel into foolishness. Never try to meet such a man on his own ground with his own weapons.

Matt. 10:9. God will never give you wisdom to make up for your own studies and searchings to know His will when He has given you opportunity to make such; but if you are put in an emergency, cast yourself upon God and it shall be given you what you shall say. He will give you better thoughts, better plans, better sermons, than you could get up yourself. God works wondrously. Never attempt to do anything else but rest upon His promises.

II Cor. 2:4. Paul said he would not speak in "enticing words of man's wisdom, but in demonstration of the Spirit and of power." This and other passages teach that true wisdom is not intellectual, but is spiritual; that it is therefore not to be got from books nor from men nor from mental culture. It means insight into the truth of God as only God can give it.

Rev. 3:18. This is God's way to make us wise. We must have the heavenly ointment applied to our eyes, in order to behold the wondrous things of God.

The best preparation to preach is to have the Word of God illuminated by the Holy Spirit. When Prof. Henry B. Smith, of Union Theological Seminary, a man of great learning, was traveling with others through the Holy Land, he came in contact with Dr. Simeon Calhoun, one of the most celebrated eastern missionaries — a man who immersed himself in the Word of God and lived in the truth of the Word. And whenever these travelers touched upon a Scripture topic, or whenever the Scripture was mentioned, such streams of Scripture knowledge would flow forth from Simeon Calhoun that Henry B. Smith turned to a friend and said: "I would give all the learning of books that I have"—and I suppose he was one of the most learned men of his age—"to have the insight into the Holy Scripture that Simeon Calhoun has."

Doddridge used to go to a very plain and unlettered man in his congregation whenever in perplexity about the meaning of a passage, and say to him: "What do you think of that passage?" and he never failed to get light on it. The Lord's Spirit took such hold on that humble man that the great commentator sat down at his feet.

It is your privilege to make discoveries in the Word of God. The Holy Spirit can illuminate your mind and unfold the meaning of a passage of Scripture so that an entirely new meaning will come out of the Word of God. I think I have had a few experiences of this kind. The Lord gave me something that appeared to be new in John 3: 16. I was going to preach on that text one night while I was living in Philadelphia. It was during the summer season, and I was staying at the hotel and had no access to my books, so that I had nothing but the Bible. I got on my knees and told the Lord that I had felt moved to preach on this text and asked for some new light upon it. I read the words over from one hundred and fifty to two hundred times, and asked as I read, word by word, that the Lord would show me something new in the text. Suddenly I saw something I had never seen before. I saw that there were ten prominent words in the verse and that they belonged in five pairs, as follows:

Persons of the Godhead — God, the Father, and the Son.
Divine attitude — Loved, gave.
Object of love — World, whosoever.
Man's activity — Believe, have.
Extremes of destiny — Perish, life.

This was an entirely new discovery to me and I have never heard of anybody else that ever saw it before. It has been there all these centuries, but was revealed to this one humble student.

## Lecture 2.

There is not one of you that may not sit down before the Word of God and ask God to unfold new meanings to His Word and you will see new things. There is no real originality in preaching except of this kind — the originality that discovers what is in the Word of God. I would not give a penny for your originality of invention. What we want is discoveries in the Word of God. A fundamental lesson that I do pray I may have grace to impress upon you is that the wisdom of the world and the grace of God are opposites. A certain minister in the last century, though a brilliant scholar, had never a conversion traced to him; brilliant, but not used of God for the conversion of souls. It is possible for you to be so brilliant, to be so full of history, of science and philosophy, that you may make the grace of God of none effect.

Divine power appears in two ways: first, to give the preacher a new understanding or idea of truth, and, second, to open the eyes of the hearers to the truth presented — the getting of the message from God and the opening of the hearts of the hearers. I think Paul perhaps made one mistake in his life. He went to Athens and tried to meet the philosophers there on their own grounds, but he made very few converts. On the other hand, Peter at Jerusalem opened the simple Word and three thousand souls were converted.

5. God's independence of human power. There is a custom that prevails in Great Britain, and I think in this country, too, and that is what is called "patronage." They cannot have an orphan asylum, or anything of that kind, without its being under the patronage of Earl so-and-so, or Lord so-and-so. But George Muller said: "I am not going to have any patron except God." In the second Psalm we have the kings conspiring against God. They were going to break in pieces God's rule; but they are suddenly broken in pieces themselves by the very scepter they sought to destroy. There are two great instances of this in Siam and Turkey. In 1831 the Siamese monarch was about to expel all missionaries from Siam. He would not even let them have a place to lay their heads — he would not allow them a foot of ground. It was just so in Turkey in 1850. The Sultan was going to expel all the missionaries from Turkey. But just as the decrees were going into effect both these kings died — right at the very time when they were going to enforce these decrees. Since then there have been no two countries where so little hindrance on the part of the governments has been placed in the way of missionary effort as in these two countries.

Isa. 59:1: "The Lord's hand is not shortened." If you do not have God's power it is because something hinders contact and coöperation — something hinders the transfer of God's power to you. Look out that you are in contact with God.

Jer. 32: 17, 27. "Nothing too hard for God." Note that God's response is in the very language of Jeremiah.

Zech. 4:6. "Not by might, nor by power, but by my Spirit, saith the Lord of hosts." And hear Micah say, "I am full of power by the Spirit of the Lord." In Daniel 2:35 we read that the aggregations of the kings of this world are as chaff that the wind blows away. The wind, we know, is a symbol of the Spirit.

Matt. 26 : 53. "Twelve Legions of angels!" What a number that was! In Psalm 34 : 7, "The angel of the Lord encampeth around about them that fear Him," and if our eyes were opened we would, like Elisha's servant, see the mountains full of horses, and chariots around about us. Our eyes are too gross to see these things. We are surrounded by the host of God and nobody need be afraid if he is in league with God.

Rom. 8 : 31. "Who can be against us?" As John Wesley said: "One with God is a majority." How prone we are even after the most wonderful exhibition of the power of God to depend upon man. I called your attention yesterday to Asa as to how wonderfully he was helped of God; and yet, see what he did. Compare IJ Chron. 14 : 9-11 with II Chron. 16 : 7-9. In the first passage, what a wonderful lesson, and then in the last passage see what a fool he made of himself. It seems impossible that men should forget these lessons, and yet they do.

II Kings 19 : 35. Sennacherib came with his army and sent an insulting letter to Hezekiah; Hezekiah spread it out before the Lord and prayed that God would interpose; and God sent forth his angel that night and 185,000 of the Assyrians were turned into dead corpses. Omnipotence was behind human weakness. He always wins who sides with God.

6. God's independence of natural laws. Natural law is merely God's way or process of working. Law cannot make itself. It is absurd to talk about natural law. Some people think that anything can be done that is in accordance with natural law and that nothing can be done that is opposed to natural law. Ex. 14 : 22. At the passage of the Red Sea the waters piled up on either side. At Joshua's passage of the Jordan the waters were held back and they all went over on dry land, but the waters did not recede until the feet of the priests touched the edge of the river.

I Kings 17 : 6. God is going to feed Elijah, and feed him by birds. That is not incredible. But he sent ravens. Now, ravens are birds of prey; but instead of eating up the meat they bring it to Elijah. What about natural law in that case? In the Book of Daniel we read about the three holy children going into the fiery furnace and coming out without the smell of fire on their clothes. Those that believe only in natural law might perhaps be put into the fiery furnace, and see if they would come out without the smell of fire on their clothes. How about the lions' den? Daniel went into the den of lions and the lions' mouths were shut. A recent writer explains that Daniel mesmerized the lions; that he had wonderful mesmeric power and thus held the lions in control. It was very unfortunate that the politicians who were cast in afterwards did not have any such mesmeric power. It is blasphemy to come to the Word of God and thus refine away all the miracles. Lazarus had been dead four days; there is no mistaking the fact that he was dead, that he was buried and that the ordinary process of disintegration would have taken place, and yet, he rose from the dead at the call of Jesus Christ. What is a miracle? I think it is an assumption to say that a miracle is an inversion of the order of nature. We do not know much about nature, but we know something about the ordinary processes of nature. Here is my watch. According to the laws of motion of this watch the hands are always turning in a certain direction. But now if the hands point to twenty minutes to twelve, and the correct time is twenty-five minutes to twelve, I pull out the stem and reverse the hands, and there is no interruption to the workings and no harm done to the watch. By the ordinary processes that watch could never turn its hands back five minutes, but it is so made that an intelligent and higher power can reverse it without interfering with the mechanism. Suppose what we call natural laws are represented by the ordinary motion of the watch, and the reverse motion be represented by a *higher plane of law* where God intervenes; perhaps this universe was so made that God can step in and reverse ordinary motions without interfering with the mechanism. This helps us to understand the miracles. In the Holley system of water works there is an arrangement that whenever a hydrant is opened in the city, and the water lowers in the reservoir, a signal is given to the engineer at the pumping station and he gears on another set of machinery that increases the force and flow of the water. The ordinary working of the machinery may represent the ordinary working of nature, and the extra gearing may represent what we call miracles; but who shall dare to say that a miracle is an inversion of nature's laws. We should take the whole system into consideration. Philosophers are like a fly on the walking beam of a great engine, criticising the working of the vast machinery.

7. God's independence of all ordinary means. He works His pleasure with or without the ordinary means. Num. 21:9. Whers did the power lie? Not in the look of the Israelite, not in the serpent, but in God's decree. Entire indifference to ordinary means. Judges 6:16. God said, I will be with you, Gideon. Take this Book of Judges and study it through and you will be surprised to see how the weakness of man is supplemented by the power of God. We read that the Spirit of the Lord came upon Othniel. The Lord strengthened the king of Moab against them. The Lord raised them up a deliverer. And every time they got into trouble the Lord raised up a deliverer. In every one of these deliverers the weakness of man is supplemented by the power of God. One of these deliverers, Ehud, was a left-handed man. The word which refers to the peculiar skill in the use of the hand is taken from the word which means right (dexterity), and this man was left-handed. Shamgar slew six hundred men with an ox goad. What is that as a weapon? Nothing but a stick with a fork of iron in the end of it. The idea of slaying six hundred men with it! But God wanted to show the weakness of men and the power that lay back of it. Just think of going to Deborah, a weak woman, for deliverance when everything was in dismay and disorder." Read what Gideon says of himself and his father's house—weakness in man. But God says: "Surely I will be with thee." See how Gideon's forces were reduced, and see the weakness of his instruments of war. Samson's strength was in his vow as a Nazarite, and his long hair distinguished him as a Nazarite. When his hair was cut off his strength went from him. His strength lay in his relations to God, and when he broke his vow God's strength departed from him. How did he rend the lion? By taking hold of it with his hands. How did he slay the great multitude? With the jawbone of an ass. There is a play on words in the verse, "heaps upon heaps." In the original the literal reading is, "With a jawbone of an ass a mass on masses." God disdains all ordinary means.

## Lecture 3.

II Kings 5. Naaman was directed to dip in the River Jordan seven times. There was nothing in the Jordan to cure a man of leprosy; it was the decree of God.

II Chron. 20. A great host came against Jehoshaphat. He fasted and prayed and the Lord went before him and caused the invading hosts to destroy each other. II Chron. 32:7, 8. The arm of flesh only was the strength of the invaders, but God was with His people.

I want to give you, as a general conclusion to all that I have said, these six words or mottoes:

1. *Every one of us must be in league with Almighty God.* The phrase that underlies the whole New Testament is that one little phrase, "In Christ." It interprets every book in the New Testament. In Matthew, "In Christ" prophecy is fulfilled. In Mark, "In Christ" God's mighty works are done. In Luke, "In Christ" we have the faithful human counsellor. In John, "In Christ" we have the divine Son of God. In Acts, "In Christ" we have the Spirit of God governing His church. In Romans, "In Christ" we are justified. In Galatians, "In Christ" we are sanctified. In Philippians, "In Christ" we are satisfied. In Colossians, "In Christ" we are complete, and so on to Revelation, where "In Christ" we are glorified. Everything moves about Christ. When you get into Christ there is nothing that you lack, and "In Christ" you are in God. He makes us one with God. The love of God is shed abroad in our hearts, the power of God manifested in our weakness, and the glory of God in our humility. We have practically no idea of the boundless treasures that there are in Christ.

2. In the second place, *make a practical surrender of yourself* this very day to the will of God. The will is the center of all being. Make the center of God's being the center of yours. Every child of God should be like our planet moving around the sun and receiving its light from it. Just as soon as you surrender yourself entirely to God, you are in the place of light, you are in the divine harmony. All things work together for good to them that love God. You can say with John Wesley, "I am immortal until

my work is done." A man said to Abraham Lincoln: "Well, Mr. Lincoln, I do hope that the Lord is on our side." "That is not giving me the least anxiety," said Mr. Lincoln. "The only anxiety I have is whether we are on the Lord's side." To have God's will revealed to me is enough. You remember Peter's vision on the housetop. It was for the day right before him, and he did not understand it. And while he meditated, three men came and asked for him. Are you willing to have just so much of God's will let down, just for to-day, and leave to-morrow in His hands. It is the most blessed life that a man can live. To be content just to-day, to go where He sends to-day, and not be anxious about to-morrow. A gunner said when he was in the crisis of the battle of Waterloo, he did not know which way the battle was going; there were such clouds of dust and smoke that he could not tell foes from friends. He was asked: "What did you do?" "Do," said he, "there was but one thing to do, *stand by my gun.*" He stood there firing his gun; he was obeying orders and not responsible as to whom he was shooting at. Are you ready to stand by your gun in the heat of the battle? No matter whether you know which way the battle is going, stand by your gun where God places you. If you are not sure as to where God wants you, wait until you are. God is not in a hurry. Just as soon as you know the will of God, move. When the Lord opens the way, then you follow.

3. In the third place, *do the work of God — not your own work*, but the work of God. This is very much misunderstood, but if you will study the life of Christ, who was the type of every believer, you will know what God's work is. Christ began His earthly activity, doing His Father's business, until the close in John 17, where He said: "I have finished the work that thou gavest me to do." You are to be about your Father's business, and let your last words be: "I have finished the work that thou gavest me to do."

It is not my work, it is His work I am to be busy at. God takes me up as a rod, uses me as a hammer, moves me as a saw, fills me as a vessel. Nothing but a rod, a hammer, a saw, or a vessel. Just an instrument, a tool of God.

Do not try to get any place for yourself. If I were at the beginning of my life again, I would resolve never to ask either man or woman to get me into any position on earth. I want to be appointed by God, and not by men, and if I go anywhere, then I am sure that God is there ahead of me, and has fitted me for the work. It is a great thing for a man to be able to say, Now, Lord, you have put me here, and you must stand by me; but a man is weak if he put himself there, when he comes to a crisis. I have sometimes thought that God never puts a man in a conspicuous position if the man wants to go. It is the man that does not want to go, it is the man who shrinks back that God wants, not the man that works himself into a place. All work of God implies divine fitness for the work. God does not take the saw to do the work of the rod, nor the rod to do the work of the hammer, nor the hammer to do the work of the vessel. Would you expect God to take a hammer to convey water with? When God wants you as the saw, you are not responsible for sharpening yourself or for setting your own teeth. God is bound to take care of all that. Remember that you are associated with God, and everything that you are doing is God's work, that you are the rod, that you are the hammer, and with them He shall do His own signs and wonders. In I Cor. 7: 20, we read: "Let every man abide in the same calling wherein he was called." It is not necessary for you to change your sphere, but get a new partner into your sphere; take God into your work. If I am working with God there is no occasion for anxiety on my part. Cannot God take care of His own work? Just think of the impudence of a man being anxious about God's work. If God sends me into His vineyard, I am not responsible if the vines die. All I have to do is to dig about them and enrich them. I am not to worry about the rain or sunshine. Cannot God provide the rain and sunshine? Yet, we are always worrying about the Lord's work. If it is your work, you may well be worrying about it. "Be careful for nothing, but in everything by prayer and supplication, with thanksgiving, let your requests be made known unto God. And the peace of God which passeth all understanding shall keep your hearts and minds through Christ Jesus." I believe just this, we are to be *anxious for nothing*. The only right solicitude is that I shall see with a clear eye what God requires of me, and shall fall into my place in God's plan. No other anxiety is right. As David said, when he went against Goliath: "I come to thee in the name of the Lord God of Hosts." What boldness when a man comes in the name of the Lord God of Hosts; what authority in a crisis.

This work of God is different from every other work. "My word shall not return unto me void." Constantly resort to prayer; never rely on your own wisdom, never rely on your own strength. Keep a record of answered prayers. When you put a thing distinctly before God mark it down; and on the opposite page leave a space for answered prayer; and whenever you get into difficulty and distress, you turn back and see how the Lord has blessed you, and how marvelously He has answered your prayers. For twenty years I have kept such a little book of answered prayers. In the front of the book I have God's promises. Mr. Muller has been praying for one thing for fifty years; and although the prayer is not yet answered, he still keeps on praying. During all the fifty years this is the only particular prayer that has not yet been answered.

4. "Study to *show thyself approved unto God*. We are to be independent of man's approval. Do not accept any human standard of success, but only God's standard of success. When Christ came among men and began to rebuke their sins they cast Him out, and would have thrown Him down the precipice. If any of you had undertaken the work as He did, people would have said it was a failure, that you lacked good common sense. After Christ had labored three and a half years, only one hundred and twenty disciples waited for Pentecost. Stephen had just begun his work when he was stoned. His life seemed an awful failure. Paul seemed to have made a bad failure in Macedonia.

Depend upon God for everything. Get physical strength and mental vigor to sustain you in your work from God. And do not have any anxiety about *money*. There is an awful peril in greed. Be the servant of God and the Lord Jesus Christ. The believer's bank-note is described in Phil. 4:19.

"My God " — the banker.

"All your needs " — the amount guaranteed.

"Riches in glory " — the assets of the bank.

"By Christ Jesus ",— the cashier.

# Jesus Christ in the Two Testaments.

By Rev. Arthur T. Pierson, D. D.

Bible Institute, Chicago.

## Lecture 1.

This morning I will endeavor to show the unity of the two Testaments with regard to the *person of Jesus*, which I regard as the most wonderful of all.

Psalm 40 : 7 : "In the volume of the book it is written of Me." The "volume of the book" is the Holy Scriptures of the Old Testament and the "Me" is the person of the Messiah. When you remember that four hundred years before Christ was born the Old Testament Scriptures were completed, you will see how remarkable it is that this Scripture should treat of Jesus at all; that any book should treat of the coming of a man four hundred years before he appeared. We get so accustomed to thinking of these things as a fact that we do not understand the stupendous character of them. Supposing that I could write a book to-day telling about a man that was to appear four hundred years from now, giving all the details, indicating the place of birth, stating the character of the man, of his career, the way in which he should work, his name, the way in which he should die; and then history moving forward four centuries, he should come exactly as I had written, in this year 1893!

You see the overwhelming character of this argument from prophecy which I have already touched upon. Notice that Jesus is the center of all prophecy. From Genesis third chapter, to Malachi third, where there is the last reference in the Old Testament to Christ, you have just one continuous prophecy or unfolding of the character of the Messiah. And just so from Matthew, first chapter, where we have the first reference to Jesus, to Revelation twenty-second, where we have the last reference to Him. There are three hundred and thirty-three prophecies about Christ in the Old Testament. Canon Liddon divides the prophetic period into three: the Mosaic, the Davidic and the Prophetic. The Mosaic includes the Pentateuch and all books until David; the Davidic includes all the indications in the Psalms and in the history of David, and the Prophetic includes all in the major and minor prophets.

1. *Direct* prophecy of Christ in the Old Testament. When I tell you that I have been thirty years getting ready to give this lecture you will not be surprised if I emphasize the importance of it. I think it is by far the most important of anything I have said to you. Let us get a careful view of the whole subject. I want you first of all to understand the argument which is founded in prophecy. You understand the laws of simple and compound probability. Whenever a single prediction is made it has a chance of being fulfilled or not being fulfilled; that is, it has *half a chance* of being fulfilled. Suppose I should say, we are going to have very cold weather. That may be so or it may not be so. There is half a chance of its proving true; that is what is called simple probability. The prediction may be true or it may not. There is half a chance of its becoming true. The moment you introduce a second particular, which particular has also a half chance probability, we come to compound probability. Suppose, for instance, I say December will be a very cold month. There are two particulars: first, severe cold, and, second, in December. Each of these has half a chance probability. How do you get the compound chance probability? Multiply $\frac{1}{2}$ by $\frac{1}{2}$ and the result is $\frac{1}{4}$, which is the compound chance. That is to say there is one chance in four that both particulars will be true. Suppose I add a third particular and say that the 15th of December will be the coldest day. What is the compound chance now? Multiply $\frac{1}{4}$ by $\frac{1}{2}$ and the result is $\frac{1}{8}$; that is, one chance in eight of the prediction coming true. Supposing I add nine o'clock on the 15th of December: you see the result is one chance in sixteen of the prediction coming true. Supposing I have three hundred and thirty-three predictions terminating on one man, what is the probability that

all those things shall come to pass without divine knowledge? It is ½ raised to the 332d power! I will give you the rest of the day to figure out what the result would be. Why is it that infidels never attack the argument of prophecy? They dare not. It is the one great key to the Holy Scripture. Jesus could not be other than the Son of God when three hundred and thirty-three prophecies center in Him and nobody else. Any man that carries this argument around with him will be a walking encyclopedia. It convinced me years ago when I was in doubt, and I have never had any doubt since. Supposing I could settle all of you with a confidence in God and in Jesus Christ that in the darkest hours your faith would never be shaken, it would pay me well for having come here. It is this compound probability that I want you to appreciate. It is marvelous. Here is a single prophecy in Genesis that the seed of the woman shall bruise the serpent's head. This prophecy is a plant from which all other Messianic prophecies branch. Supposing we are going to find out in prophecy what is the family of Jesus Christ. He is to come four thousand years after this prophecy was uttered; and during those four thousand years there were generations that averaged forty years, so that you have nearly one hundred generations from Adam to Christ. Every generation puts forth a new branch and each of these branchings makes more impossible any guesswork. For instance, this Messianic line is to be in the seed of Seth. Adam had many children, but here is the branch out of several branches. Then that branches out again in the family of Noah. Noah has three sons. One of the three must be chosen. Shem is chosen; Shem branches out and we come to Abraham. In the family of Abraham Isaac is chosen; Isaac had two sons and Jacob is the chosen one. Jacob has twelve sons and you have to choose one of the twelve, and it is Judah. Again, there is the place of birth. On the face of the earth there were thousands and millions of places that He might be born at. Bethlehem is chosen. But there may be many Bethlehems. Any common village might get the name of Bethlehem. But it is Bethlehem in Judea. Now we have also the time. Here are the four thousand years, and during any part of this time Christ's birth might occur. In the ninth chapter of Daniel seventy times seven—four hundred and ninety years after the restoration of Jerusalem — is the time. We have three hundred and thirty-three twigs to our Messianic tree, and if one twig fails prophecy goes to the wall. If Jesus Christ is not born of the line of Joseph and Mary, of the line of David; if He is not born after the four hundred and ninety, or seventy times seven, years; if His birth does not occur within the limits, and if all these predictions are not fulfilled, the plant ceases to be a "plant of renown," something is wrong about it. But history goes on and touches his twig of the place of Christ's birth, and Bethlehem becomes light with the glory of God; it touches the precise year of his birth, and that twig becomes light with the glory of God; it touches the line of descent and that twig becomes light with the glory of God, and at last this whole Messianic tree becomes a "burning bush." Observe in the second of Luke, we read of the taxing of the Roman world. Eight years were required to carry out that taxing. The whole world had to be set in motion to bring Mary, the virgin mother, to Bethlehem, where the prophets said the Christ was to be born, and to bring her there at the precise time in order to the fulfillment of prophecy. So the whole world was set revolving in order to bring this one virgin mother to the precise place where she was to be enrolled when the birth took place. It is perfectly unanswerable.

Another remarkable thing is the paradoxes of prophecy. A paradox is an apparent contradiction which is not a real contradiction, but which is only apparent because we do not know how to reconcile the disagreement. It presented a lock which men could not unlock, and when history comes along it furnishes a key that unlocks the wards and bolts of this old mechanism. God put the paradoxes in prophecy so that men could not unlock them until He furnished the key, and then men would be compelled to say that the same hand that made the lock made the key.

## Lecture 2.

You will find some of these paradoxes in Isa. 53. This is perhaps the most remarkable instance in the Old Testament. I have marked twelve in this one chapter. It only has twelve verses and it averages a contradiction to each verse.

1. "A root out of a dry ground," and yet He is a fruitful vine.
2. He has no form nor beauty, and yet He is the servant of God.
3. He is despised and rejected of men, and yet He is the Messiah.
4. He suffers unto death, and yet He is the Saviour of men.
5. He has no natural offspring, and yet He has numerous seed.
6. He made His grave with the wicked, and yet with the rich in His death.
7. He is a man of sorrows, and yet a divine person.
8. All His life was adversity, and yet in God's sight He prospered.
9. Defeated, and yet He has triumphed.
10. He was cut off in the midst of His days, and yet prolonged His days.
11. He was spoiled by men, and yet He divided the spoil.
12. He was condemned, taken from judgment, yet a justifier of the condemned.

Could you imagine a group of paradoxes more utterly irreconcilable than these? But in these days we understand the paradoxes. Christ died without natural offspring, but became the parent of innumerable spiritual seed. Condemned, yet taken from judgment. Slain, yet raised from the dead, He led captivity captive.

Notice the growth of Messianic prophecy. First we have an outline, as if a man drew a rough outline of a face and afterward fills in tint after tint and hue after hue, thus making the complete portrait; so that when Malachi closes the Old Testament canon we have a magnificent portrait of the Messiah.

But there is a more remarkable thing than this, and that is *indirect* prophecy. I have spoken of direct prophecy as in Isaiah and Daniel, but how about that indirect, that is, prophecy that does not seem to be such? When you take up Isa. 53 you say it refers to the Messiah, but how about Psalm 22? You will find there a reference to a man whose hands and feet are pierced and whose enemies come around him like wolves. You see a man lifted up before the people in a naked condition. You hear a man cry, "I thirst," and they gave Him vinegar. There is no intimation that it is the Messiah, and it has to wait a thousand years to be understood. But when Jesus Christ is on the cross, every intimation of that Psalm is fulfilled in Him.

The first verse of the Psalm is the atonement cry.

The words "I thirst," representing the cry amid the agonies of crucifixion. The Psalm refers to a human mother but never refers to a human father, because He had no human father. At the end of the Psalm are these words: "Shall declare His righteousness unto a people that shall be born, that He hath done this." The Hebrew is: "They shall speak or proclaim, to an unborn generation, *it is finished.*" The Psalm begins with the atonement cry and ends with the cry of our Lord when the atoning suffering is complete. Every one of the seven sentences of Christ on the cross will be found hinted at in Psalm 22. A more remarkable fact about it is this: If you read that Psalm you will find that it is broken up — it is fragmentary; there was a man on the cross very near to death, His blood having been poured out, His whole nervous energy wasted, and the most torturing agony inflicted upon Him. His strength giving way, He could not utter one solitary sentence properly. He just gasps a word at a time, unable to finish a sentence. It is a Psalm of fragments; it is called the "Psalm of sobs." "My God, — my God, — why hast thou forsaken me! — far from helping — from words of my roaring —." Not a complete sentence.

Piercing of the hands and the feet was not a Jewish punishment. It was a Roman punishment. This could not have been known in advance; and even with the Romans the hands and the feet were not always pierced. But in His case His hands and His feet were pierced. Then again, His side was pierced. "I am poured out like water." "My heart is like wax; it is melted in the midst of my bowels." You could not understand that until you know that the Roman soldiers pierced His side. "All my bones are out of joint." It was like dislocating a victim on the rack. "He trusted on the Lord," etc. This is exactly what they said at the cross. Just put yourself thus in twenty-second Psalm and take Christ with you. It is a dark cavern until you put Christ into it; then it is full of the light of the glory of God.

Then again, what are you going to do with still other indirect prophecy, such as is found in the rites and ceremonies, as in the Passover. Jesus Christ is to save you from your sins, and He is the strength by which you live. See how this is beautifully expressed in the lamb. The Passover lamb was roasted and eaten. It was first slain as an expression of expiation and then eaten to give strength. Christ is first slain for you and then partaken of by you. It is an anticipation of Christ all the way through. The paschal lamb was roasted on a cross. One long spit crossed another shorter one, so that every lamb roasted was turned on a cross-spit. Moses lifted up the serpent on a pole,—a banner pole and the banner pole is a cross; and so when Moses put the serpent on the pole it wound around the arm of a cross.

Take the historical events of the characters of the Old Testament and see the indirect prophecies of Christ. Take Joseph in Egypt; sold by his brethren into slavery, thrown into prison and interpreting the dreams of the chief baker and the chief butler. He comes out of prison and ascends the throne of Pharaoh and becomes a dispenser of bread. Jesus was sold by His brethren into captivity to death, went into the prison of the grave, stayed there three days, came up from the grave and ascended the throne of the universe and became the dispenser of bread to a famishing people.

Take Joshua. He comes to deliver. He crosses the Jordan and captures Jericho, the first great stronghold of the Canaanites. The priests encompassed the city seven times. That is preaching the Gospel, surrounding the whole world with the story of redemption. Joshua saw the walls of Jericho fall by the power of God.

Take Jonah and the fish. He was thrown overboard and taken into the stomach of a great fish, then thrown out on the land. Jesus said that as Jonah was three days in the fish's belly so shall the Son of Man be in the earth. In some of these prophecies we have an indication of what it means. But if you will take other passages and follow them to many Old Testament scriptures, how perfectly they fit. Beneath the history there is a wonderful unfolding of spiritual truth. I believe there is not a character in the Old Testament that has not some reference to Christ and does not become a forecast of things to come; so that if you read the Old Testament and put Christ into it you will find Him everywhere. There are thirty-two or thirty-three resemblances between Christ and Joseph, more than that between Christ and Moses, and more than twenty instances in which Daniel is a type of Christ.

## Lecture 3.

Take two things in the Old Testament — the priesthood and the tabernacle. The Messiah is the center of them all. There are indirect prophecies of Christ in the Levitical ceremonies and in the great structure built by the command of God — one of the most marvelous things in the Holy Scripture. If the Bible be a revelation of God we should expect two objects to be accomplished. First, it will reveal God as the object of worship; second, it will reveal Christ as the means of redemption. We want to know how we can draw near to God, being sinful, and how we can be delivered from sin. Christ is revealed as the hope of salvation. In other words, Christ comes down to man in order that men may draw near to God. That figure in John 1 : 51 is Jacob's ladder; the angels coming down and going up. God comes down to man in Christ and man goes up to God in Christ; Christ brings God down to man and then, as the representative of man, carrying man up to God.

Notice that God is revealed as holy — the first great revelation about God; second, as perfect; third, as love, not in the sense that any other being exercises love, because the secrets of love are in God. The first thought, holiness, implies that the sinner will be driven away from God; the second, that, with all His perfection, the imperfect man cannot be acceptable in His sight; and the third, love, implies that everything that has to do with sin is foreign to love and repulsive to God. This will interpret the whole Old Testament. Everything about the tabernacle has to do with the setting forth of the holiness and perfection of God. Next comes the high priesthood of Jesus Christ. The sinner is repelled from the holy, the imperfect from the perfect, and the dead from the living. Jesus Christ, an absolutely perfect man, becomes the mediator by which the sinner draws near and is not repelled by the holy God, his imperfection invested with perfection, and God looks upon the imperfect just as if it were perfect. This is common to the whole Old Testament. I wish I had been told this twenty years ago just to give me the key to the wonderful Old Testament scriptures. Let us dwell upon this a moment. Look at the high priesthood of Christ. You cannot think of high priesthood without meditation. The priest comes between man and God and represents man to God and God to man; and therefore we have, in Christ, God and man in one. The Jews called the Scriptures the book of the law. What is the object of law? Paul tells us that by the law is the knowledge of sin. The law imparts the knowledge of two things, God's holiness and our sin. It shows us the holiness of God and the sinfulness of man. Man is polluted and mediation is by blood. Notice the double fact: the kingly tribe not in Levi but in Judah, and the priestly tribe not in Judah but in Levi. There being two tribes to express Christ's double nature—Levi as the priest and Judah as the king—thus representing Him as priest and king. The prophets did not belong to any particular tribe; they belonged to the people of Israel; so you need two tribes to represent Christ as priest and king, and all the tribes to represent His prophetical character. Observe that the priest had no political power and was not self-appointed, and so Christ was apart from all human kingdoms, and was no self-appointed. "My father appointed me to this work; I came to finish His work." He was not made a priest by man, but by God. The priest had no right to make the law, but to carry it out; so did Christ in His high priestly office; and the high priest stood for the whole nation as Christ stands for the whole body of believers. Now there was one priest distinct from all his brethren. He was called the high priest, and while they were all dedicated to God, he was especially dedicated. The high priest alone, and only on one day in the year, entered the Holy of Holies, and there applied the blood of propitiation to the mercy seat. All that refers to Jesus Christ the only high priest. He took the blood of atonement in behalf of man and once for all sprinkled the mercy seat with the blood of propitiation.

The whole apex of the priesthood is found in the high priest and in his work on the great day of atonement. In fact the whole apex of the Levitical code is found, in this, that through blood is the only atonement, and through atonement is the only access and acceptance with God. The high priest on the day of atonement took the blood of the victim and passed in through the holy place to the holiest, touching all the vessels as he passed; then he came into the innermost part of the tabernacle, where was the oblong structure called the ark, with the law of God within, over which the mercy seat with the cherubim. Touching that with the blood, he signified that there is no atonement except through blood. Look at the great truth about Jesus Christ. There is no atonement without blood and there is no acceptance without atonement; so the apex of the great pyramid of Levitical ceremonies is these two truths —atonement through blood and access and acceptance through atonement.

The tabernacle was a perfect object lesson. Outside were two objects; the first was an altar and the second was the laver. Inside was the golden candlestick with its seven branches, and the table of shew bread and altar of incense, and then, still within, the mercy seat. Was there ever such a building? Thirteen chapters in Hebrews are devoted to the description of that house, the only house God ever directed the building of, while there is only a chapter devoted to the creation of the universe. What does it all mean? First, the brazen altar represents blood; second, the laver represents washing. Blood is connected with expiation; water is connected with regeneration; the altar may represent Christ's work, and the laver represent the Spirit's work in connection with the Word of God. Here you have the *terms* of communion. You want to know how to draw near to God. First of all by the blood, secondly, seeing that Jesus Christ died for sinners and I have accepted Him, I come to the Holy Spirit to be renewed; and hence the laver is connected with the Spirit. We are born of the Spirit. Peter says, God has begotten us by the Holy Ghost. You get the Spirit through the Word; you get the Word through the Spirit. After you have learned the terms of communion you come to the *forms* of communion.

The table of shew bread represents subsistence, food and drink; consecrated substance. What does the candlestick mean but consecrated time? The next thing we come to is the altar of incense, and what does that mean but a consecrated heart? This is more noble than consecrating your substance. You come to the blood and accept it; you come to the Spirit and get renewed, and then you give your substance, and time, and your heart itself, by the consecration of your whole soul to God. In the most holy place is the ark and the cherubim bending over it, representing the harmony of all God's attributes. The wings of the Cherubim touch the walls on either side as if to indicate the two great periods of history of believers in the Old and New Testaments, reaching back to the beginning of the world and forward to the end of time.

God puts this picture of the tabernacle before the race so that, when a poor sinner wants to draw near to God, he comes to be sprinkled in the blood, to be washed in the water of regeneration; and if he wants to enjoy divine communion, he consecrates his soul and his substance to God, and finally he will come within the veil, where union and communion are perfected.

## Lecture 4.

The connection between the Old and New Testaments will still occupy us, especially as to how they revolve about Jesus Christ.

1. The Old Testament is prophetic even to its history. The historians were prophets, and they wrote prophetically, hence they dwelt upon that which a mere historian would not have dwelt upon, and they magnified that which a mere historian would have passed over, because these things were written for our learning, and because historical characters were typical of events and character, and because they can only be interpreted by the Lord Jesus Christ Himself. From Isaiah to Matthew we have links of prophecy all the way through and reaching far beyond Isaiah to the time of Moses. Prophecy and history bear the relation to each other of lock and key; neither is complete without the other. The lock is incomplete without the key and the key is incomplete without the lock. It is remarkable how all these prophetic inti-

mations have been fulfilled. I have already spoken of how the tax was first made, and how it was not collected until eight years after the enrollment. Christ must be born at a given time, and Mary did not live in Bethlehem, and so she must be brought, at the crisis of the sorrow of her sex, when this infant Christ was mature for birth, to Bethlehem, and so the whole world was set in motion that He might be born when and where prophecy indicated.

In John, nineteenth chapter, we read that, in order that the Scripture might be fulfilled, He said, "I thirst," and it was the only thing that remained, in order to complete the portrait given in the Old Testament; and so, even in the midst of the agonies crucifixion this divine God man said, "I thirst," to fill up the prophetic prediction. One of the sweetest and most pathetic verses in the New Testament is this verse, John 19 : 38.

2. Mystery and solution. There are seven mysteries in the New Testament. The word mystery does not mean that which cannot be known. Mystery in the New Testament means an open secret, something that was a secret, but is now revealed. Read I Cor. 2 : 9, 10.

The seven mysteries of the New Testament are as follows:

1st. The mystery of God (Col. 2 : 2).

2d. The mystery of godliness, the incarnation of Christ (I Tim. 3 : 16).

3d. The mystery of Christ and the church (Eph. 5 : 32).

4th. The mystery of God's will (Eph. 1 : 9; Col. 1 : 26).

5th. The mystery of the kingdom of God (Matt. 13).

6h. The mystery of iniquity, or of the man of sin (II Thess. 2 : 7).

7th. The mystery of the resurrection (I Cor. 15 : 51.)

Now observe that these seven mysteries could not be understood until the whole Word of God was complete, and from that time forth there is no reason for not understanding them. Notice that there are five of these that have to do with certain unities. The first has to do with the unity of the Father and the Son; the second, has to do with Christ's union with human nature; the third has to do with the union of Christ and the church; the fourth concerns the union of the Jew and the Gentile, and the mystery of the resurrection has to do with the union of body and spirit. This book — the Bible — is worth all the books in the world to greaten a man or a woman and expand the heart. All these scriptures center in Christ. Christ is in God and God is in Christ, and Christ is in the church. He is in Gentile believers; He rules even in the kingdom of Satan; is in the bodies of saints as the assurance of resurrection.

3. Type and anti-type. I have spoken on this before. An anti-type is that which corresponds to the type and fulfills and explains it. I question whether there is one single feature of the Old Testament economy without a typical value as related to Jesus Christ. Take even so insignificant a thing as the high priest's garment. We are told that there was run through the hem of it a blue ribbon. Blue is, in the Bible, a type of divine fidelity; it is the color of heaven, where the greatest expanse of blue has always been since the foundation of the earth. The great color of the earth is green, the color of the heaven is blue. You cannot look at heaven without thinking of blue and you cannot think of heaven without thinking of God. God is faithful and true, the great Promiser. From the blue heavens, God has poured down rain and sunshine and all blessings; because of the blue of heaven there is a green earth. If blue represents divine fidelity it stands for divine promises. Did you ever ask yourself why the woman having the issue of blood touched the hem of Christ's garment. Is it not because it was connected with the blue ribbon and it represented taking hold of the promise? This was instinct in the woman who probably understood something of the typical value of high priestly garments. Sometimes people talk of this woman as if she were the only one that ever touched Christ's garments. You read in the Gospels how they pressed about Christ's garments, and it was a common thing to touch the hem. Look at the shoulder clasps of the high priest; the stones on the shoulder and on the breastplate. On the shoulders were the onyx stones and on the breastplates were twelve stones, each containing the name of one of the tribes of the children of Israel. To keep a name before you is to keep a friend before you. They had no photographs in those days, but they kept the name in the place of the photograph. And so in these

two places on the high priest's garments were these names inscribed. The shoulder is the symbol of strength and the breast is the symbol of love. You carry the likeness of a friend on your heart, and so the Lord Jesus Christ, the great high priest, bears us on His heart. He carried the lamb that was lost on His shoulders, and so our great Intercessor at the throne of God lifts our names upon His breast. I am on His heart, for He loves me; I am on His shoulder, for He bears me. I do not think there is a more wonderful symbol of Jesus Christ in the whole Old Testament than that.

The bush that Moses saw was burning, but it was not consumed. That is to say, the bush was not in the fire, but the fire was in the bush. To me that is an exhibition of the union of the human and divine in Jesus Christ. A mysterious fire is burning in the bush; it conveys the idea of the mystery of Jesus Christ. Moses said I will turn aside to see this great sight, and he stood and contemplated it. The burning bush in the desert place is a type of Jesus coming down from heaven to abide in the desert of sin on earth. A voice came out of the bush. Jesus Christ is the Word of Life. A flame could not speak, but Jesus Christ was the voice in the fire. The ground was hallowed, and wherever Jesus Christ comes the ground is hallowed. The fire in the burning bush was a practical communication to Moses to teach him his duty with regard to Himself and the children of Israel. The Lord Jesus Christ has appeared like a pillar of fire in human form to lead us like the pilgrims through the desert to the land of promise.

I made a discovery last week, and have been asked to give it to you. It came from a little study on the expression "He bare our sins." I question whether there are four words in the New Testament more important than these. It is very seldom you find a repetition in the word of God, but this, or a like expression, is found from eight to ten times in the New Testament, and you will know there must be some reason for it.

1. "He bare our sins" (I Peter 2:24).
2. "He bare the sins of many" (Heb. 9:28.)
3. "He suffered for us" (I Peter 2:21).
4. "Once suffered for sins" (I Peter 3:18).

5. "He gave Himself for us" (Titus 2:14).
6. "He gave Himself for our sins" (Gal. 1:4).
7. "He died for us" (I Thess. 5:10).
8. "Made sin for us" (II Cor. 5:21).
9. "Christ died for our sins" (I Cor. 15:3).
10. "Christ died for the ungodly" (Rom. 5:6).

You will notice that these are in pairs. Here is the wonderful thing about all this repetition. You see God wanted to make it emphatic. Back in the Old Testament there are certain luminous points in the history of God's people, standing out with great conspicuousness. For instance, here is the *exodus* from Egypt, the first great event in the history of God's people; secondly, the institution of *sacrifices* in the desert; and all those sacrifices were of two sorts, the first including the sin and trespass offerings, and then the sweet savor offerings. The next great thing is what may be called the law of Levitical *cleansing*, the whole ceremonial which found its apex or summit in the cleansing of the *leper*. The next thing was the great day of *atonement* in which the whole ritual found its summit. Next the year of *jubilee*. Then the *pilgrimage* of the children of Israel accomplished through the desert and completed on entrance into the Holy Land. That finishes the Old Testament. The great events in the New Testament are the *life*, *death*, and *resurrection* of Jesus Christ. I think you will agree with me that these are the great points in the Old and New Testament history. These are exactly related to the passages I have named above.

The statement is made, "He gave Himself for our sins, that He might deliver us from this present evil world," or evil age. Egypt is the type of this present evil age and it is always referred to in the Bible as "this present age." Here we have a reference to the Exodus.

## Lecture 5.

"He was made sin for us," has reference to the sin offering. Notice this; it is not said that He took the sinner's place only, but that He was *made sin*. The word sin is singular. Notice the distinction between sin and sins. In Rom. 6 it is "sin" over and over again. Sin is the root and the source of sins just as the pear tree is the source of the pear. You may pluck off poor pears from a pear tree, but if the tree is a good tree it will bring forth good fruit some time; but if the tree never brings forth anything but bad fruit you will know that the tree itself is corrupt. There needs to be some one made sin for us. We will, as children of God, be emancipated entirely from the power of sin. I may be dead to sin and love the things I once hated and hate the things I once loved. To Christ was made a sin offering for us. There were five great divisions of the offerings. Sin and trespass offerings go by themselves, and peace and burnt offerings, etc., by themselves. The last three are sweet savor offerings. Sin and trespass offerings are different from the sweet savor offerings. God cannot forgive sin, it has to be "*put away.*" Christ appeared to put away sin. God forgives your sins, but He must "put away" your sin. The sin and trespass offerings were utterly turned to ashes, but the sweet savor offering went up in flame. The word "burnt" in the first instance means that the offering was utterly turned to ashes, and the last, that the offering went up in the fire. Christ was made sin for us that we might live unto righteousness. The victim was believed to die and live again; as it were going up in flame to God. Being dead like the victim slain, the true disciple ascends up in fire as a sweet savor offering unto God.

Take the leper's cleaning. Christ has also once suffered for sins that He might bring us to God. Study the cleansing of the leper. You will find that he could not come into the camp of Israel. He had to be examined by the priest outside of the camp, and if the priest decided that he was clean, he led him by the hand to the altar and permitted him to take part in the sacrifice; that is, the leper being pronounced clean was led to God. Just so Christ suffered that He might lead us to God, that He might put away our leprosy, that He might conduct us unto God and there assure us of access.

"He bare the sins of many." On the day of atonement two kids were brought forth. They were exactly alike in every particular excepting that one was marked by a red ribbon around its neck. One was called "Azazel," or the kid of "removal." The two parts of Christ's work in bearing our sins were here presented to the people in figure. The first, expiation by blood; second, confession and removal of sin before God. You want to have your sins forgiven, but more than that, you want them to be forgotten. God says, "I will remember their iniquities no more." The idea is that when you come to God in Christ Jesus your sins are not only pardoned but annihilated. While in the Alps last June I saw a cloudy mist, but the sun rose up and shone upon it and it disappeared in a moment. The Lord God shines upon our sins as on a cloud of mist, and they immediately disappear. He puts them behind His back; He puts them in the depths of the sea where they cannot be dredged up. First the kid slain and then the kid taken away into the wilderness. And so we read in the beautiful and touching Epistle of Paul, "He bore the sins of many "—*bore them away.*

Jesus Christ gave Himself for our sins that He might deliver us from this present evil age; that is the exodus from Egypt. Second, He was made sin for us, that we might be made the righteousness of God in Him; that is the sin offering. Third, He bare our sins in His body on the tree; there is the sweet savor offering.

Christ has "once suffered for sins" that He might bring us to God. I Peter 3:18. The cleansing of the leper is there fulfilled.

"He bare the sins of many;" that is the great day of atonement.

Ce gave Himself that He might redeem us from all iniquity. The climax of redemption was the year of jubilee. Three things occurred on that day. All debts were canceled; second, every servant was released from bondage; third, all forfeited estates were restored to their original owners. The year opened with the close of the day of atonement. If a creditor had a document for which another man owed him he went and nailed it on the post of his neighbor's doorway; hence we are told that Jesus Christ took the handwriting of ordinances out of the way, nailing it to His cross. That is, the debt was canceled forever in the crucifixion of Jesus Christ. Again, deliverance from bondage. If a man had been a slave on the year of jubilee he went free If he chose to remain a servant his ear was bored with an awl and fastened to the post the same as the document was. Compare Psalm 40. "Mine ears hast thou opened," or bored. Jesus Christ came to preach deliverance to the captives. Again, restoration of lost estates. What you lost through judgment you will get back through Jesus Christ.

He suffered for us, leaving us an example. This refers to the pilgrimage. Wherever the pillar of fire went the children of Israel pitched their tent. They had a divine example to follow. Last, He died for us, that whether we wake or sleep we shall live together with Him.

4. Latent and patent, the hidden and apparent things.

We all agree that the Trinity is clearly revealed in the New Testament, but is it revealed at all in the Old Testament? I think I have found many marks of the Trinity in the Old Testament. The name Elohim is plural, but always connected with the singular verb as though to indicate the three persons all belonging to one God. In that Levitical benediction in the Book of Numbers you can see the Trinity. That is the one fixed form of words in the Old Testament. It was pronounced by the high priest when he came out of the holy place on the great day of atonement, and lifted up his hands in blessing on the people. "The Lord bless thee and keep thee." Here is God the Father. Second, "The Lord make his face to shine upon thee and be gracious unto thee." We have never seen the face of God, but in Jesus Christ, and His face shines on us in Christ. Christ is the manifestation of God the Father, and all we know about God is through Jesus Christ. Here we have the second person of the Trinity. Third, How is God's face to be seen in Christ unless the Holy Spirit opens blind eyes? The only way for God to lift up His countenance upon us is to give us His Spirit. The only way for peace to come to our minds and hearts is by the surrender of our hearts to the Holy Spirit. God is revealed in the Old Testament only in part — might, power, knowledge, holiness — but we have very few hints of His love and of His grace. This had to wait for the New Testament to be fully understood.

In the Old Testament we have man put conspicuously before us, but we have to wait for the New Testament to see woman at her proper sphere and service for Jesus Christ.

5. There is a difference between the two testaments as to the ideas of preservation and promulgation. In the Old Testament the main thing is to *guard* the truth; in the New Testament the main thing is to *spread* the truth. In the Old Testament is the flock of sheep and the shepherd on guard; in the New Testament it is the fishermen catching the fish and bringing them to the land.

6. There is a difference between the two Testaments as to law and grace. Law came by Moses, but grace and truth by Jesus Christ. I presume every one of you have been troubled by the prominence of law and the absence of grace in the Old Testament, while in the New Testament it is all grace and very little law. The Old Testament opens with law and ends with a curse; the New Testament opens with salvation begun by the coming of Christ and ends with a picture of the second coming to complete salvation.

The Old Testament closes with a malediction and the New Testament with a benediction. The law knows for disobedient souls only penalty. It knows nothing of pardon; it makes no provision for salvation and knows nothing but wrath from heaven upon evil doers. The penalty must be in exact proportion to the act committed; an eye for an eye and a tooth for a tooth. Hence the Old Testament emphasizes justice. In Jer. 51:56 God takes to Himself the name of "the Lord God of Recompenses," and says He will surely requite. In the Old Testament is the scale of judgment; if you put the slightest weight on one side you must put a counterweight on the other side. God weighs the actions of men in His scales. He weighs our words, thoughts and acts, and there is no possible appeal from that judgment, any more than there is from a pair of mechanical scales. The law of penalty is that whatsoever you inflict shall be inflicted upon you.

In Judges 1:6, 7, we read that as Adonibezek cut off the thumbs and great toes of others so his thumbs and great toes were cut off. That is the law of justice. Retribution must be in precise accord with the wrong committed. Haman built a gallows for Mordecai, and his sons and himself were strung upon it. Ahab by vile treachery got possession of Naboth's vineyard, but Elijah, the prophet, came unto him and said: "In the place where the dogs licked the blood of Naboth shall dogs lick thy blood." Exact retribulation. David committed an awful sin and sapped the life of another man's family, and his own son committed a like sin with his wives. Some people stumble over the imprecatory Psalms, but the judgment called down upon evildoers is precisely in accordance with what was due them — what they had done to others was to be done to them. If you take another man's life your life shall be taken; if you cut off the ear of another, your ear shall be cut off. If you betray another man, your family shall be betrayed. If you commit murder, you shall be murdered or slain. This is by the exact mechanical scale of the law of justice; it is perfectly right. God is under no obligation whatever to exercise grace. Grace is not properly an attribute of God, but a voluntary exercise of love. God *must* be just, but is not compelled to be gracious. The Old Testament is not a revelation of grace, but of justice. Proper justice demands that no evil shall go unpunished, that reward and retribution shall have their full measure of desert — exact correspondence between every act and every penalty.

Under the law alone, holy anger is right, exact penalty is perfect justice; it is all meant to drive us to Christ for grace. There is no hope for us except as God exercises grace toward us through Christ. Law makes us conscious of sin and of the awful consequences of sin. Under the law we are penniless under a great debt of sin, and if thrown into prison shall never come out thence until we have paid the utmost farthing. You can never get to where the whole debt has been paid. If at any time in eternity all the evil that you have done could be expiated, then you could have a restoration, but you could never pay that utmost farthing. On the other hand grace comes in to teach such a thing as forgiveness with God — to teach me that there is justification by faith in Christ through grace. The law is my schoolmaster to bring me to Christ. The Greek word " paidagogos," translated " schoolmaster," means foot-leader, child-conductor, one who came to the door of the house of the parents, took the children from the house and led them along the streets to the house of their teacher. So the law is our schoolmaster to bring us to Christ. The law knocks at the door of our house and says, are there any poor, wretched, burdened sinners here? I will take you to one who will atone for sin. The law of God thunders at the door of our house of bondage and condemnation, and says, if you will follow me I will lead you to Jesus?

www.ingramcontent.com/pod-product-compliance
Lightning Source LLC
Chambersburg PA
CBHW021829230426
43669CB00008B/912